Pareto's 80/20 Rule for Corporate Accountants

Pareto's 80/20 Rule for Corporate Accountants

DAVID PARMENTER

John Wiley & Sons, Inc.

This book is printed on acid-free paper.

Published by John Wiley & Sons, Inc., Hoboken, New Jersey
Published simultaneously in Canada.

Wiley Bicentennial Logo: Richard J. Pacifico

Library of Congress Cataloging-in-Publication Data:

Parmenter, David.
Pareto's 80/20 rule for corporate accountants / David Parmenter.
p. cm.
Includes index.
ISBN: 978-0-470-12543-4 (cloth)
1. Corporations—Accounting. I. Title. II. Title: Pareto's eighty/twenty rule for corporate accountants.
HF5686.C7P27 2007
657—dc22 2006038752

Printed in the United States of America

10 9 8 7 6 5 4 3 2 1

CONTENTS

ACKNOWLEDGMENTS

The writer would like to acknowledge the commitment and dedication of ***waymark solutions*** staff, both past and present, Ian Niven, and Wayne Morgan (leading CFOs), Bill Cotton, clients and peers who have commented on drafts, Matthew Clayton, Jeremy Hope, and Harry Mills for their wise counsel over the years, and my two daughters, Alexandra and Claudine, who have put up with my many late nights at the office.

I am grateful to all those accountants who have shared their better practices with me during workshops I have delivered around the world.

A special thanks goes to my parents who through their unique style of parenting and continuous support have given me the confidence and the platform to undertake the mission I am now on.

INTRODUCTION

All corporate accountants need to leave a legacy before they move on; in other words, they need to have made a permanent improvement to the organization. Yet many corporate accountants are not producing enough added value to their organization—they are failing to make a difference. I know this, from observation and my own personal experience. How many accountants on leaving receive an outpouring of loss from the senior management team and budget holders?

Most of us have done a good job as a processing machine, but little time has been invested in being a business partner to budget holders and senior management. I believe we have "lost the plot" through not applying Pareto's 80/20 principle in our work, because without it we can get buried in the details, only surfacing on retirement! This book is designed to transform your contribution, increase your job satisfaction and profile in the organization, and help you leave a legacy in every organization you work for.

The better practices in this book are ignored at your peril, because they are based around the wisdom and better practices of more than 4,000 accountants who I have met through my workshops in Ireland, United Kingdom, Australia, and New Zealand. I use the word "better" instead of "best" because what is best for one size of organization may not be appropriate for an organization that is much smaller or larger. It is also supplemented by the teams that have participated in the ***waymark solutions*** better practice study of finance functions. The word participants used in this book refers to all these aforementioned people and we owe them a great deal of gratitude for showing us the way forward.

I would like to add that few, if any, of these practices were used by me when I was a corporate accountant thus senior management did not shed a tear when I left the organization. It is my mission to ensure corporate accountants worldwide have a fate that is different from mine—that they leave a legacy that stays around a long time after they have left the organization.

EMBARKING ON IMPLEMENTING BETTER PRACTICES

The goal of this book is to help corporate accountants implement better practices that will make a difference to the finance team's performance, creating permanent improvements in their organization's processes.

It is my wish that the material in this book, along with the workshops I deliver around the world, will increase the likelihood of success. In order for both you and your finance team to succeed, I suggest that you:

- Read the Introduction carefully, a couple of times.
- Seek an outside mentor—see Chapter 6—who will guide you in this transformation.
- Scan the material in the subsequent chapters so you know what is there.
- Focus, the next 3 to 6 months, on implementing the content in the chapters in Part One.
- Visit www.waymark.co.nz and www.davidparmenter.com Web sites.
- Commence the team-building initiatives exercises in Chapter 6 and undertake any training to plug those identified skill gaps in the finance team.

HOW TO USE THE BOOK

This book is divided into four sections. The table below explains the purpose of each section.

	Section	Significance
Introduction	Covers the foundation stones which will facilitate change. The corporate accountants need to improve the	Failure to understand and implement these suggestions will limit how

	Section	Significance
Introduction *(continued)*	the way they sell change, sort out their personal baggage they carry (we all carry some), maintain a 80/20 helicopter view, and improve the work-life balance.	effective the rest of the book can be.
Part One	Focuses on the areas where the finance team can score the easy goals in the next 6 months.	The better practices in Part One, if implemented, will free up time so Part Two initiatives can be attempted successfully.
Part Two	Focuses on more wide-ranging changes such as "introducing winning KPIs" and "quarterly rolling planning" which will require a heavy investment of time from the finance team.	These initiatives will make a profound impact.
Appendices and Exhibits	The templates, checklists, and diagrams in the book will take take some time to absorb. Discuss these amongst the corporate accountants in the finance team and with your mentor.	Once understood, these templates, checklists, and diagrams will have a significant impact.

GETTING THE RIGHT WORK BALANCE

The impact of the efficient and effective practices listed in the book will, if implemented, make a major change to the nature of work performed by the accounting team. There will be a migration away from low-value processing activities into the more value-added areas such as advisory, being a business partner with budget holders, and implementing new systems. As Exhibit 1 shows, the change in focus should mean we are working smarter, not harder. This change in workload will, over time, lead to the formation of a smaller but more experienced accounting team and a better work–life balance.

Exhibit 2 shows the impact of this shift away from processing into more service delivery work. The key change is to reduce radically the time the accounting team spends in month-end reporting, the annual accounts, and the annual planning process. I call these three activities

Exhibit 1 Getting the Balance of Work Right

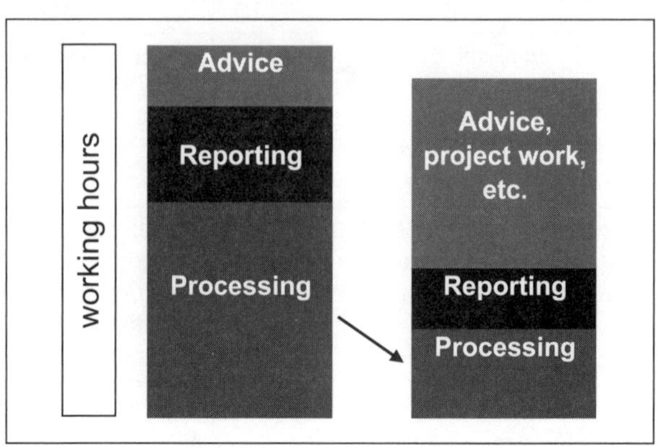

the trifecta of lost opportunities for the accounting team. When were you last thanked for any of these tasks?

The better practices in this book will approximately double the amount of "added value time" you and your team have!

Exhibit 2 Year's Planner for Better Practice Finance Function (Based on a June Year-End)

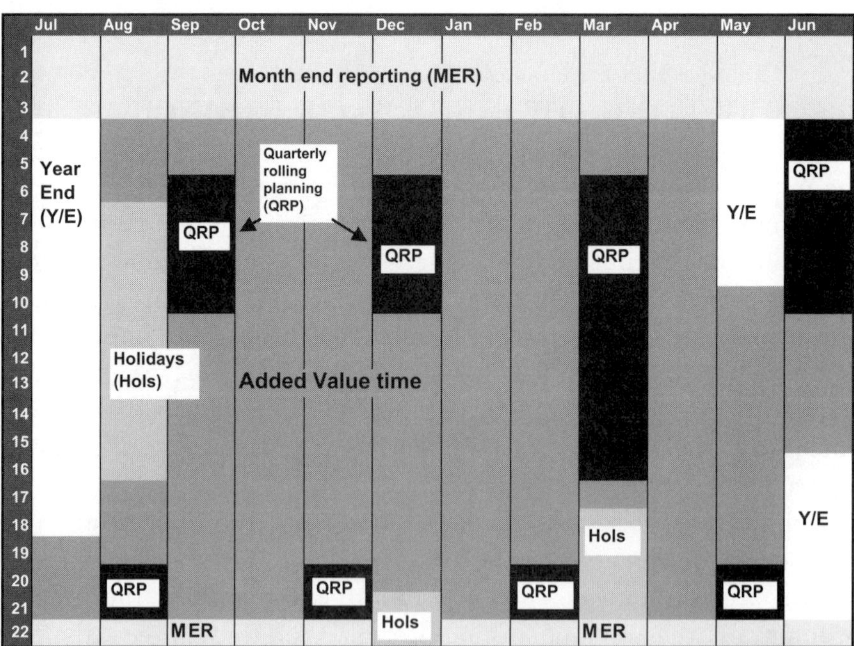

PARETO'S 80/20 PRINCIPLE

As accountants we are all aware of Pareto's principle, but unfortunately seldom apply it. Why is it that we spend months on an annual planning process that we know is flawed? Why is it we spend days preparing a monthly report that is informing management well and truly after the horse has bolted? Why do we produce a 30+ page month-end finance report for the senior management team? Why do we spend a couple of months preparing an annual report when we had the final numbers in the first five working days of the new year?

This book is based around the principle that as corporate accountants we need to spend more time on what matters, and be more efficient with the time we spend on less important issues.

Wilfred Pareto, an economist, published *Cours d'economie politique* (1896–97), which included his famous law of income distribution. It was a complicated mathematical formulation in which he attempted to prove that the distribution of incomes and wealth in society is not random and that a consistent pattern appears throughout history, in all parts of the world and in all societies. When he discovered the principle, it established that 80% of the land in Italy was owned by 20% of the population. Later, he discovered that the Pareto principle was valid in other parts of his life, such as gardening: 80% of his garden peas were produced by 20% of the pea pods. The principle provides rough approximations and recognizes that effort and reward are not linearly related.

It applies in business, as rough approximations:

- Approximately 80% of process defects arise from no more than 20% of the process issues.
- Approximately 20% of the sales force is likely to produce 80% of the company's revenues.
- Approximately 80% of sales are likely to come from 20% of the product/service range.

The law applies in the finance team's work:

- Approximately 80% of purchase invoices will be for small amounts (e.g., under $2,000).
- Approximately 80% of the time spent by the finance team is not adding much value.

- About 80% of the chart of account's codes are not worthwhile having.
- About 80% of all month-end reporting is adding little or no value.
- About 80% of the total debt will reside with about 20% of the customers.

SELLING A NEW PROCESS THROUGH THE "EMOTIONAL DRIVERS"

The contents of this book will encourage you to change the way you do things. Because this book is a compilation of better practices that you will want to adopt, it is thus appropriate to talk about selling change.

Remember, nothing was ever sold by logic! You sell through emotional drivers. Remember your last car purchase—the car salesperson would have worked overtime on your emotional drivers! Many initiatives driven from the finance team fail at this hurdle because we attempt to change the culture through selling logic, writing reports, issuing commands via email. It does not work.

All major projects need a public relations (PR) machine behind it. No presentation, email, memo, or paper related to a major change should be distributed unless it has been vetted by your PR expert. All presentations should be road-tested in front of the PR expert. Your PR strategy should include selling to staff, budget holders, senior management team (SMT), and the Board.

We need to alter radically the way we pitch a sale to the SMT and the Board. We first have to ensure we have a good proposal with a sound focus on the emotional drivers that matter to them. We then need to focus on selling to the thought leader on the SMT and Board before we present the proposal. This may take months of informal meetings, sending copies of appropriate articles, telling better practice stories, and so forth to awake the interest.

It is worth noting that the thought leader of the SMT and Board may not be the CEO or Chairman. Having pre-sold the change to the thought leader watch, after delivering your presentation, how the meeting turns to listen to the thought leader's reaction. Your proposal now has the best possible chance of a positive vote.

The following are some of the emotional drivers around the annual planning process which you would use if selling the need to streamline the process and eventually migrate to quarterly rolling planning:

- Meaningless month-end reports (e.g., "it is a timing difference")
- Lost evenings/weekends producing meaningless variances comments
- Lost months! Lost weekends with family! Producing the annual plan
- Huge cost associated with the annual plan—estimate on the high side, as costs motivate Boards
- Time spent by the Board and SMT second guessing the next year—it is more efficient on a rolling quarterly basis
- It is a better practice to implement quarterly rolling forecasting and planning (e.g., 80% of major U.S. companies expect to be doing quarterly rolling forecasts, etc.)

SORTING OUT PERSONAL BAGGAGE

This section is in the front for good reason. We will always be running with a few cylinders misfiring unless we fully understand our behavior patterns and those around us. Skip this section and I promise you that you will never reach your potential. You will never be able to successfully implement large change because this requires advanced interpersonal skills.

We inherit baggage from our ancestry, along with many great things. This baggage is added to by our parents, with too much smothering, too little attention, too much criticism, too little quality time—need I go on? One course I attended called "turning point" stated that we all have baggage; our role in life is to lighten the load so that it is not crippling when we decide to start "management summiting."

It is important to understand that to be a leader today you do not have to have handled all of your personal baggage; the key is the awareness of your weaknesses. There are plenty of "crippled CFOs" causing havoc with every organization that they work for. Yet there are those icon CFOs who are a pleasure to work with.

My point is you owe it to your colleagues, your staff, your suppliers, contractors, family, partner, and offspring, to do something about it.

Here are some suggestions:

- Understand yourself by attending workshops on the Myers-Briggs, the Enneagram, and Hermann think style preferences. These are a must for a better understanding of oneself. (Useful places to search are www.enneagraminstitute.com/ennagram.asp, www.myersbriggs.org, and www.ledgehill.com/default.asp.)
- Develop a decent toolkit so you learn to handle disappointment, anger, loss; if not there will be plenty of opportunities for these events to mess up your life.
- Invest in some personal development (PD) courses; the ones that are of a longer duration have the most chance of changing behaviors. The experts in behavioral change say that it takes up to 12 to 16 weeks of weekly exercises to change a behavior.
- Periodically rate yourself against (for an example checklist, see Exhibit 3).

Exhibit 3 Personal Baggage Checklist

	Tick Your Answer
Focus	
Have you made management aware of the problem of late month-end reporting?	❑ Yes ❑ No
Do you allocate the major chunks of your time to the major goals in your life? (as per your treasure map)	❑ Yes ❑ No
Have you determined what your goals are for the next two to three years?	❑ Yes ❑ No
Do you treat e-mails, as you would mail, by reading them at an appropriate time? (you can set up e-mail filters to help manage them and better channel your time)	❑ Yes ❑ No
Do you avoid being sucked into “nonurgent, not important” issues?	❑ Yes ❑ No
Do you inoculate yourself from the diversion disease?	❑ Yes ❑ No

Exhibit 3 *(Continued)*

	Tick Your Answer
Focus *(Continued)*	
Do you have a clear understanding of all the loose ends that are outstanding?	❑ Yes ❑ No
Do you carefully check the purpose and intent of a meeting before you agree to attend?	❑ Yes ❑ No
Ability to finish	
Do you have specific times for finishing (e.g., a finishing week or two each month)?	❑ Yes ❑ No
Do you minimize your involvement in new projects until your previous ones are finished?	❑ Yes ❑ No
Do you occasionally work away from your office (from home or a a quiet location) so that you can focus on projects uninterrupted?	❑ Yes ❑ No
Interpersonal skills	
Are you able to make sufficient eye contact at least 50% of the time the conversation is taking place?	❑ Yes ❑ No
Are you able to demonstrate "humility" when you consider yourself an expert in the subject matter? (showing that you are open to others' suggestions and opinions)	❑ Yes ❑ No
Can you remain open to ideas, which initially you would like to reject out of hand?	❑ Yes ❑ No
Do you listen to tone and context of the spoken words so as to ascertain what the person is really meaning? (the poor choice of words commonly leads to misunderstandings)	❑ Yes ❑ No
Do you allow others to complete their conversations?	❑ Yes ❑ No
Are you using your mind to create more linkages from the conversation?	❑ Yes ❑ No
Do you show interest and give back verbal and non-verbal signals that you are listening?	❑ Yes ❑ No
Are you aware of all the non-verbal cues you are giving from your body language?	❑ Yes ❑ No
Can you be courteous with people and ruthless with time?	❑ Yes ❑ No
Can you be as patient with other people as you would wish them to be with you?	❑ Yes ❑ No

(continues)

Exhibit 3 *(Continued)*

	Tick Your Answer
Calm in adversity	
Can you avoid taking adversity personally?	❑ Yes ❑ No
Can you look at the funny side when adversity strikes?	❑ Yes ❑ No
Can you realize that adversity is part of life and deal with it?	❑ Yes ❑ No
Can you still be courteous to people when you are on a tight deadline?	❑ Yes ❑ No
Addiction management	
Do you limit stimulants that adversely affect your behavior? (e.g., caffeine can make a substantial impact on how argumentative we become especially if you have more than two strong coffees during the working day)	❑ Yes ❑ No
Have you controlled your addiction to the adrenaline rush of completion in the 11th hour?	❑ Yes ❑ No
Have you controlled your desire to work harder (or longer) than anyone else on your team?	❑ Yes ❑ No
Anger management	
Do you see anger as a negative trait?	❑ Yes ❑ No
Do you handle the feelings for anger in a safe way?	❑ Yes ❑ No
Are you aware that you have a choice and alternatives? (there are many good behavioral change programs)	❑ Yes ❑ No
Are you aware that frustration with one's self is one of the great initiators of anger?	❑ Yes ❑ No
Do you use the time-out technique when angry?	❑ Yes ❑ No
Do you view events as challenges to be overcome rather than roadblocks to your progress?	❑ Yes ❑ No
Personal learning and growth	
Have you attended any personal development courses to overcome the defense mechanisms that you have put in place from childhood onward that may be limiting your effectiveness?	❑ Yes ❑ No
Have you attended any personal development courses to challenge your negative behavior traits? (we all have them)	❑ Yes ❑ No

Exhibit 3 *(Continued)*

	Tick Your Answer
Personal learning and growth *(Continued)*	
Do you know where you lie on the Enneagram? (a worldwide program to help individuals understand their behavioral weaknesses)	❑ Yes ❑ No
Do you know your Myers-Briggs personality type? (a worldwide program to help individuals understand their personality type)	❑ Yes ❑ No
Have you done the Myers-Briggs team wheel?	❑ Yes ❑ No
Creating win-win situations	
Do you analyze the situation from the other side?	❑ Yes ❑ No
Can you honestly say you are focused on a mutual win-win?	❑ Yes ❑ No
If your suppliers, customers, and so forth were contacted do you think they would say you are fair and reasonable?	❑ Yes ❑ No
Functioning team member	
Are you able to curb your own desires in order to function fully as a team member?	❑ Yes ❑ No
Are you able to put other team members' needs alongside yours?	❑ Yes ❑ No
Does the administration staff willingly help you? (because you have connected well with them)	❑ Yes ❑ No
Do you share praise from others with the team rather than "bag it" for yourself?	❑ Yes ❑ No
Your score	
Your staff scoring you	

Yes count

Less than 20	Treat it as an urgent priority to attend some PD courses
20–25	Time to get serious with personal development
25–30	Still more could be done
Over 30	Congratulations, you have made good progress minimizing your personal baggage (suggest you get a number of your staff to score you—there may be a difference)

We have a choice. To grow and challenge those behavior traits that will create havoc in the workplace, or ignore and seek new jobs like we do new partners, hooked on the romance period and leaving when the going gets tough. To make a major contribution, you will need to achieve through the contribution of others. This means acquiring a suite of appropriate behavioral skills.

PART ONE

Areas to Focus on in the Next Six Months

There are some steps that you can take to get started very quickly in changing the way you handle the processes within your company. They are:

Goal	Reason
1. Invest in accounts payable technology.	The accounts payable team is the center of the accounting team. Investing in accounts payable technology pays high dividends for the finance team, the budget holders, and their administrators. This will take about a six-month time frame and thus you need to start now.
2. Get month-end reporting to the senior management team (SMT) down to three working days post month-end.	If you are not this quick too much time is being absorbed by this low-value task. Time needs to be freed up in order to provide decision-based reports during the month, which are much more valuable.
3. Introduce daily and weekly financial and nonfinancial reports that help management make decisions on a timely basis.	You need to provide information so the barn door can be shut as soon as it is left open.

(continues)

Goal *(Continued)*	**Reason**
4. Draft a dashboard with your key resource indicators (KRIs) for your Board of Directors.	This will revolutionize the Board's finance report and can be set up very quickly (e.g., one person did it over one evening).
5. Start work on your annual reporting cycle so that it can be completed and signed off by the auditors in ten working days post year-end.	You never get thanked for this activity so streamlining annual reporting is a must.
6. If your annual planning cycle is to be completed within the next six months, plan now to complete it within a ten working day time frame.	Your annual plan takes too long, undermines reporting, creates dysfunctional budget holders, and smart organizations do not do it anymore. You need to adopt some of the practices suggested, which will speed up the process and prepare the way for quarterly rolling planning (see Part Two).
7. The CFO and the staff reporting directly to the CFO should each have their own mentor.	A mentor will not only progress your career, they will save your career time and time again.
8. Start marketing the accounting team as of tomorrow.	This will be a challenge but one you cannot delay—the profile of the finance team has been too low for many years.
9. Plan for some team building events in the next three months.	Your team deserves this: it is a better practice, productivity will improve, and you will feel good about creating an improved work environment.

A checklist has been developed covering the major steps. This is set out in Appendix A.

CHAPTER 1

Accounts Payable in the 21st Century

An accounts payable (AP) team is the center of an accounting function, for without its smooth operation:

- Monthly accounts cannot be prepared promptly.
- An organization does not, at any point in time, know of its total liabilities.
- Budget holders spend too much of their valuable time processing orders and approving invoices for payment.
- Low level of accuracy in the monthly accounts due to missed liabilities and posting errors.
- Processing procedures are more akin to the Charles Dickens era than the 21st century (Charles Dickens had a checkbook and received paper-based invoices).
- Suppliers are forever on the phone chasing up payment.
- Expense claims are a nightmare for claimants and the accounts payable team.

The discussion in this chapter provides better practices on how to improve the accounts payable department.

MOVE TO A PAPERLESS AP FUNCTION

As mentioned, many accounts payable processing procedures are more akin to the Charles Dickens era than the 21st century. How do we go from an electronic transaction in the suppliers' accounting system to a Charles Dickens paper-based invoice? Surely we should be able to change this easily with our major suppliers.

Many U.S. multinationals have achieved this already. It requires an investment, skilled AP staff, and retraining of the budget holders. The rewards are immense. To appreciate the benefits, the AP team should regularly visit the website of The Accounts Payable Network (www.TAPN.com).

The 21st century paperless AP includes:

- Invest in an electronic ordering system (procurement system) so control is at the order stage, receipting is electronic, and supplier payments are automatically processed once matching has been done (in some cases not requiring the supplier invoice!) (see the following section).
- Introduce the purchase card to all staff with delegated authority so all small-value items can be purchased through the purchase card, thereby saving thousands of hours of processing time by both budget holders and the accounts payable teams (see the following section).
- All major suppliers are required to provide electronic invoices, which will include the general ledger account codes—this requires liaison between your information technology (IT) team and the supplier's IT team.
- Electronic expense claims processed through a web-based system so employees, wherever they are, can process their claim. These expense claim systems can be integrated with the purchase card system so there is one on-line system accounting for cash and card expenses.
- Eliminate all check payments, framing the last check on the CEO's office wall (see following section).

- Introduce scanning technology for all those paper-based invoices from your minor suppliers (all major suppliers will become electronic feeds over time). The electronic image can then be sent to the budget holder for approval if there is no purchase matching order.
- Post remittances electronically onto your website in a secure area so that suppliers with their password can download them. This removes the need to send them by email or post.

INVEST IN AN ELECTRONIC ORDERING SYSTEM (PROCUREMENT SYSTEM)

Most accounting systems come with an integrated purchase order system. Some systems even enable the order to be priced using the suppliers' online price list and then e-mailed automatically to the preferred supplier providing the order is within the budget holder's delegated authority.

These systems should be purchased and implemented before the accounting team ever considers upgrading the general ledger (G/L). Increasingly today the G/L is only the holder of actuals with the targets, reporting, and drill down being provided in auxiliary systems.

This is a major exercise and one that should be researched immediately. There will be an organization that has your accounting system where the purchase order system is working well. Visit them and learn how to implement it.

INTRODUCE PURCHASE CARDS

It has been estimated that the average cost of the whole purchase cycle is between $65 and $85 per transaction. Pretty horrific when you realize that a high portion of your transactions are for minor amounts. Exhibit 1.1 shows a typical profile of AP invoices. The bulk of invoices can be for low value amounts, especially if consolidation invoices have not yet been organized. Remember it costs the same to process a $10 transaction as it does a $100,000 transaction. In addition, is it appropriate

Exhibit 1.1 AP Invoices That a Purchase Card Is Targeting

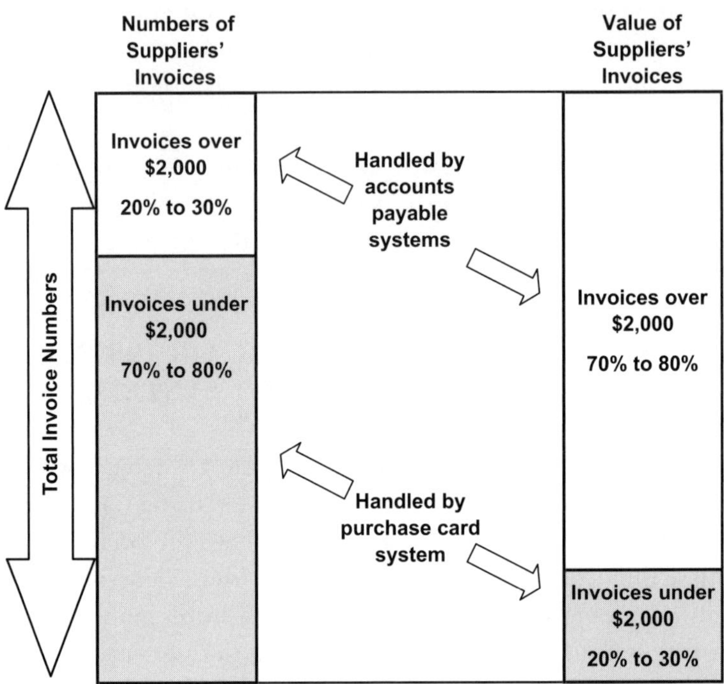

to request budget holders to raise an order in your purchase order system for a $20 transaction? Surely the system is designed around 100% compliance on material invoices.

Purchase cards are different from credit cards and are here to stay. There are three liability options (limited to genuine business, company has sole liability, and individual has sole liability). They offer more features than a standard credit card and often come with a Web-based expense claim system, free of charge! Purchase cards can have a variety of limits put on them (e.g., transactions types, total spend in a month, maximum amount of any one transaction). They work particularly well with high-value/low-volume items where you are purchasing through the same suppliers, because the supplier will be able to insert G/L code information on the transaction (e.g., organizations have told their national suppliers the relevant G/L code and department codes associated to each purchase card).

The purchase card is certainly a way for you to take control of processing these minor-value/high-volume transactions, where they cannot be organized through an electronic consolidated invoice.

For more information search the web for "purchase card" + "name of your bank."

> *My financial controller lobbied hard for a purchase card for all staff with all expenditures under $2,000 being processed via the card. The staff entered coding for purchases that were not already precoded by the supplier, and the approval process was on-line. Thousands of transactions were replaced by one electronic feed and one direct debit.*
>
> —CFO with blue chip international experience

The statements are sent electronically with additional vendor spend analysis and can be loaded directly into the G/L.

These systems have been working well in many companies for a number of years. All you need to do is contact your bank; they will have many better practice examples.

CUT OFF AP ON THE LAST WORKING DAY

If AP is held open you will find it difficult to complete prompt month-end reporting. What benefit does holding the AP open for one or two days do? A better practice is to cut off accounts payable at noon on the last working day. There are some organizations that cut off AP even earlier, e.g., day − 2 (see Exhibit 1.2). They manage this by more reliance on recurring reversing accruals supplemented by budget holders' accruals for the larger one-off amounts. They place timeliness above preciseness. This requires good communication to budget holders, and suppliers

Exhibit 1.2 Month-End Time Key

Day − 2	Day − 1	Day + 1	Day + 2
2nd to last working day	Last working day	First working day	2nd working day of new month

with the latter sending their invoices earlier through changing the billing timings (e.g., invoicing from 28th to 27th of following month).

> *Your month-end result doesn't become more accurate the longer you leave it. It just becomes more expensive to produce.*
>
> —CFO with blue chip international experience

CLOSING ACCRUALS ON DAY – 2

One accountant I have come across worked out that budget holders know little more about month-end purchase invoices at day + 2 than at day – 2. So, the accountant introduced accrual cut-off on day – 2, the day before month-end. Budget holders were required to send their last invoices for processing to meet the month-end AP cut-off by noon day – 2, which gave AP 24 hours to process them before the day – 1 AP cut-off. He also told them to prepare their accruals in the afternoon of day – 2, directly into the G/L. Cutting off accruals early recognizes that month-end invoices will not arrive miraculously by day + 1 or day + 2, so staff will need to phone some key suppliers to get accrual information regardless of when the cut-off is. Another point to note is that the accrual cut-off does not need to be after the AP cut-off. All that is required is a guarantee that all invoices approved for payment by budget holders within the deadline will be processed prior to the AP cut-off, or accrued directly by the AP team.

THROW AWAY THE COMPANY CHECKBOOK

For some time many companies have tried to change their suppliers' preferences for checks. The benefits from using direct credits (electronic funds transfers) as a payment method include lower costs, predictable cash flows, and fewer supplier phone calls over late payment. The question is how do you get the suppliers to give you their bank details? Some progressive companies are realizing that mail is not often read let alone acted upon. They have hired temporary staff to call suppliers. A participant with 99% of accounts paid by direct debit (and they are still not happy) calls suppliers and says "we would like to pay you but we cannot . . . pause . . . we are a modern company and pay all our accounts electronically. We have thrown away the checkbook and are at a loss as to how we can pay you because you have ignored our requests for your bank account details!" They say it is amazing to see the prompt response from the supplier's accounts receivable section.

In fact, one company cancelled its next check payment run and was able to obtain all suppliers' bank details who were in the payment run, within four hours of phoning! Do not believe a supplier's accounts receivable officer who says their organization does not accept electronic payments. A call by your CFO to the supplier's CFO will sort this out in ten minutes!

FREQUENT DIRECT CREDIT PAYMENT RUNS

Perform frequent direct credit payment runs; a better practice is to do these daily. This does not mean you are paying earlier because you still stipulate the agreed future payment date. All those suppliers who insist on written checks should be part of a once-in-every-six-week process. If I had my way they would also be requested to personally collect their checks. If they want a Dickens era method of payment, they should witness the Dickens era process!

MOUNT THE LAST SIGNED CHECK ON THE CEO'S OFFICE WALL

When I am giving a seminar I often paint the picture of a final closing ceremony for a company's checkbook. The checkbook is brought in on a black cushion on a silver platter, with a student dressed as Black Rod walking in front; you could even get musicians from a local music college. The supplier's checks are written and then the last check is written payable to "A.N. Other" for 99 cents and is then ceremoniously mounted in a golden frame and handed to the CEO for their office wall. The CEO will get much fun from this as they tell the story when their visitors ask "what is a check doing in a frame?" To make the final point to suppliers who insist on checks you can invite them all to come to the "last signing" function. See Appendix I for an example of a letter you may wish to send suppliers notifying them of the "mounting of the last check."

SPEED UP BUDGET HOLDER TURNAROUND ON APPROVING INVOICING

One company reports that it now has a 24-hour turnaround for all branches to approve all invoices that cannot be matched to order and have not been electronically receipted. If a branch manager does not achieve this on one single day in the month, they lose one month's performance bonus. The CEO was approached and got behind this initiative. This takes clever marketing, and is well worth the effort.

This change along with streamlining of supplier invoice timings will make a profound impact on processing volumes, helping smooth out the workload as shown in Exhibit 1.3.

SEND A WELCOME LETTER TO ALL NEW BUDGET HOLDERS AND PROVIDE THEM TRAINING

Imagine the goodwill created when a new employee, who is a budget holder, receives a welcome letter from the AP department asking for a slot to deliver a brief 20-minute training session for them within the next few weeks. See Appendix I for a draft letter.

Why wait till new employees are educated by the uneducated (budget holders who do not know or do not comply with the AP procedures)? Get in there first. Deliver a brief training presentation, including:

- Procedures to comply with
- Forms to complete
- Problems the AP systems can have when procedures are not followed and why they create a lot of wasted time
- How budget holders and the AP team can work most effectively together
- Presence of "shame and name" lists for which you point out "but this, of course, will not affect you!"

Exhibit 1.3 AP Invoice Processing Volumes During Month

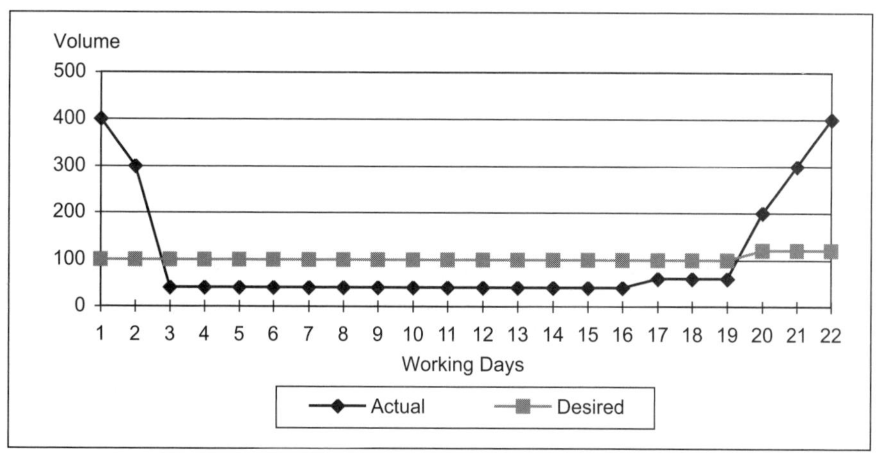

This presentation is best delivered in a casual format, on a laptop supplied by the IT function, or utilizing the budget holder's computer. You will find the laptop screen is big enough for up to four or five people.

INTRODUCE "SHAME AND NAME" LISTS TO FOCUS THE BUDGET HOLDERS

If you want to change human behavior you need to work on it for 12 weeks, and during this time the penny will drop. If you create a number of shame and name lists and publish these on the intranet and in a hard copy for the SMT you will, over 12 weeks, create change. I would recommend preparing a laminated card with all the league tables (i.e., lists of the culprits with the highest number of errors, exceptions, etc.) cut to fit the inside pocket of an SMT member's jacket. All the SMT needs to do is discuss the matter with the budget holders when they bump into them or, when they have time, make a few career-limiting phone calls to these non-compliant staff!

The suggested lists are:

- Budget holders with the most purchase invoices without a corresponding order
- Employees with late expense claims

- Budget holders with purchase invoices awaiting approval that are already outside the set "approval turnaround time"
- Budget holders who have missed deadlines

Remember, you will never want to invite all the budget holders to your Sunday afternoon barbeque, so do not worry about being unpopular with the non-compliant budget holder. You need to make one thing clear: Not complying with the accounting system requirements is going to be career limiting. In other words, there are three options open to these nonconforming budget holders: either you leave the organization, they leave the organization, or they change. You might, as one attendee pointed out, want to call these lists "Budget holders requiring further training."

REWARD GOOD BUDGET HOLDER BEHAVIOR

One accounting department gives a bottle of wine a month to the budget holder who provides the first complete month-end submission. This simple acknowledgment has provided the appropriate environment for timely submissions from budget holders.

HAVE A CLOSER RELATIONSHIP WITH YOUR MAIN SUPPLIERS

There are a number of ways a closer relationship with suppliers can improve processing. The more your key suppliers' systems are linked to yours the better. It is simply an issue of getting the two IT departments together around the same table.

Better practices include:

- Have all major suppliers link their systems with you. The supplier should provide electronic invoices that are already G/L coded. Set a target of receiving your top five suppliers' invoices all electronically within the next three months. You will need to get on the phone today to talk to your counterpart in the supplier. Do not leave this to the IT department to organize because they find this type of exercise personally challenging.

- Introduce consignment stock where the supplier is responsible for constant replenishment (e.g., core stock items [they need online access to relevant stock records], stationery, etc.).
- Ask for consolidated invoices from suppliers, especially utilities and stationery.
- Change invoicing cycles on all monthly accounts such as utilities, credit cards, and so forth (e.g., invoice cycle including transactions from May 26 to June 25 and being received by June 28). The accruals for these suppliers can then be a standard four or five business days depending on how the working days fall.
- Ask major suppliers to request an order from your budget holders —support this by not paying the supplier invoices unless there is a purchase order. Simply return the invoice to the supplier and ask them to attach the purchase order (they will not want to repeat this activity more than once).
- Ask large-volume, small-dollar suppliers to accept your purchase card.

USE SELF-GENERATED INVOICES (BUYER-CREATED INVOICES)

The supplier's shipping document is used to determine the quantity of goods supplied, or in the case of a weigh-bridge process, the actual weight. The agreed weight is then multiplied by the agreed purchase contract price to calculate the amount owed. The customer then direct credits the supplier, who is also sent an electronic invoice. The invoice contains all required details such as quantity, date of service, taxes, value, total payable, and a unique invoice number using, say, the first three letters of your company, two letters of their's, and four numbers (e.g., Invoice #dsbbd1234).

CHAPTER 2

Timely Month-End Reporting—By Working Day 3 or Less

It never ceases to amaze me how the senior management team (SMT) can manage a business without receiving monthly reports in a timely manner. CEOs need to demand a complete and radical change if they are to free management and accountants from the shackles of a "zero sum" process—reporting last month's results halfway through the following month. Here are the facts:

- Companies in the United States are now providing commentary and numbers by the first working day.
- Companies are migrating to closing the month on the same day each month (i.e., months are either five or four weeks ending on Friday, Saturday, etc.).
- In leading companies the SMT are letting go of report writing—they are no longer *rewriting* reports, having informed the Board that they concur with the writer's findings but it is a delegated report!

See Appendix B for the checklist of implementation steps to reduce month-end reporting time frames.

RATING SCALE FOR MONTH-END REPORTING

The following rating scale shows the time frames of month-end reporting across the 4,000 corporate accountants I have presented to in the last five years.

Exceptional	Outstanding	Above Average	Average
One working day	Two working days	Three to four working days	Five working days

BENEFITS OF QUICK MONTH-END REPORTING

As a CFO friend of mine said "every day spent producing month-end reports is a day less spent on analysis and projects." There are a larger number of benefits to management and the finance team of quick reporting, and these include:

Benefits to Management	Benefits to the Finance Team
So that reporting plays a bigger part in the decision-making process	Staff are more productive as efficiencies are locked in and bottlenecks are tackled
Reduction in detail and length of reports	Many month-end traditional processes are out of date and inefficient and thus are removed
Reduced cost to organization of month-end (m/e) reporting	Happier staff with higher morale and increased job satisfaction
Management spends more time focusing on current month's operations	Finance staff focus is now being a business partner to the budget holder, helping them to shape the future
Greater budget holder ownership (e.g., accruals, variance analysis, coding,	The team has time to be involved in more rewarding activities such as

Benefits to Management *(Continued)*	**Benefits to the Finance Team**
corrections during month, better understanding, etc.)	quarterly rolling forecasts, project work, and so forth
Budget holders forced to adopt better practices	Leads to a very quick year-end

IMPACT OF A QUICK MONTH-END ON FINANCE TEAM WORKLOAD

The significance of month-end reporting can be seen from this comparison of three companies reporting in different time frames. The analysis of more than 500 finance teams is that the quick reporting accounting teams are far more advanced in many other areas. They should be, because they have much more time on their hands, as shown in Exhibit 2.1.

It is important to cost out to management and the Board the month-end reporting process. When doing this exercise, remember that senior management barely have 32 weeks of productive time when you remove holidays, sick leave, traveling time, and routine management meetings. Thus a cost of $1,000 per senior management day is not unrealistic.

Such an analysis can be easily performed by the management accountant in 30 minutes, and will be valuable in the sale process of changing month-end reporting time frames. Exhibit 2.2 shows the time

Exhibit 2.1 Impact of Quick Month-Ends

Tasks	**Day 1**	**Quick m/e**	**Slow m/e**
	No. of working days a month		
Month-end reporting	**1**	**4**	**9**
Remaining days	**21**	**18**	**13**
Percentage of extra time for project work and daily routines	**60%**	**40%**	**0%**
Based on a 22 working day month	time	time	

Exhibit 2.2 Senior Management Time Invested in Month-Ends

	Days
Drafting papers	2 to 4
Review and redrafting	1 to 2
Total days of effort by each unit	3 to 6
Say 5 business units	15 to 30
Support function reports	10 to 15
Review by CEO etc. and redrafting	1 to 2
Total senior management effort each month	26 to 47

invested in an organization with 5 business units with around 500 to 700 staff.

TIGHTEN UP ON MONTH-END CUT-OFFS

It is difficult to have a quick month-end when one is leaving accounts payable (AP) and accounts receivable (AR) open for one or two working days into the next period. Both AP and AR should be cut-off on the last working day.

PUSHING PROCESSING BACK FROM MONTH-END

It is worth looking at the processing carried out in the last few days before cut-off. Most "quick reporting" companies have avoided payment runs at month-end that only serve to stimulate budget holders to release invoices at the last minute. Smoothing out AP and AR transactional flow and reducing AP transaction volumes have been covered in Chapters 1 and 8 respectively.

BAN SPRING CLEANING AT MONTH-END

Make it clear to budget holders that you have delegated the responsibility of maintaining their part of the general ledger (G/L) to budget holders. Budget holders are expected to monitor their department in the

G/L and ask for any reclassifications during the month. Make it clear that there is no spring cleaning at month-end for any misclassified postings.

MOVING PERIOD ENDING TO NEAREST WEEKEND

Julius Caesar gave us the calendar we use today. It is not a good business tool because it creates 12 dramas a year for the finance team, with each month being slightly different.

Between four and five months every year will end on a weekend, and you may find the month-end processes are smoother for these months. Why not close-off on the last or nearest Friday/Saturday of every month like many U.S. companies do? The benefits of this include precise four- or five-week months, which make comparisons more meaningful, and there is less impact on the working week as the systems are rolled over at the weekend.

Staff know intuitively what to do and there is no need for month-end instructions other than saying we are closing on the Friday 28th or Friday 2nd. By making this change you are beginning to create "12 nonevents a month," the "Eldorado" of all corporate accountants.

Closing off at the weekend can be done for all sectors; some will require more liaison than others. It would also make a big difference in the public and not-for-profit sectors.

You simply present to the Board June's result and balance sheet. You do not need to highlight the July 2 close. At year-end the missing two or extra two days of income and balance sheet movement will be taken up in the auditor's "overs and unders" schedule!

REFOCUS COMMENTS ON THE YEAR-TO-DATE VARIANCE (UNTIL QUARTERLY ROLLING PLANNING IS INSTIGATED)

How often do you find that the variance commentary is not very useful? Companies are now focusing variance analysis commentary more on the year-to-date variance. The only companies that get meaningful, month variance, commentary are those that have migrated to quarterly rolling planning, where targets for the next three months are set the last month before the quarter starts. This is explained in Chapter 14.

How we as accountants thought one could set realistic targets month by month for periods as far as 15 months forward is beyond reason. Monthly variances reporting is a storytelling activity in most organizations, taking budget holders too much time. Budget holders often have no idea of the real reasons for the variance because they do not know what makes up the monthly target. In many cases, the commentary often starts with "this is a timing difference."

LIMIT BUDGET HOLDERS' MONTHLY "VARIANCE TO BUDGET" REPORT TO ONE PAGE

How big would the pile of reports be if every month-end report was stacked up? How much would this pile represent in management and staff time? How much does it cost the organization every month? In many cases the cost is horrific. I once walked into a CFO's office to find a pile of reports over one foot high. "What are these?" I asked. "They are the budget holders' month-end reports" was the reply. "Wow, there is a lot of information and would have cost over $60,000 to prepare, what do you do with it?" "Nothing." "Surely you must use it for the consolidated variance analysis!" "No, it is too much information; I simply ring them up."

Thus $60,000 of management time was spent simply as a stewardship function. You have a budget so you must do a report.

A better practice is a one-page budget holder report, taking no more than half an hour to prepare. Why prepare any more when the CEO should be discussing important issues during a month rather than at the end of the month when the horse has well and truly bolted?

ISSUE A "FLASH REPORT" AT THE END OF DAY ONE

Issue a flash report on the profit and loss statement (P/L) bottom-line to the CEO stating a level of accuracy of, say, ±5%. Immediately inform the CEO of any real problems with the flash report numbers in the next couple of days. You may find that a flash report is not required if you can report within three working days. (See Exhibit 2.3 for an example of a flash report.)

It is important not to provide too many lines because you may find yourself with another variance report on your hands if you are unlucky to have a CEO who fails to look at the big picture. Remember to state your degree of accuracy (e.g., ±5%, ±10%). Never attempt a flash report until the AP, AR, and accrual cut-offs have been successfully moved back

Exhibit 2.3 Flash Report Given to the CEO During the First Working Day

		This month $000s			
		Act	**Target**	**Var**	
Revenue					
	Revenue 1	5,560	5,660	(100)	⇔
	Revenue 2	3,560	3,450	110	⇔
	Revenue 3	2,450	1,800	650	✓
	Other revenue	2,250	2,350	(100)	⇔
Total Revenue		13,820	13,260	(100)	⇔
	Less cost of sales				
		(11,500)	(11,780)	280	⇔
Gross Profit		2,320	1,480	180	✓
Expenses					
	Expense 1	780	760	(20)	⇔
	Expense 2	540	520	(20)	⇔
	Expense 3	220	200	(20)	✖
	Expense 4	180	160	(20)	✖
	Other expenses	470	620	150	✓
Total Expenses		1,790	1,860	70	⇔
Surplus/(Deficit)		530	(380)	910	✓

Highlights:

1. Xxxxxxxxxxxxxxxxxxxxxxxxxxxxxxxxxxxxxxxx xxxxxxxxxxxxxxxxxxxxxxxxxxxxxxxxxxxxxxxxxxxxxxxxxxxxxxxxxxxxxxxxxxxx xxxxxxxxxxxxxxx xxxxxxxxx xxxxxxx xxxxxxxxxxxx xxxxxxxxxxxxxxxxxxxxxxxxxxxxxxxxxx
2. Xxxxxxxxxxxxxxxxxxxxxxxxxxxxxxxxxxxxxxxx xxxxxxxxxxxxxxxxxxxxxxxxxxxxxxxxxxxxxxxxxxxxxxxxxxxxxxxxxxxxxxxxxxxx xxxxxxxxxxxxxxx xxxxxxxxx xxxxxxx xxxxxxxxxxxx xxxxxxxxxxxxxxxxxxxxxxxxxxxxxxxxxx
3. Xxxxxxxxxxxxxxxxxxxxxxxxxxxxxxxxxxxxxxxx xxxxxxxxxxxxxxxxxxxxxxxxxxxxxxxxxxxxxxxxxxxxxxxxxxxxxxxxxxxxxxxxxxxx xxxxxxxxxxxxxxx xxxxxxxxx xxxxxxx xxxxxxxxxxxx xxxxxxxxxxxxxxxxxxxxxxxxxxxxxxxxxx
4. Xxxxxxxxxxxxxxxxxxxxxxxxxxxxxxxxxxxxxxxx xxxxxxxxxxxxxxxxxxxxxxxxxxxxxxxxxxxxxxxxxxxxxxxxxxxxxxxxxxxxxxxxxxxx xxxxxxxxxxxxxxx xxxxxxxxx xxxxxxx xxxxxxxxxxxx xxxxxxxxxxxxxxxxxxxxxxxxxxxxxxxxxx

to the last working day of the month. Otherwise you will be using the accruals to change final numbers so they can closely match your flash numbers! A practice I would not recommend.

RUN A WORKSHOP TO "POST-IT" RE-ENGINEER MONTH-END REPORTING

Re-engineering month-end reporting can be a complex and expensive task or a relatively easy one; the choice is yours. Many organizations start off by bringing in consultants to process map the existing procedures. This is a futile exercise, because why spend a lot of money documenting a process you are about to radically alter, and when it is done only the consultants will understand the resulting data-flow diagrams!

The answer is to "Post-it" re-engineer your month-end procedures in a workshop (see Exhibit 2.4 for an outline of the workshop).

Exhibit 2.4 Workshop on Implementing Quick Monthly Reporting

Agenda and Outline of the Quick Month-End Workshop

Date and Time: xxxxxx

Location: xxxxxx

Suggested Attendees: All those involved in month-end including accounts payable, accounts receivables, financial and management accountants, representatives from teams who interface with month-end routines, e.g., someone from IT, payroll, etc.)

Learning Outcomes:

Attendees after this workshop will be able to:

- Discuss and explain to management why their organization should have quicker month-end reporting
- Use better practices to streamline their current bottlenecks
- Use a step-by-step implementation framework
- Describe better practice month-end routines
- Recall all agreements made at the workshop (these will be documented)

9:00 A.M.	Welcome by Financial Controller
9:10 A.M.	**Setting the scene**—a review of better practices among accounting teams that are delivering swift reporting, topics covered include: • What is quick reporting?

Exhibit 2.4 *(Continued)*

9:10 A.M. *(continued)*	• Benefits of quick reporting to management and the finance team • Better practice month-end procedures—stories • Current performance gap between xxxxxxxxx and better practice • Precision versus timeliness • Latest developments—day one reporting and virtual closing **Senior management and a selection of budget holders (who are based locally) will be invited to attend this session "setting the scene"**
9:50 A.M.	**Agreement on the current key bottlenecks of month-end reporting presented by Financial Controller** • Current cost estimate of month-end reporting • Human costs • What we are doing well • We need to work within existing systems • Goal is "twelve nonevents" each year
10:05 A.M.	**Workshop 1 on when activities should start and finish** where separate teams look at the different issues (we will cover month-end close-off of the various teams, listing bottlenecks within and between teams, reporting and forecasting issues, reconciliation issues, etc.)
10:30 A.M.	Morning break
10:45 A.M.	**Workshop 1** continues
11:00 A.M.	Feedback from work groups and action plan agreed (date and responsibility)
11:20 A.M.	**Workshop 2** to analyze the month-end procedures using Post-its (yellow—accounts payable, red—production, green—accounts receivable, purple—management accounting team, blue—financial accounting team, pink—CAPEX, etc.)
12:30 P.M.	Lunch
1:15 P.M.	**Workshop 2** to analyze the month-end procedures using Post-its continues
2.00 P.M.	Feedback and pulling it together, participants will document agreed changes and individuals will be encouraged to take responsibility for implementing the steps
2:30 P.M.	Afternoon break
2:45 P.M.	**Implementing a quick month-end—the implementation plan, the typical steps, and the issues to look at**

(continues)

Exhibit 2.4 *(Continued)*

3:00 P.M.	**Workshop 3 to set out the appropriate implementation steps to implement quick reporting.** Each team prepares a short presentation of the key steps they are committed to making (teams will use PowerPoint on laptops)
4:00 P.M.	Each team presents reports to the group on what changes they are going to implement and when. They can also raise any issues they still have. **Those senior management teams and budget holders who attended the first session will be invited to attend this session**
4:45 P.M.	Wrap up of workshop by Financial Controller
5:00 P.M.	Finish

The "Post-it" re-engineering process is simple—all it requires is:

- Each team lists all their processes on to the "Post-it" stickers allocated to them (as set out in Exhibit 2.5) prior to the workshop and documented as set out in Exhibit 2.6.
- In a workshop environment the teams gather together and start off by explaining what better month-end procedures are.
- The "Post-its" are placed in time order under column headings day − 2, day − 1, day + 1, day + 2, and so forth using a white board (the "Post-its" do not stick well to walls!).
- A movie voucher is given to each workshop attendee who points out a process that can be removed as it is not necessary (they were

Exhibit 2.5 Allocation of "Post-it" Stickers

AP	Yellow
AR	Green
Production	Red
Financial Accounting Team	Blue
Management Accounting Team	Purple
Capex	Pink
Payroll	Etc.

Exhibit 2.6 "Post-it" Stickers

+2 Close-off
Accounts Payable

done because they were done last month)—each one removed is like finding gold because it means less work, fewer steps.

- Reorganize the key processes and bottlenecks based on better practice (e.g., AP close-off occurring at noon on the last working day) and now reschedule tasks that can be done earlier. You will find it hard to justify any task needing to be done after day 3!

Rules for "Post-it" stickers include:

- One procedure per "Post-it" sticker
- State when it is done—time scale is −2, −1 (last working day), +1 (first working day), +2, etc.
- Write in big letters (must be seen from 15 feet)

KEY ACTIVITIES OF A THREE WORKING DAY MONTH-END

The key activities of a three working day month-end include:

Day − 3 and earlier	Day − 2	Day − 1	Day + 1	Day + 2 and 3
Payroll accrual finalized Depreciation finalized G/L accounts reconciled Daily bank a/c reconciliation (DBR)	Close off accruals DBR	Close off AP, AR, work in progress (WIP), WIP to finished goods, production for last day, time sheets by noon First close of G/L Numbers available to budget holders by 5 P.M. DBR	Flash report by 5 P.M. to CEO Second close of G/L Budget holders complete their two-page report DBR	Draft report Quality assurance procedures Report preparation Issue report DBR

CASE STUDY: HOW QUICK CHANGE CAN BE IF YOU FOLLOW THESE LESSONS

The CFO of a famous entertainment center in Australia brought 20 of his team along to a session I ran in September. They all went back and re-engineered their month-end. On November 3, we were talking over the phone and he had the final accounts in his hand—day three reporting within six weeks! The CFO had for years been used to very quick reporting with a U.S. company, so you can imagine his frustration when he first arrived at his new position. The "Post-it" re-engineering process unlocked the potential he knew was there.

A Financial Controller, of a radio station conglomerate, flew all her management accountants from around the country for a one-day "Post-it" re-engineering workshop. For some it was the first time they had met. The workshop was a fun day and members could laugh at the bottlenecks that they in some cases had created. Excel spreadsheets were tossed out along with other low-value month-end activities. I rang the CFO two weeks later on June 2 and asked how the month-end was going, she replied, "What do you mean going? It is finished." The team had achieved two-day month-end reporting, down from day 8 reporting in two weeks.

CHAPTER 3

Make the Monthly Reports Worth Reading

Many management reports are not a management tool; they are merely memorandums of information. As a management tool, management reports should encourage timely action in the right direction, by reporting on those activities the Board, management, and staff need to focus on. The old adage "what gets measured gets done" still holds true.

USEFUL RULES ON REPORTING

What is good monthly reporting? Good month-end reporting should:

- Not be delayed for detail—finished by the third working day is the better practice mark (exceptional organizations are doing this in one working day)
- Be consistent between months—with judgment calls and reporting formats
- Be a "true and fair" view and be error free
- Be concise—less than nine pages
- Report major category headings only writing to no more than 10 to 15 lines

- Have an icon system to highlight major variances
- Be a merging of numbers, graphs, and comments on the one page, thus doing away with the essay in front of the financial statements
- Have graphs that say something—a title that describes the main issue, a trend going back at least 15 months (neither your operations nor your graphs should start at the beginning of the year)
- When finished make them available to all the finance team!

Board members and the senior management team (SMT) have complained for years that they are sent too much information, yet we still insist on preparing 20+ page month-end financials. The cost of preparing, analyzing, and checking this information is a major burden on the accounting function, creating significant time delays and consequently minimizing the value of these financials.

Have a separate reporting line if the category is over 20% of total revenue or expenditure, whichever is relevant (e.g., show the revenue line if revenue category is over 20% of total revenue). If the category is between 15% and 20%, look at it and make an assessment as to whether a separate reporting line is merited.

Set up an icon system to highlight variances. A suggested way is to ignore all variances less than a certain amount. For all variances over this amount, allow a tolerance of, say, plus or minus 10% and show an icon for this, and then show as a positive or negative any variance over 10%. For example, if threshold is $10,000, then an $8,000 negative variance would not have an icon; if the variance is $15,000 over spent but it is only 3% of total expected, then show it is within tolerance; if variance is $15,000 over spent and is 12% of total expected, show a negative icon.

REPORTING A BUSINESS UNIT'S PERFORMANCE

Exhibit 3.1 is an example of a business unit's report. The profit and loss statement (P&L) is summarized in 10 to 15 lines. Two graphs are shown: One looks at the trend of the major expenditure items, and the other looks at revenue of a profit center typically contrasting financial and nonfinancial numbers is useful (e.g., tourist numbers against personnel costs). The notes are the main highlights and action steps to take.

Exhibit 3.1 Reporting a Business Unit's Performance

Operating Statement for the period ending 31 January 20XX

Month $000s					Year-To-Date $000s				Full Year $000s	
Act	Bud	Var			Act	Bud	Var		Budget	Forecast
				Revenue						
1,430	1,380	50	⇔	Revenue 1	5,720	5,520	200	⇔	17,200	16,600
1,430	1,380	50	⇔	**Total Revenue**	5,720	5,520	200	⇔	17,200	16,600
				Less						
267	215	(52)	✖	Commissions	1,066	860	(206)	✖	3,200	2,600
1,164	1,165	(2)		**Gross Profit**	4,654	4,660	(6)		14,000	14,000
				Expenses						
278	262	(16)	⇔	Expense 1	1,240	1,046	(194)	✖	3,300	3,100
218	212	(6)		Expense 2	672	848	176	✓	2,600	2,500
188	182	(6)		Expense 3	752	728	(24)	⇔	2,300	2,200
158	152	(6)		Expense 4	632	608	(24)	⇔	1,900	1,800
128	122	(6)		Expense 5	512	488	(24)	⇔	1,500	1,500
51	60	9		Expense 6	673	642	(32)	⇔	1,000	1,200
1,020	990	(30)	⇔	**Total Expenses**	4,080	3,960	(120)	⇔	12,200	11,900
144	175	(32)	✖	**Surplus/(Deficit)**	574	700	(126)	✖	1,800	2,100

Major Costs ($000s)

Commissions, Expense 1, Expense 2, Expense 3

Visitor numbers, Operational wages

Highlights:

1. Xxxxxxxxxxxxxxxxxxxxxxxxxxxxxxxxxxxxxxxxxx xxxxxxxxxxxxxxxxxxxxxxxxxxxxxxxxxxxxxxxxxxxxxxxxxxxxxxxxxxxxxxxxxxxxxxxxxx xxxxxxxxxxxxxxx xxxxxxxxx xxxxxxx xxxxxxxxxxx xxxxxxxxxxxxxxxxxxxxxxxxxxxxxxx
2. Xxxxxxxxxxxxxxxxxxxxxxxxxxxxxxxxxxxxxxxxxx xxxxxxxxxxxxxxxxxxxxxxxxxxxxxxxxxxxxxxxxxxxxxxxxxxxxxxxxxxxxxxxxxxxxxxxxxx xxxxxxxxxxxxxxx xxxxxxxxx xxxxxxx xxxxxxxxxxx xxxxxxxxxxxxxxxxxxxxxxxxxxxxxxx
3. Xxxxxxxxxxxxxxxxxxxxxxxxxxxxxxxxxxxxxxxxxx xxxxxxxxxxxxxxxxxxxxxxxxxxxxxxxxxxxxxxxxxxxxxxxxxxxxxxxxxxxxxxxxxxxxxxxxxx xxxxxxxxxxxxxxx xxxxxxxxx xxxxxxx xxxxxxxxxxx xxxxxxxxxxxxxxxxxxxxxxxxxxxxxxx
4. Xxxxxxxxxxxxxxxxxxxxxxxxxxxxxxxxxxxxxxxxxx xxxxxxxxxxxxxxxxxxxxxxxxxxxxxxxxxxxxxxxxxxxxxxxxxxxxxxxxxxxxxxxxxxxxxxxxxxx xxxxxxxxxxxxxxx xxxxxxxxx xxxxxxx xxxxxxxxxxx xxxxxxxxxxxxxxxxxxxxxxxxxxxxxxx

No other commentary is provided on the business unit's P/L. The business unit manager can discuss other issues in person with the CEO.

Each business unit may have up to five different graphs, and the two graphs that show the most pertinent information are shown in that month's report. Each business unit report will look slightly different. The titles of the key lines and graphs may be different.

REPORTING A CONSOLIDATED PROFIT AND LOSS ACCOUNT

Exhibit 3.2 is an example of reporting a consolidated P&L. This report summarizes the P&L in 10 to 15 lines. Instead of looking at consolidated costs such as personnel, premises, and so forth, the report summarizes the divisions'/business units' expenditure. The graphs look at

Exhibit 3.2 Reporting a Consolidated P&L

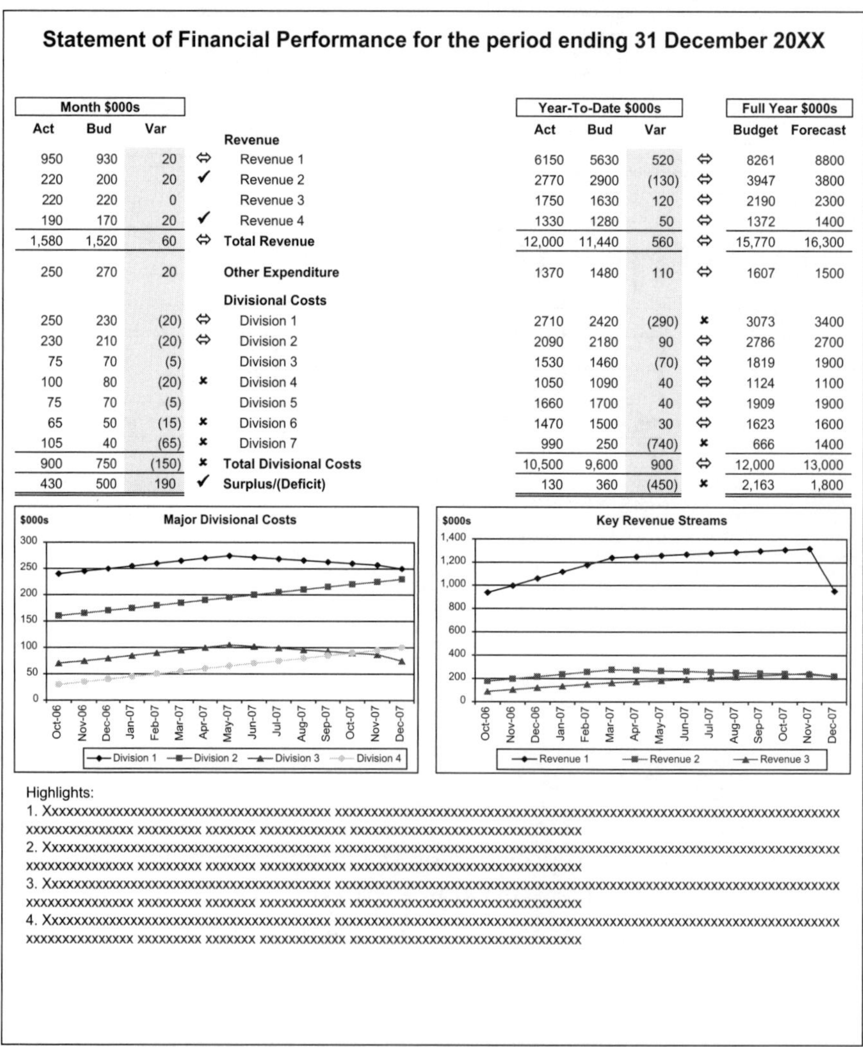

Statement of Financial Performance for the period ending 31 December 20XX

Month $000s					Year-To-Date $000s				Full Year $000s	
Act	Bud	Var			Act	Bud	Var		Budget	Forecast
				Revenue						
950	930	20	⇔	Revenue 1	6150	5630	520	⇔	8261	8800
220	200	20	✓	Revenue 2	2770	2900	(130)	⇔	3947	3800
220	220	0		Revenue 3	1750	1630	120	⇔	2190	2300
190	170	20	✓	Revenue 4	1330	1280	50	⇔	1372	1400
1,580	1,520	60	⇔	**Total Revenue**	12,000	11,440	560	⇔	15,770	16,300
250	270	20		**Other Expenditure**	1370	1480	110	⇔	1607	1500
				Divisional Costs						
250	230	(20)	⇔	Division 1	2710	2420	(290)	✗	3073	3400
230	210	(20)	⇔	Division 2	2090	2180	90	⇔	2786	2700
75	70	(5)		Division 3	1530	1460	(70)	⇔	1819	1900
100	80	(20)	✗	Division 4	1050	1090	40	⇔	1124	1100
75	70	(5)		Division 5	1660	1700	40	⇔	1909	1900
65	50	(15)	✗	Division 6	1470	1500	30	⇔	1623	1600
105	40	(65)	✗	Division 7	990	250	(740)	✗	666	1400
900	750	(150)	✗	**Total Divisional Costs**	10,500	9,600	900	⇔	12,000	13,000
430	500	190	✓	**Surplus/(Deficit)**	130	360	(450)	✗	2,163	1,800

Highlights:

1. Xxxxxxxxxxxxxxxxxxxxxxxxxxxxxxxxxxxxxxxx xxxxxxxxxxxxxxxxxxxxxxxxxxxxxxxxxxxxxxxxxxxxxxxxxxxxxxxxxxxxxxxxxxxxxxxx xxxxxxxxxxxxxx xxxxxxxxx xxxxxxx xxxxxxxxxxx xxxxxxxxxxxxxxxxxxxxxxxxxxxxxxx
2. Xxxxxxxxxxxxxxxxxxxxxxxxxxxxxxxxxxxxxxxx xxxxxxxxxxxxxxxxxxxxxxxxxxxxxxxxxxxxxxxxxxxxxxxxxxxxxxxxxxxxxxxxxxxxxxxx xxxxxxxxxxxxxx xxxxxxxxx xxxxxxx xxxxxxxxxxx xxxxxxxxxxxxxxxxxxxxxxxxxxxxxxx
3. Xxxxxxxxxxxxxxxxxxxxxxxxxxxxxxxxxxxxxxxx xxxxxxxxxxxxxxxxxxxxxxxxxxxxxxxxxxxxxxxxxxxxxxxxxxxxxxxxxxxxxxxxxxxxxxxx xxxxxxxxxxxxxx xxxxxxxxx xxxxxxx xxxxxxxxxxx xxxxxxxxxxxxxxxxxxxxxxxxxxxxxxx
4. Xxxxxxxxxxxxxxxxxxxxxxxxxxxxxxxxxxxxxxxx xxxxxxxxxxxxxxxxxxxxxxxxxxxxxxxxxxxxxxxxxxxxxxxxxxxxxxxxxxxxxxxxxxxxxxxx xxxxxxxxxxxxxx xxxxxxxxx xxxxxxx xxxxxxxxxxx xxxxxxxxxxxxxxxxxxxxxxxxxxxxxxx

the trends in major revenue and expenditure. A number of different graphs will be maintained and the most pertinent will be shown. The notes are the main highlights and action steps to take. There is no other commentary on the P/L. The icons are fully automated based on preset criteria.

REPORTING THE BALANCE SHEET

Exhibit 3.3 is an example of a summarized balance sheet with rounded numbers in millions. Surely the key is to give management a clear view of the relative sizes of the major assets and liabilities rather than precision (e.g., tell management debtors are $28 million rather than

Exhibit 3.3. Balance Sheet Example

Statement of Financial Position as of 30 April 20XX

	Month-End Actual	Last Month Actual
Bank and Cash	4,000	5,800
Accounts Receivables	2,000	1,800
Inventory	2,000	1,800
Fixed Assets	9,000	8,800
Other Non-Current Assets	1,000	800
Total Assets	18,000	19,000
Accounts Payable & Accruals	(3,500)	(2,500)
Other Liabilities	(1,000)	(800)
Net Assets	13,500	15,700
Funded by		
Current Year Profit	2,700	2,500
Accumulated Funds	10,800	13,200
Total Equity	13,500	15,700

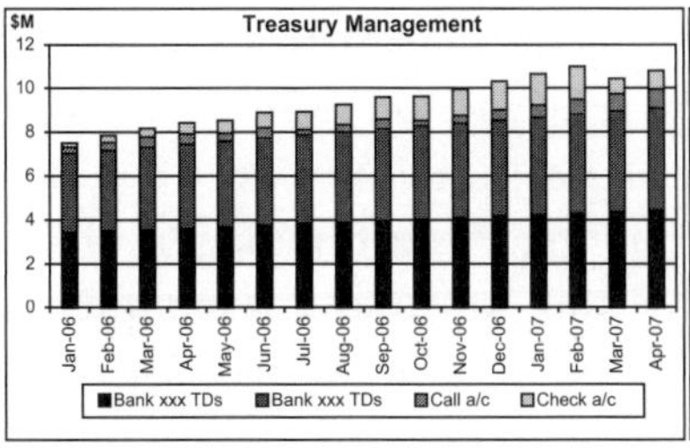

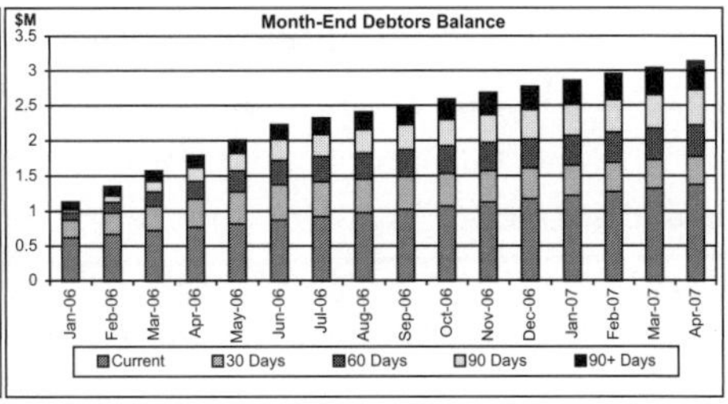

Highlights:

$27,867,234; they will remember $28 million but will have forgotten the other number). The detailed balance sheet, balanced to the cent, should be left to the accountants' working papers.

The balance sheet should have no more than ten categories. Each additional category serves to confuse management and benefits only the accountants. If you can draft the balance sheet in less than ten categories, all the better.

The graphs focus on the main balance sheet issues such as debtors aging, stock levels, and cash. The notes cover the main highlights and action steps to take. There should be no other commentary about the balance sheet.

REPORTING A QUARTERLY ROLLING ACCRUAL FORECAST

Exhibit 3.4 shows the year-end position and the remaining 18 months forward. The expenditure graph looks at the three primary expenditure lines and highlights where budget holders are playing the old game of locking in slack. The revenue graph highlights the reasonableness of the sales teams' projections.

SNAPSHOT OF ALL PROJECTS CURRENTLY STARTED

Project reporting can be a huge burden on a project team, consuming significant amounts of time, creating documents that are too long, poorly structured, and often lacking quick reference action points.

Project management software was first designed for very complex projects such as "putting a man on the moon." Project managers charging in excess of $200 per hour for their time can spend it completing endless progress schedules. As a rule of thumb, if more than 5% of the project time is spent on reporting, balance has been lost. Project reporting is best managed by progressively updating a PowerPoint presentation. This means that at any time the project team can give an interesting and informative progress update.

Exhibit 3.4 Quarterly Rolling Forecast

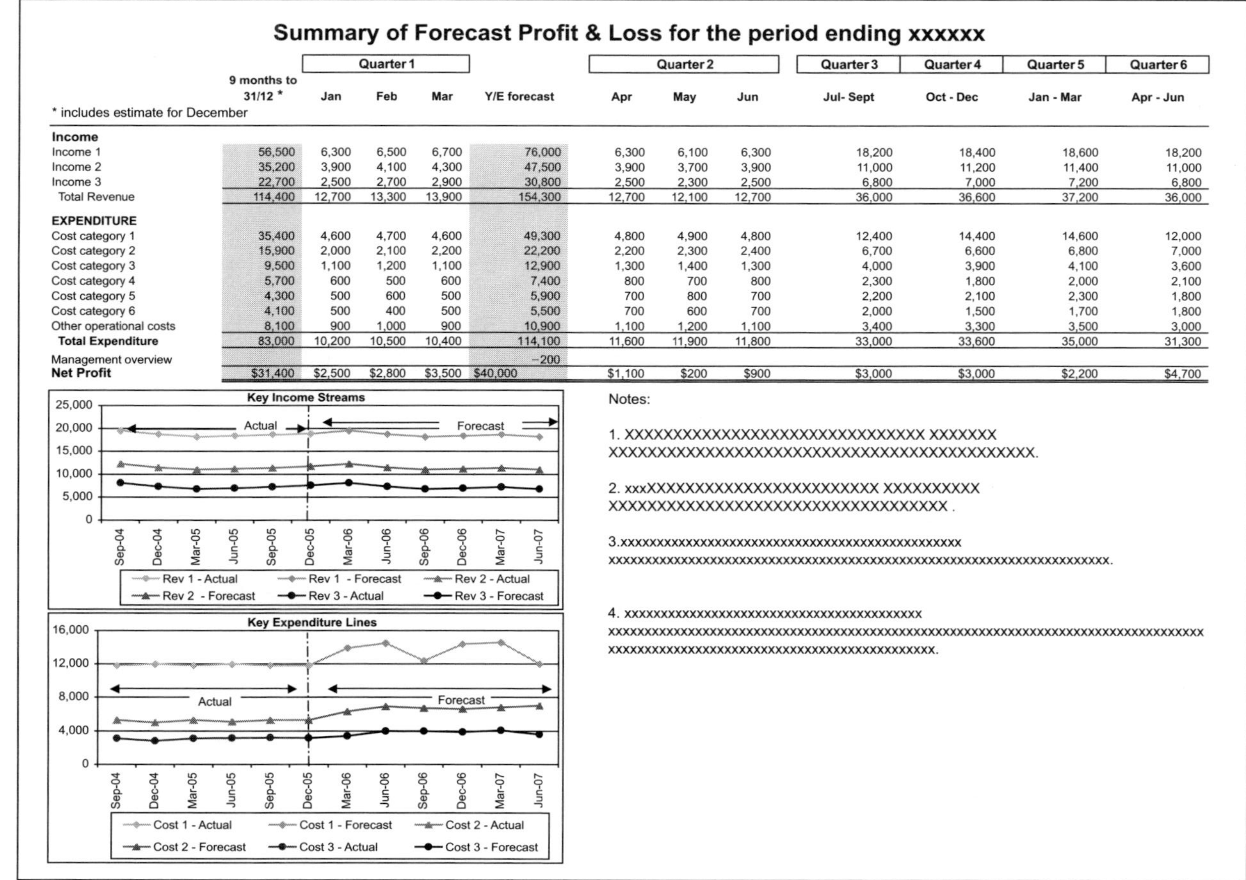

Summary of Forecast Profit & Loss for the period ending xxxxxx

	9 months to 31/12 *	Quarter 1 Jan	Feb	Mar	Y/E forecast	Quarter 2 Apr	May	Jun	Quarter 3 Jul- Sept	Quarter 4 Oct - Dec	Quarter 5 Jan - Mar	Quarter 6 Apr - Jun
* includes estimate for December												
Income												
Income 1	56,500	6,300	6,500	6,700	76,000	6,300	6,100	6,300	18,200	18,400	18,600	18,200
Income 2	35,200	3,900	4,100	4,300	47,500	3,900	3,700	3,900	11,000	11,200	11,400	11,000
Income 3	22,700	2,500	2,700	2,900	30,800	2,500	2,300	2,500	6,800	7,000	7,200	6,800
Total Revenue	114,400	12,700	13,300	13,900	154,300	12,700	12,100	12,700	36,000	36,600	37,200	36,000
EXPENDITURE												
Cost category 1	35,400	4,600	4,700	4,600	49,300	4,800	4,900	4,800	12,400	14,400	14,600	12,000
Cost category 2	15,900	2,000	2,100	2,200	22,200	2,200	2,300	2,400	6,700	6,600	6,800	7,000
Cost category 3	9,500	1,100	1,200	1,100	12,900	1,300	1,400	1,300	4,000	3,900	4,100	3,600
Cost category 4	5,700	600	500	600	7,400	800	700	800	2,300	1,800	2,000	2,100
Cost category 5	4,300	500	600	500	5,900	700	800	700	2,200	2,100	2,300	1,800
Cost category 6	4,100	500	400	500	5,500	700	600	700	2,000	1,500	1,700	1,800
Other operational costs	8,100	900	1,000	900	10,900	1,100	1,200	1,100	3,400	3,300	3,500	3,000
Total Expenditure	83,000	10,200	10,500	10,400	114,100	11,600	11,900	11,800	33,000	33,600	35,000	31,300
Management overview					−200							
Net Profit	$31,400	$2,500	$2,800	$3,500	$40,000	$1,100	$200	$900	$3,000	$3,000	$2,200	$4,700

Notes:

1. XXXXXXXXXXXXXXXXXXXXXXXXXXXXXXXXXX XXXXXXX XXXXXXXXXXXXXXXXXXXXXXXXXXXXXXXXXXXXXXXXXXXXX.

2. xxxXXXXXXXXXXXXXXXXXXXXXXXXX XXXXXXXXXX XXXXXXXXXXXXXXXXXXXXXXXXXXXXXXXXXXXXXX .

3.xxxxxxxxxxxxxxxxxxxxxxxxxxxxxxxxxxxxxxxxxxxxxxxxxx xxxxxxxxxxxxxxxxxxxxxxxxxxxxxxxxxxxxxxxxxxxxxxxxxxxxxxxxxxxxxxxxxxxxxxxxxxxxxxxxxxxxx.

4. xxxxxxxxxxxxxxxxxxxxxxxxxxxxxxxxxxxxxxxxxxxxxx xxxxxxxxxxxxxxxxxxxxxxxxxxxxxxxxxxxxxxxxxxxxxxxxxxxxxxxxxxxxxxxxxxxxxxxxxxxxxxxxxxxxxxxxxxxxxxxxxxxxxxx xxxxxxxxxxxxxxxxxxxxxxxxxxxxxxxxxxxxxxxxxxxxxxxxxxxx.

It is only worthwhile measuring metrically—by that I mean measuring accurately without estimate—those performance measures that are so fundamental to the organization that they affect nearly every aspect of its operation (e.g., the key performance indicators which are explained in Chapter 18).

"Project progress" certainly does not fit into this category and hence I promote two simple types of project reporting, as shown in Exhibits 3.5 and 3.6: One to give a snapshot of all projects currently started and the other to focus on the progress of the top ten projects.

Using this report enables management and the SMT to see the overall picture and answer the questions: Have we got too many projects on the go? What projects are running late? What projects are at risk of noncompletion?

REPORTING PROGRESS OF THE TOP TEN PROJECTS

To minimize the time spent reporting progress, a four-quadrant (showing project quartile) and four-color (showing project status) graph should be used. Using this method a project is either 0%, 25%, 50%, 75%, or 100% complete, and it is either at risk of noncompletion, behind, on-track, or finished.

A project that is 15% complete would be shown as 25% complete, and next month when it might be 30% complete it would still stay at the 25% quartile. Project managers are simply asked which quadrant and what color best reflects progress to date.

Managers at first may try and hide lack of progress. This soon becomes apparent when a project has been at the 25% quadrant for 3 months and supposedly is still "on-track." This method is applying Pareto's 80/20 principle and also acknowledges that progress reports, by their very nature, are arbitrary and no two project managers would come up with the same progress evaluation.

The key message for projects in the last quadrant is to finish the project no matter what the sunk cost is. It is thus not particularly helpful for the accounting team to constantly focus on the over-run. It would be far better to focus on the remaining cost to complete and compare

Exhibit 3.5 Project Report Example

Project Office Status Report—June xx

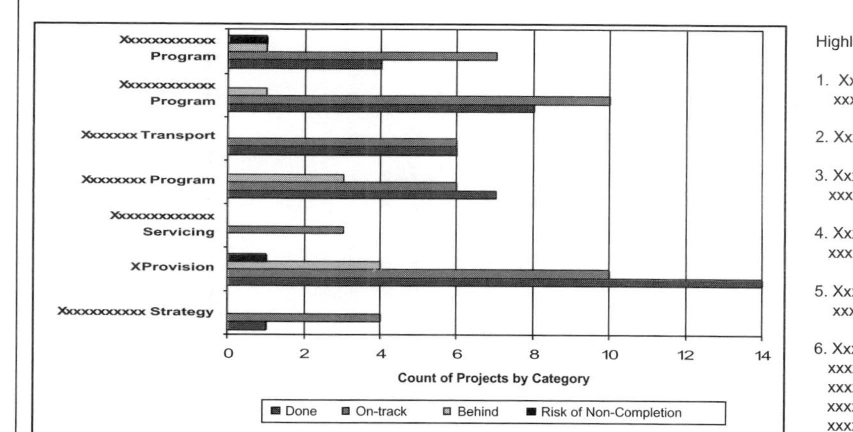

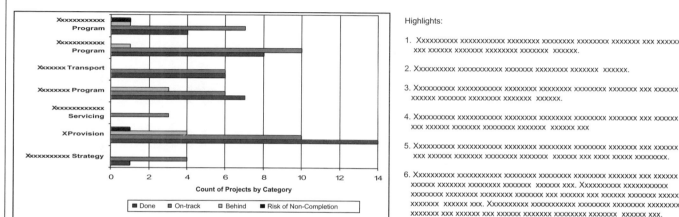

Highlights:

1. Xxxxxxxxxx xxxxxxxxxxx xxxxxxxx xxxxxxxx xxxxxxxx xxxxxxx xxx xxxxxx xxx xxxxxx xxxxxxx xxxxxxxx xxxxxxx xxxxxx.

2. Xxxxxxxxxx xxxxxxxxxxx xxxxxxx xxxxxxxx xxxxxxx xxxxxx.

3. Xxxxxxxxxx xxxxxxxxxxx xxxxxxxx xxxxxxxx xxxxxxxx xxxxxxx xxx xxxxxx xxx xxxxxx xxxxxxx xxxxxxxx xxxxxxx xxxxxx.

4. Xxxxxxxxxx xxxxxxxxxxx xxxxxxxx xxxxxxxx xxxxxxxx xxxxxxx xxx xxxxxx xxx xxxxxx xxxxxxx xxxxxxxx xxxxxxx xxxxxx xxx

5. Xxxxxxxxxx xxxxxxxxxxx xxxxxxxx xxxxxxxx xxxxxxxx xxxxxxx xxx xxxxxx xxx xxxxxx xxxxxxx xxxxxxxx xxxxxxx xxxxxx xxx xxxx xxxxx xxxxxxxx.

6. Xxxxxxxxxx xxxxxxxxxxx xxxxxxxx xxxxxxxx xxxxxxxx xxxxxxx xxx xxxxxx xxx xxxxxx xxxxxxx xxxxxxxx xxxxxxx xxxxxx xxx. Xxxxxxxxxx xxxxxxxxxxx xxxxxxxx xxxxxxxx xxxxxxxx xxxxxxx xxx xxxxxx xxx xxxxxx xxxxxxx xxxxxxxx xxxxxxx xxxxxx xxx. Xxxxxxxxxx xxxxxxxxxxx xxxxxxxx xxxxxxxx xxxxxxxx xxxxxxx xxx xxxxxx xxx xxxxxx xxxxxxx xxxxxxxx xxxxxxx xxxxxx xxx.

Projects at Risk of Non-Completion at Year-End
Xxxxxxx xxxxxxx xxxxxxx xxxx xxxxx,
Xxxxxxxxx xxxxxx xxxxxxxx xxxxx.
Xxxxxxxxxxxx xxxxxxxxx xxxxxxxxxxxx xxxxxxxxx xxxxxxxxxxxxxx xxxxxxxx xxxxxx xxxxxxx xxxxx xxxxxx xx.

Previously Reported Project at Risk of Non-Completion
Xxxxxxxxxxx xxxxxxxx xxxxxxxx xxxxxxxxxx xxxxxxxxxx xxxxxxxx xxxxxxxx xxxxxxxx xxxxxx xxxx xxxxxx xxxxxxxxx.

Exhibit 3.6 "Top Ten" Projects Report Example

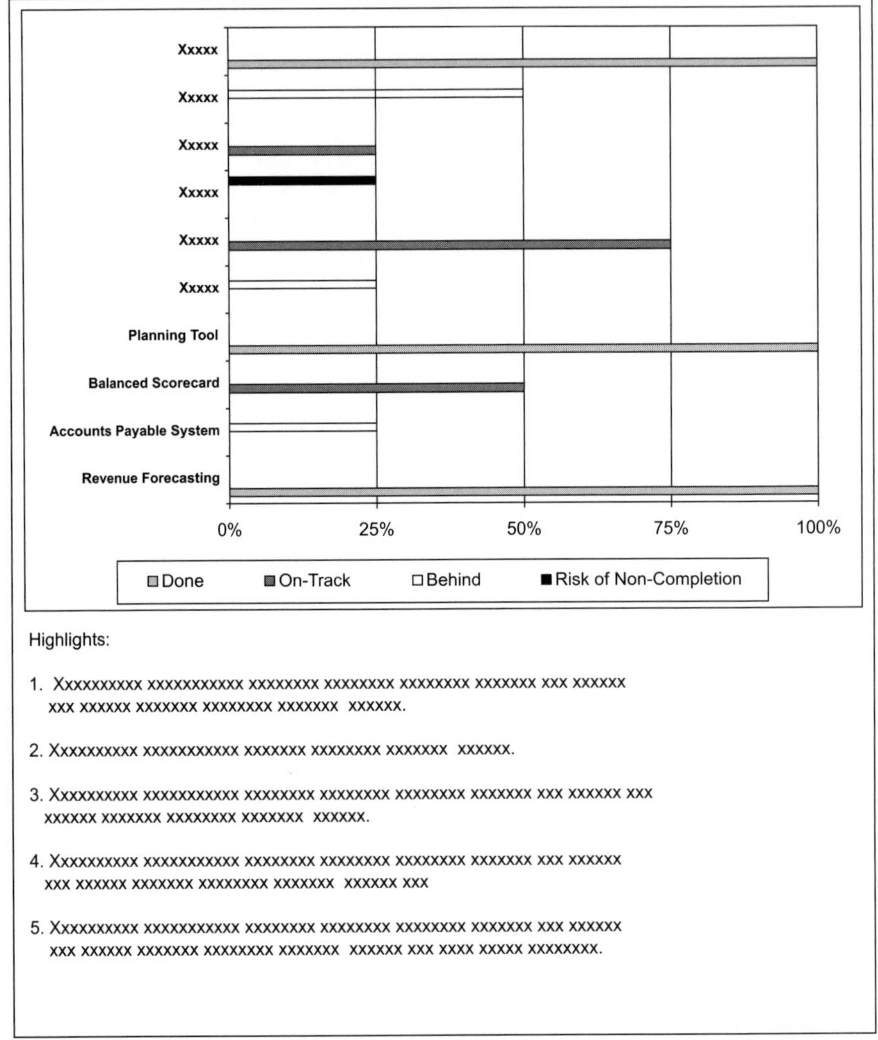

Highlights:

1. Xxxxxxxxxx xxxxxxxxxxx xxxxxxxx xxxxxxxx xxxxxxxx xxxxxxx xxx xxxxxx xxx xxxxxx xxxxxxx xxxxxxxx xxxxxxx xxxxxx.

2. Xxxxxxxxxx xxxxxxxxxxx xxxxxxx xxxxxxxx xxxxxxx xxxxxx.

3. Xxxxxxxxxx xxxxxxxxxxx xxxxxxxx xxxxxxxx xxxxxxxx xxxxxxx xxx xxxxxx xxx xxxxxx xxxxxxx xxxxxxxx xxxxxxx xxxxxx.

4. Xxxxxxxxxx xxxxxxxxxxx xxxxxxxx xxxxxxxx xxxxxxxx xxxxxxx xxx xxxxxx xxx xxxxxx xxxxxxx xxxxxxxx xxxxxxx xxxxxx xxx

5. Xxxxxxxxxx xxxxxxxxxxx xxxxxxxx xxxxxxxx xxxxxxxx xxxxxxx xxx xxxxxx xxx xxxxxx xxxxxxx xxxxxxxx xxxxxxx xxxxxx xxx xxxx xxxxx xxxxxxxx.

Notes:

0–25% quadrant: Key decision is do we still need this project, if we are too busy let's stop it now.

26–50% and 51–75% quadrant: This is where the main "cost over-run" damage is done and hence a high degree of control is needed.

76–100% quadrant: At this stage any substantial over-run is history, it is a sunk cost. The focus of management should be on completion almost regardless of cost.

these against the benefits of finishing. Post project is the place for post-mortems. This will help reduce the tendency of the staff to remove them-sselves from an over-running project to a project with a new budget.

CASH FLOW FORECASTING

Cash flow forecasting is error prone for many of us. It is very hard to get right for the following reasons: lack of information—we do not know when major customers are paying us, no historic analysis of daily cash flows, no historic tracking of the large receipts, a lack of use of electronic receipts and payments, and often a lack of understanding and coordination with the organization's buyers and sales staff.

> *The most important part of a forecast is not the prediction of what is likely to happen, but the strength of the logic behind the forecast—even a broken clock is right twice a day.*
>
> *The best way to gauge the present against the future changes is to look back twice as far as you look forward.*
>
> —Paul Saffo of the Institute of the Future

Building Blocks of a Better Practice Daily Cash Flow Forecast Process

The building blocks of a better practice daily cash flow forecast process include:

Enter the certain figures first	• Rent, rates, leases, loan repayments, loan interest, payroll, taxes are all certain payments • Track cash flow of major customers; they are more certain • Track cash flow of all other customers who have signed up for a direct debit (DD)—offer continuing discounts to customers to go onto direct debits • Track payment of major suppliers paid by DD or direct credit (DC) • Track payment of minor suppliers paid by DC

(continues)

Building Blocks *(Continued)*	
Track the history of your daily cash flows	• Need at least the last 24 months of cash flow data in the same categories that you are forecasting—the best place for storing this historic data is in a forecasting application • Use trend graphs in your forecasting application to help understand seasonal fluctuations—remember you need to go back twice as far as you look forward
Appropriate time frame	• Look forward at least to week 5 in working days and to week 13 in weeks—the month-end is irrelevant for cash flow forecasting because a cash flow crisis comes at any time • It is usually okay to cash flow model in months from month 4 onward—this modeling can be automated from the accrual forecasting model and in some cases is taken out a rolling 24 months
Automatic feeds to cash forecasting application	• Daily major receipts from accounts receivable • Tax payment calculations can be automated • For key customers—cash flows can be accurately predicted in the short term
Cash flow forecast built on a planning application—not Excel	• Put the cash flow on an appropriate forecasting application—Excel is best left to non-core activities such as expense claims at airports or one-off diagrams.

Exhibits 3.7 and 3.8 show the short-term cash flow predicted by day and the longer ranged one going out in months, which typically would be generated from the accrual forecast via standard timing amendments. Exhibit 3.9 shows an alternative graph for the longer range cash flow report.

CAPITAL EXPENDITURE REPORTING

There are two main issues with the reporting capital expenditure (CAPEX). First and most important, the extent of the CAPEX slippage—for as sure as night follows day, there will be CAPEX slippage. Worse still is

Exhibit 3.7 Short-Range Cash Flow Example

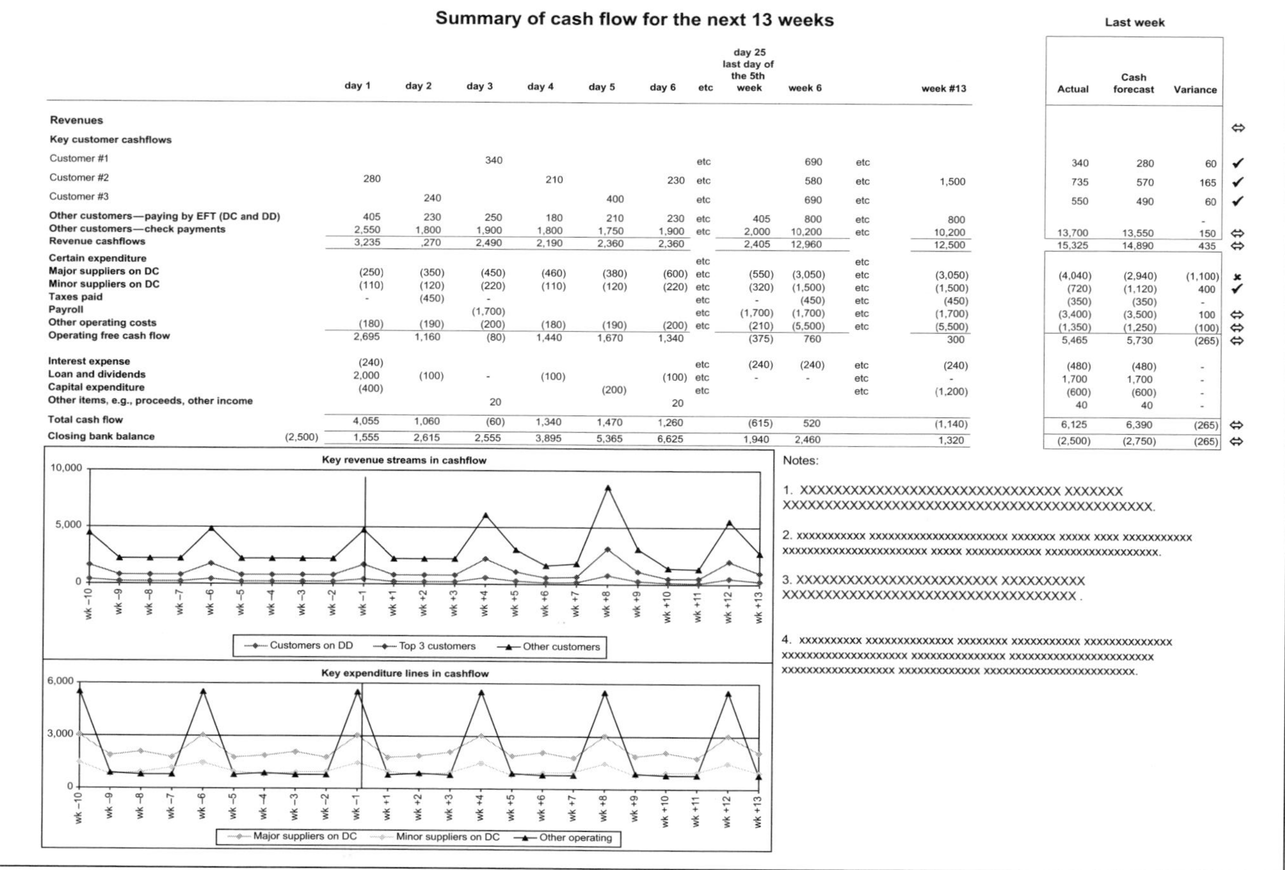

Summary of cash flow for the next 13 weeks

		day 1	day 2	day 3	day 4	day 5	day 6	etc	day 25 last day of the 5th week	week 6		week #13	Last week: Actual	Last week: Cash forecast	Last week: Variance	
Revenues																
Key customer cashflows																⇔
Customer #1				340				etc		690	etc		340	280	60	✔
Customer #2		280			210		230	etc		580	etc	1,500	735	570	165	✔
Customer #3			240			400		etc		690	etc		550	490	60	✔
Other customers—paying by EFT (DC and DD)		405	230	250	180	210	230	etc	405	800	etc	800			-	
Other customers—check payments		2,550	1,800	1,900	1,800	1,750	1,900	etc	2,000	10,200	etc	10,200	13,700	13,550	150	⇔
Revenue cashflows		3,235	,270	2,490	2,190	2,360	2,360		2,405	12,960		12,500	15,325	14,890	435	⇔
Certain expenditure								etc			etc					
Major suppliers on DC		(250)	(350)	(450)	(460)	(380)	(600)	etc	(550)	(3,050)	etc	(3,050)	(4,040)	(2,940)	(1,100)	✖
Minor suppliers on DC		(110)	(120)	(220)	(110)	(120)	(220)	etc	(320)	(1,500)	etc	(1,500)	(720)	(1,120)	400	✔
Taxes paid		-	(450)	-				etc	-	(450)	etc	(450)	(350)	(350)	-	
Payroll				(1,700)				etc	(1,700)	(1,700)	etc	(1,700)	(3,400)	(3,500)	100	⇔
Other operating costs		(180)	(190)	(200)	(180)	(190)	(200)	etc	(210)	(5,500)	etc	(5,500)	(1,350)	(1,250)	(100)	⇔
Operating free cash flow		2,695	1,160	(80)	1,440	1,670	1,340		(375)	760		300	5,465	5,730	(265)	⇔
Interest expense		(240)						etc	(240)	(240)	etc	(240)	(480)	(480)	-	
Loan and dividends		2,000	(100)	-	(100)		(100)	etc	-	-	etc	-	1,700	1,700	-	
Capital expenditure		(400)				(200)		etc			etc	(1,200)	(600)	(600)	-	
Other items, e.g., proceeds, other income				20			20						40	40	-	
Total cash flow		4,055	1,060	(60)	1,340	1,470	1,260		(615)	520		(1,140)	6,125	6,390	(265)	⇔
Closing bank balance	(2,500)	1,555	2,615	2,555	3,895	5,365	6,625		1,940	2,460		1,320	(2,500)	(2,750)	(265)	⇔

Notes:

1. XXXXXXXXXXXXXXXXXXXXXXXXXXXXXXXX XXXXXXX XXXXXXXXXXXXXXXXXXXXXXXXXXXXXXXXXXXXXXXXXXXXXX.

2. xxxxxxxxxxx xxxxxxxxxxxxxxxxxxxxxxx xxxxxxx xxxxx xxxx xxxxxxxxxxx xxxxxxxxxxxxxxxxxxxxxxx xxxxx xxxxxxxxxxxx xxxxxxxxxxxxxxxxxx.

3. XXXXXXXXXXXXXXXXXXXXXXXXX XXXXXXXXXX XXXXXXXXXXXXXXXXXXXXXXXXXXXXXXXXXXXX .

4. xxxxxxxxxx xxxxxxxxxxxxxx xxxxxxxx xxxxxxxxxxx xxxxxxxxxxxxxx xxxxxxxxxxxxxxxxxxxx xxxxxxxxxxxxxxx xxxxxxxxxxxxxxxxxxxxxx xxxxxxxxxxxxxxxxxx xxxxxxxxxxxxx xxxxxxxxxxxxxxxxxxxxxxx.

Exhibit 3.8 Longer Range Cash Flow Forecasting Example

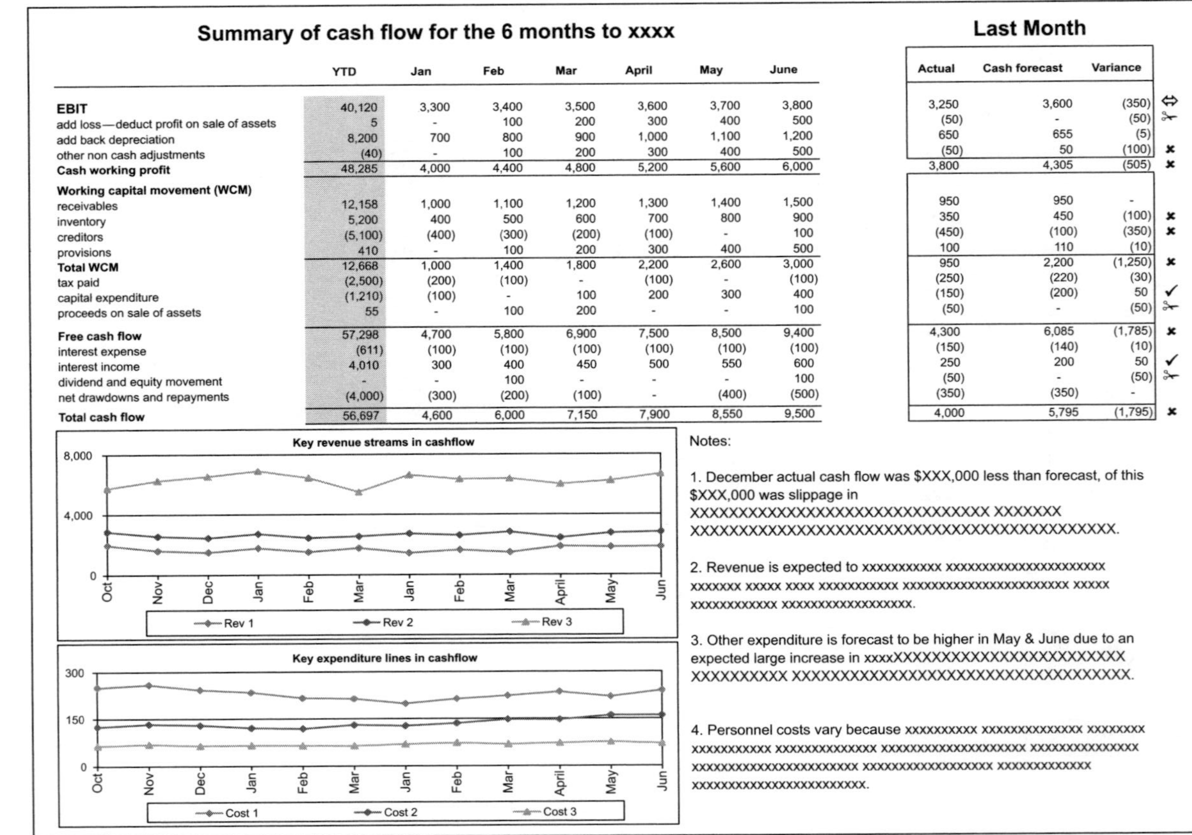

Summary of cash flow for the 6 months to xxxx

	YTD	Jan	Feb	Mar	April	May	June	Last Month: Actual	Cash forecast	Variance	
EBIT	40,120	3,300	3,400	3,500	3,600	3,700	3,800	3,250	3,600	(350)	⇔
add loss—deduct profit on sale of assets	5	-	100	200	300	400	500	(50)	-	(50)	✂
add back depreciation	8,200	700	800	900	1,000	1,100	1,200	650	655	(5)	
other non cash adjustments	(40)	-	100	200	300	400	500	(50)	50	(100)	✖
Cash working profit	48,285	4,000	4,400	4,800	5,200	5,600	6,000	3,800	4,305	(505)	✖
Working capital movement (WCM)											
receivables	12,158	1,000	1,100	1,200	1,300	1,400	1,500	950	950	-	
inventory	5,200	400	500	600	700	800	900	350	450	(100)	✖
creditors	(5,100)	(400)	(300)	(200)	(100)	-	100	(450)	(100)	(350)	✖
provisions	410	-	100	200	300	400	500	100	110	(10)	
Total WCM	12,668	1,000	1,400	1,800	2,200	2,600	3,000	950	2,200	(1,250)	✖
tax paid	(2,500)	(200)	(100)	-	(100)	-	(100)	(250)	(220)	(30)	
capital expenditure	(1,210)	(100)	-	100	200	300	400	(150)	(200)	50	✓
proceeds on sale of assets	55	-	100	200	-	-	100	(50)	-	(50)	✂
Free cash flow	57,298	4,700	5,800	6,900	7,500	8,500	9,400	4,300	6,085	(1,785)	✖
interest expense	(611)	(100)	(100)	(100)	(100)	(100)	(100)	(150)	(140)	(10)	
interest income	4,010	300	400	450	500	550	600	250	200	50	✓
dividend and equity movement	-	-	100	-	-	-	100	(50)	-	(50)	✂
net drawdowns and repayments	(4,000)	(300)	(200)	(100)	-	(400)	(500)	(350)	(350)	-	
Total cash flow	56,697	4,600	6,000	7,150	7,900	8,550	9,500	4,000	5,795	(1,795)	✖

Notes:

1. December actual cash flow was $XXX,000 less than forecast, of this $XXX,000 was slippage in XXXXXXXXXXXXXXXXXXXXXXXXXXXXXXXX XXXXXXX XXXXXXXXXXXXXXXXXXXXXXXXXXXXXXXXXXXXXXXXXXXXXX.

2. Revenue is expected to xxxxxxxxxxx xxxxxxxxxxxxxxxxxxxxxx xxxxxxx xxxxx xxxx xxxxxxxxxxx xxxxxxxxxxxxxxxxxxxxxx xxxxx xxxxxxxxxxxx xxxxxxxxxxxxxxxxxx.

3. Other expenditure is forecast to be higher in May & June due to an expected large increase in xxxxXXXXXXXXXXXXXXXXXXXXXXXX XXXXXXXXXX XXXXXXXXXXXXXXXXXXXXXXXXXXXXXXXXXXXX.

4. Personnel costs vary because xxxxxxxxxx xxxxxxxxxxxxxx xxxxxxxx xxxxxxxxxxx xxxxxxxxxxxxxx xxxxxxxxxxxxxxxxxxxx xxxxxxxxxxxxxxxx xxxxxxxxxxxxxxxxxxxxxxx xxxxxxxxxxxxxxxxxx xxxxxxxxxxxxx xxxxxxxxxxxxxxxxxxxxxxxxx.

Exhibit 3.9 Alternative Cash Flow Graph

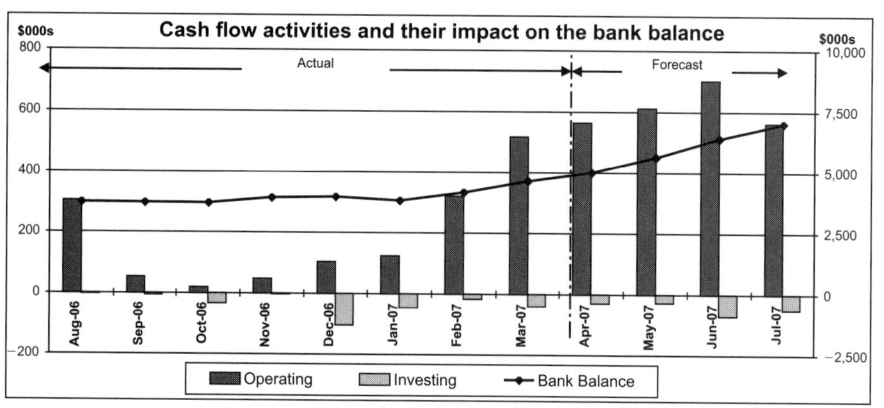

the fact that this CAPEX was to improve the working conditions, improve quality of products/services, increase profitability, and so forth. If an office renovation has been approved why is it completed in the last week of the year? Surely it would have been better for it to have been completed in the first couple of months so the staff would have the benefit of it! We therefore need a report (see Exhibit 3.10) that contrasts the percentage of capital spent by divisions against the percentage of the year gone. The aim is for status of the CAPEX projects to beat the year gone progress bar.

Second, it is important to control the CAPEX approval process. During the life of a CAPEX project there may be signs that it may be going over budget. Normally this is hidden from the Board until management is sure there is a problem. If you have a system in which the Board is informed about the possibility of CAPEX exceeding the budget as soon as it recognized, it gives the Board a choice. They can make the decision as to whether they want a formal application for the additional expenditure or decide to defer and wait until more information is known about the magnitude of the over expenditure. In Exhibit 3.11 the Board would typically not request immediate additional information because there is still half the project to go, so the over expenditure may not occur. The Board may instead flag that a progress brief is required by the project manager or request for a new CAPEX approval application be prepared for the next Board meeting.

Exhibit 3.10 CAPEX Approval Report

CAPEX

Capital Expenditure for the period ending 31 December XX

	Unspent CAPEX b/f	Current Year Budget	Approved Changes	Total Approved	CAPEX Spent YTD	Forecast to Complete	Forecast Underspend	Forecast Unapproved CAPEX
	$000s							
Project #1	10	100	50	160	80	70		0
Project #2		450	700	1,150	590	400	(160)	0
Project #3		1,700	(700)	1,000	550	600		150
Project #4								
Project #5								
Other								
Total	**10**	**2,250**	**50**	**2,310**	**1,220**	**1,070**	**(160)**	**150**

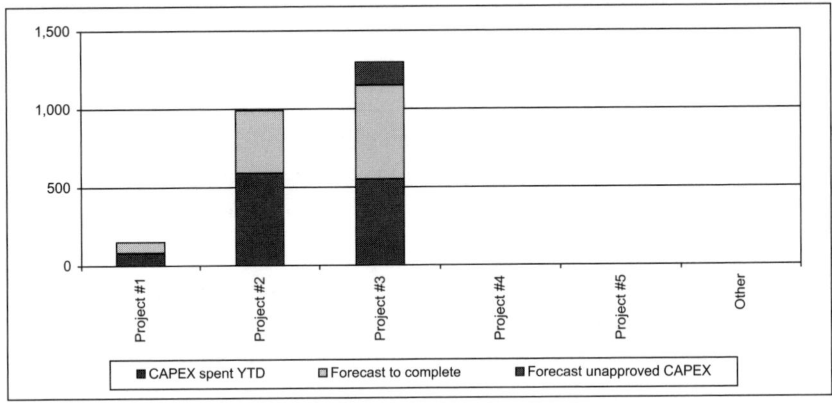

Unapproved items:
xxxxxxxxxxx
xxxxxxxxxxxxx

Issues:
xxxxxxxxxxx
xxxxxxxxxxx
xxxxxxxxxxxxx

Actions to be taken:
xxxxxxxxxxx
xxxxxxxxxxxxxxxxxxxxxxxx
xxxxxxxxxxxxx

Exhibit 3.11 CAPEX Slippage Report

CAPEX
Capital Expenditure for the period ending 31 December 20XX

	% Spent	YTD Actual	Annual Budget	Outstanding
Div 1	50%	45	90	45
Div 2	31%	25	80	55
Div 3	70%	63	90	27
Div 4	72%	93	130	37
Div 5	56%	25	45	20
Other	58%	105	180	75
Average	56%			
% of Year Gone	75%			
Total		356	615	259

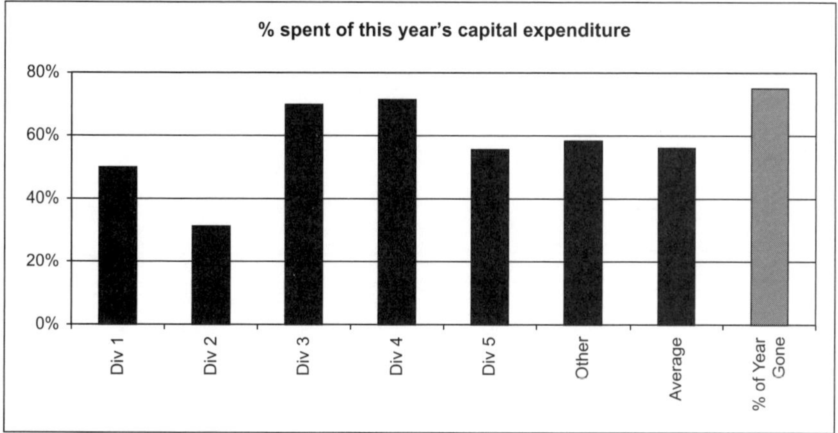

Highlights:

1. xxxxxxxxxx xxxxxxxxxxxxxx xxxxxxxx xxxxxxxxxxx xxxxxxxxxxxxxx xxxxxxxxxxxxxxxxxxxx xxxxxxxxxxxxxxxxxxxxxxx xxxxxxxxxxxxxxxxxx xxxxxxxxxxxxx xxxxxxxxxxxxxxxxxxxxxxxx.

2. xxxxxxxxxxx xxxxxxxxxxxxxxxxxxxxxx xxxxxxx xxxxx xxxx xxxxxxxxxxx xxxxxxxxxxxxxxxx xxxxxxxxxxxx xxxxxxxxxxxxxxxxxx.

3.xxxxxxxxxx xxxxxxxxxxxxxx xxxxxxxx xxxxxxxxxxx xxxxxxxxxxxxxx xxxxxxxxxxxxxxxxxxxx xxxxxxxxxxxxxxxxxxxxxxxxxxxxxx.

4. xxxxxxxxxx xxxxxxxxxxxxxx xxxxxxxx xxxxxxxxxxx xxxxxxxxxxxxxx xxxxxxxxxxxxxxxxxxxx xxxxxxxxxxxxxxxxxxxxxxx xxxxxxxxxxxxxxxxxx xxxxxxxxxxxxx xxxxxxxxxxxxxxxxxxxxxxxx.

CHAPTER 4

Limit Time Invested in Board Reporting

Reporting to the Board is a classic "catch-22" situation. Boards complain about getting too much information too late, and management complains that up to 20% of their time is tied up in the Board reporting process. Boards obviously need to ascertain whether management is steering the ship correctly and the state of the crew and customers before they can relax and "strategize" about future initiatives. The process of assessing the current status of the organization from the most recent Board report is where the principal problem lies. Board reporting needs to occur more efficiently and effectively for both the Board and management.

SELLING THE CHANGE

Before commenting on the changes that need to be made, we need to see why the suggestions in the past have not worked. As accountants we are commonly typically thinking and judgmental people, in Myers-Briggs terms. We thus assume that as logic is our foundation stone, so it is to others, and we use logic to sell change. As already mentioned we need to sell by the emotional drivers and pre-sell them to the most influential Board member prior to the meeting.

The corporate accountants should work with the CEO and the Board to carry out the following tasks:

- Commence an education process regarding the cost versus benefit of the Board reporting process—start with costing out each Board paper, because the Board will be the first to complain about the waste!
- Ensure all requests for information are properly scoped and costed first.
- Instigate an empowerment program so reports are not rewritten unless absolutely necessary.
- Table Board papers electronically using some of the innovative Board reporting applications designed for this purpose.
- Release papers to the Board as they become available.
- Bring the Board meeting forward to the tenth working day.
- Refocus of "variance to budget" reporting to the year-to-date numbers.
- Work with the Chairman to constantly purge the number of Board papers.
- Report key result indicators in a "dashboard" to the Board.

COSTING BOARD PAPERS

Board papers can reach mammoth proportions, tying up vast amounts of management time in preparation. I have seen organizations where one week a month is written off by the senior management team (SMT) on Board reporting. The result of these excesses is often late Board meetings with the papers often being sent to the directors only a day or two before the meeting. The Board meetings themselves can then be side-tracked by the detail with the strategic overview inadequately addressed.

Directors are often a guilty party requesting changes to Board report formats, or additional analysis without first finding out what the exercise will involve, or giving staff guidelines as to how much detail is required.

What amount of senior management time is absorbed by the monthly reporting process? It is important to cost this out and report this to the

Board. They will be horrified. All you need now is to cost out each request, and the Board will soon rein in the changes.

SCOPING OF INFORMATION REQUESTS

A request for information from the Board often can take on a life of its own. A simple request soon adopts "charge of the light brigade" characteristics as the request is passed down the management tree. Often the director who asked the question had visualized a 30-minute job and now a staffer embarks on a massive exercise. How often in your organization is a lengthy report given to the Board only to receive a cursory glance when more than $20,000 of time has been invested in preparing it?

There needs to be more direct communication between the directors and the staff who are going to research the request. A discussion between the relevant director, the allocated researcher, and the relevant general manager will probably scope the exercise and ensure the likely investment is worthwhile. Failing that, all directors should be asked by the Chairperson to scope their request. "I would like to know about xxxxxxx, I would suggest we invest no more than x days and $x,xxx on this."

AVOIDING REWRITES OF BOARD REPORTS

Some organizations have made a major cultural change to report writing, committing the Board, CEO, and SMT to avoid rewrites at all costs. The Board no longer considers the quality of the Board papers as a reflection of the CEO's performance. The organizations have learned to delegate and empower their staff so that the SMT and Board papers are being written with limited input from senior managers and are being tabled with few amendments provided that the SMT agrees with the recommendations. The CEO can choose to put a caveat on each report: "while I concur with the recommendations the report was written by XXXXX."

The Board understands that the report is not written in SMT "speak." Board members are encouraged to comment directly to the writer about strengths and areas for improvement with report writing. The writers are also the presenters, where necessary. The organization thus has a much more relaxed week leading up to the Board meeting, having largely delegated the report writing and the associated stress. The rewards include motivated and more competent staff and general managers being free to spend more time contributing to the bottom line.

TABLING BOARD PAPERS ELECTRONICALLY

Many of the procedures that support a Board meeting have changed little since Charles Dickens' time. Board members, in many organizations, typically receive large Board papers that they had difficulty finding the time or inclination to read. In this century we should be using technology.

The financial report should be made available, as soon as it has been finished, via a secure area of the organization's intranet. Other Board papers likewise can then be read as and when they are ready instead of the last paper determining when all the rest are available.

The executive information system (EIS) also offers an answer to the question "How can we reduce the ridiculous size of the Board papers?" Imagine an environment where Board members would receive a 20-page document with pointers to relevant pages in the EIS. Board members then could arrive before the meeting and examine those areas of particular interest. During the Board meeting some queries could be dealt with before the meeting had finished. One manufacturing company has such a system in place and they comment that Board meetings are now more strategic, the Board papers are brief, the non-executive directors have access to the EIS, and management has better control over the business.

REFOCUS OF "VARIANCE TO BUDGET" REPORTING TO YEAR-TO-DATE NUMBERS

Board members find that the variance commentary is not very useful. The setting of monthly budgets before the year commences is a futile task and completely undermines the credibility of the reporting process. How often do your variance reports start with "it is a timing difference"?

Until common sense prevails and your organization evolves to setting the monthly targets only quarterly in advance (discussed in the quarterly rolling planning chapter, Chapter 14), reporting on monthly variances should be avoided wherever possible. The focus of variance analysis commentary should be focused on the year-to-date (YTD) variance where many timing differences will wash out. This makes for boring commentary as we recycle last month's comments and simply change the variance magnitude, hopefully taking care to note if the YTD variance has swung the other way.

CONTINUALLY PURGING BOARD PAPERS

Does it take a 200-page Board paper package to run a business? Are the key decisions a direct result of Board papers or the collective experiences of the Board members? Increasingly today Microsoft PowerPoint is used to deliver presentations to the Board so a major time savings can be made if Board members are given a copy of the slides plus notes rather than a written report. The benefit to the Board is that management has less space to cloud a problem! Management has to set out the issues clearly and concisely.

MORE TIMELY BOARD MEETINGS

The longer the period of elapsed time you allow a task to be completed within, the greater the chance of it being completed inefficiently. Thus, a prompt board meeting will ensure a more efficient preparation of board papers. Some Boards are meeting within ten working days of month-end. Why not yours?

In some cases management is meeting with the Board six weeks after month-end. There is, of course, another month-end in between so they have to be careful to talk about the correct month. This situation is ridiculous.

Boards do not need to sit every month—some sit six, others eight times a year. Changing the frequency will benefit management and the saved Directors time can be reallocated into worthwhile subcommittees.

Exhibit 4.1 Efficiency Scale in Holding Board Meetings

Exceptional	Above Average	Average	Below Average
< 5 working days	5–10 working days	10–15 working days	> 15 working days

Exhibit 4.1 shows an efficiency scale in the holding of Board meetings after the month-end in question.

REPORTING KEY RESULT INDICATORS IN A "DASHBOARD" TO THE BOARD

There is a major conflict in most organizations that have Boards as to what information is appropriate for the Board. Because the Board's role is clearly one of governance and not of management, it is inappropriate to be providing the Board with key performance indicators (KPIs) unless the company is in trouble and the Board needs to take a more active role. KPIs are the very heart of management, and used properly many of them are monitored 24/7 or at least weekly. Certainly not measures to be reported monthly or bi-monthly to the Board.

Indicators of overall performance are needed that only need to be reviewed on a monthly or bi-monthly basis. These measures need to tell the story as to whether the organization is: being steered in the right direction at the right speed; whether the customers and staff are happy; and whether the organization is acting in a responsible and environmentally friendly way. Chapter 18 on KPIs calls these measures *key result indicators* (KRIs). These KRIs help the Board focus on strategic rather than management issues.

A good dashboard with the KRIs going in the right direction will give confidence to the Board that management knows what it is doing and the "ship" is being steered in the right direction. The Board can then concentrate on what it does best, focusing on the horizon for "icebergs" or looking for "new ports to visit" and coaching the CEO, as required. This is instead of parking themselves on the "bridge" and thus getting in the way of the captain who is trying to perform important day-to-day duties.

A dashboard should be a one-page display such as the two examples in Exhibits 4.2 and 4.3. The commentary should be included on this page.

Exhibit 4.2 Nine KRI Dashboard for a Board

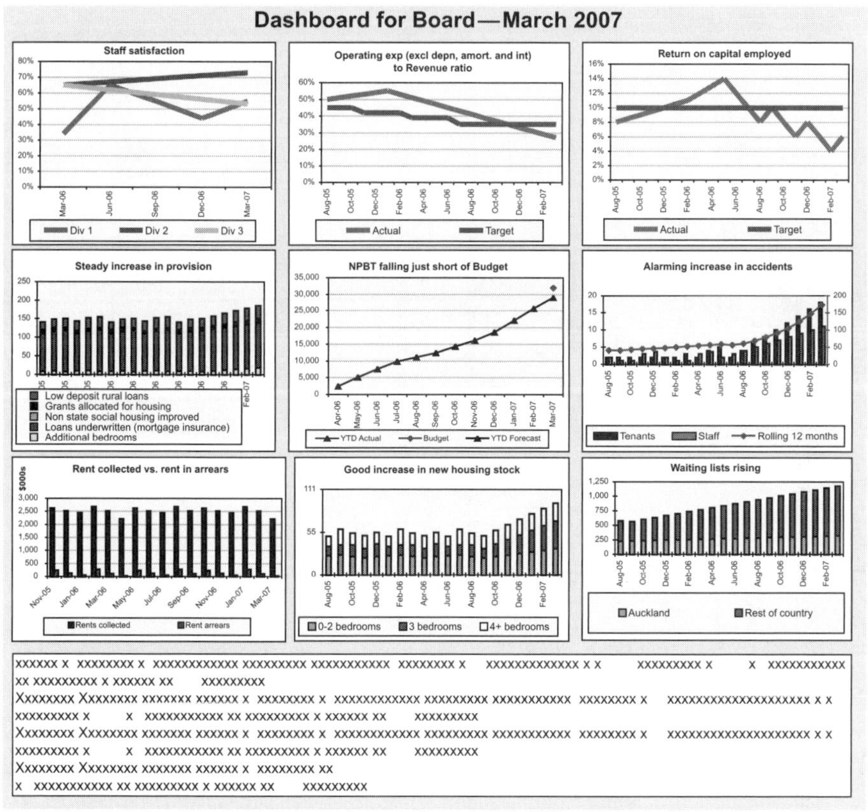

The Board's role is to supervise management as much as it is to think on strategic issues. You can't point them away from the KPIs—otherwise you will hit the icebergs. They need to challenge and measure performance in balance with the strategic direction.

—CFO with blue chip international experience

In response to the preceding quote, I understand this point of view and agree that once the ship is in dangerous waters the Board will want to see and should see more detail. However, if sailing on flat calm water, wind behind, with the sun setting, there should be no need for the Board to see the KPIs!

The key features of the two dashboards (Exhibits 4.2 and 4.3) include:

- They are one-page documents with brief commentary covering the issue and what is being done about it.

Exhibit 4.3 Six KRI Dashboard for a Board

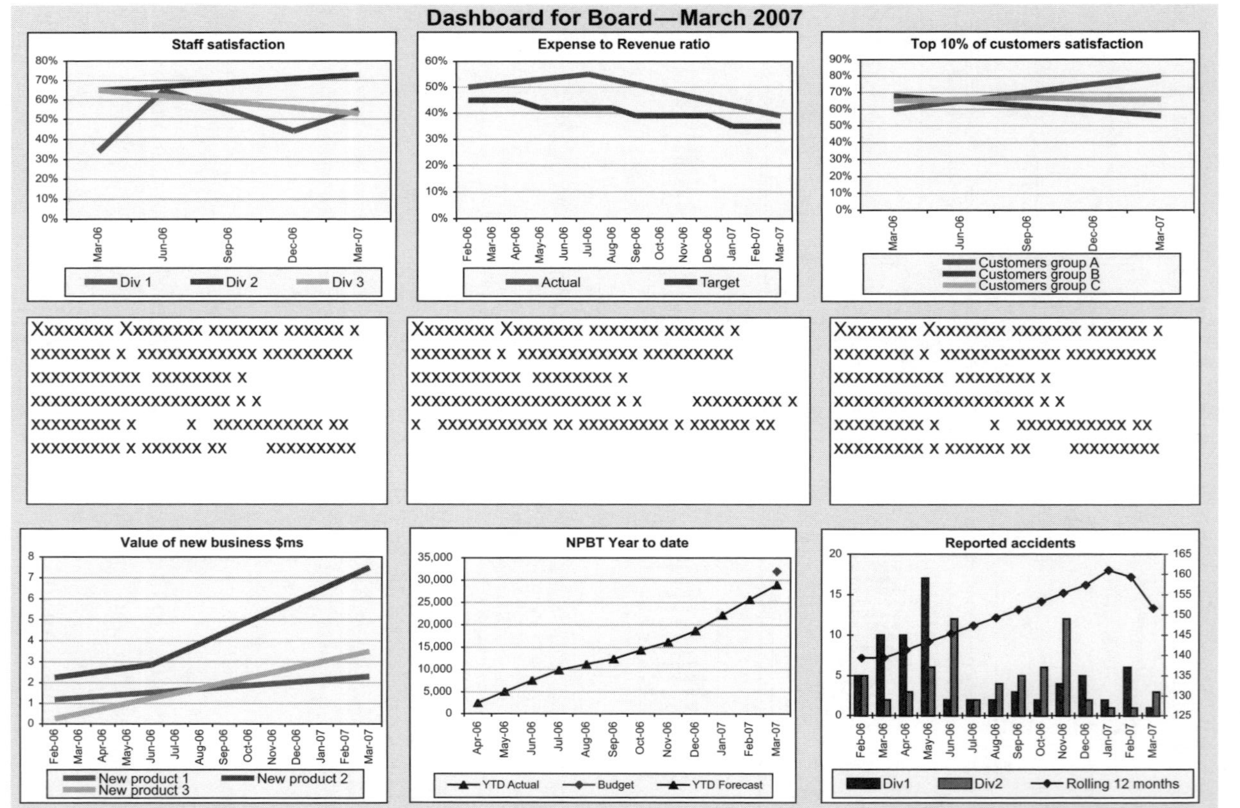

- The trend analysis goes back at least 12 months (some businesses need to go back a rolling 15 to 18 months). Remember business has no respect for your year-end; it is merely an arbitrary point in time.
- You can use the title of the graph to explain what is happening. "Return on capital employed" becomes "return on capital employed is increasing."
- You may need to maintain somewhere between 8 and 12 graphs, and report the most relevant ones to the Board.
- These KRI measures need to cover the six perspectives of a balanced scorecard in order to show whether the organization is being steered in the right direction at the right speed. See www.bettermanagement.com and search under "Parmenter" to listen to presentations on KPIs and read the whitepapers.
- To find your KRIs you need to ascertain the critical success factors first.[1]

Exhibit 4.4 provides an example of KRIs for a board dashboard.

Exhibit 4.4 Key Results Indicators for a Board Dashboard Example

Customer satisfaction: This needs to be measured at least every three months by using statistical samples and focusing on your top 10% to 20% of customers (the ones that are generating most if not all of your bottom line). This process does not need to be overly expensive. If you think once a year is adequate for customer satisfaction, stick to running a sports club because you are not safe in the public or private sectors.

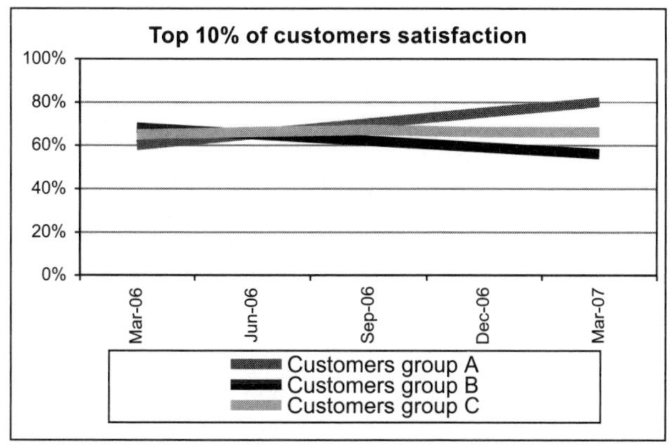

(continues)

Exhibit 4.4 *(Continued)*

Employee satisfaction: No different or less important than customer satisfaction. As one person said, happy staff make happy customers that make a happy bottom line. If you believe in this connection, run a survey now! A staff satisfaction survey need not be expensive and should never be done covering all staff; instead, it should be replaced by a rolling survey with a vertical and horizontal slice of the management and staff. (See "How to Seek Staff Opinion and Not Blow Your Budget," *Human Resources,* June 2002, www.waymark.co.nz.)

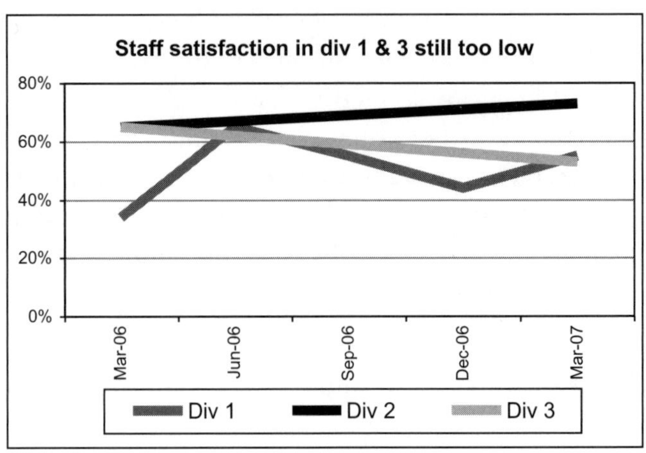

Value of new business: All businesses in the private sector need to focus on the growth of their rising stars. It is important to monitor the pickup of this new business, especially among the top 10% to 20% of customers.

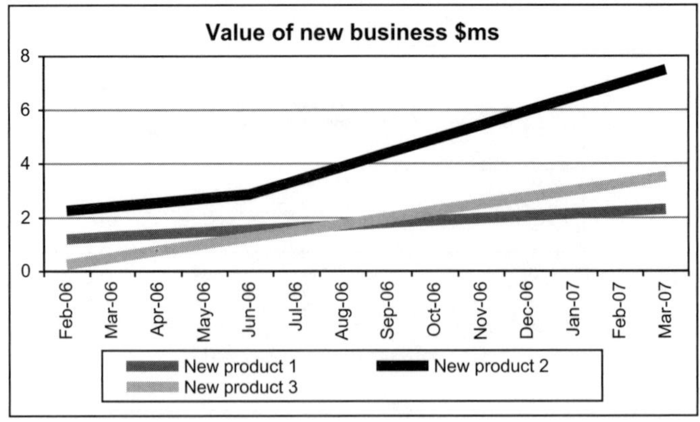

Exhibit 4.4 *(Continued)*

Net profit before tax: Since the Board will always have a focus on the year-end, it is worthwhile to show the cumulative net profit before tax (NPBT). This graph will include the most recent forecast, which should be updated on a quarterly basis bottom-up.

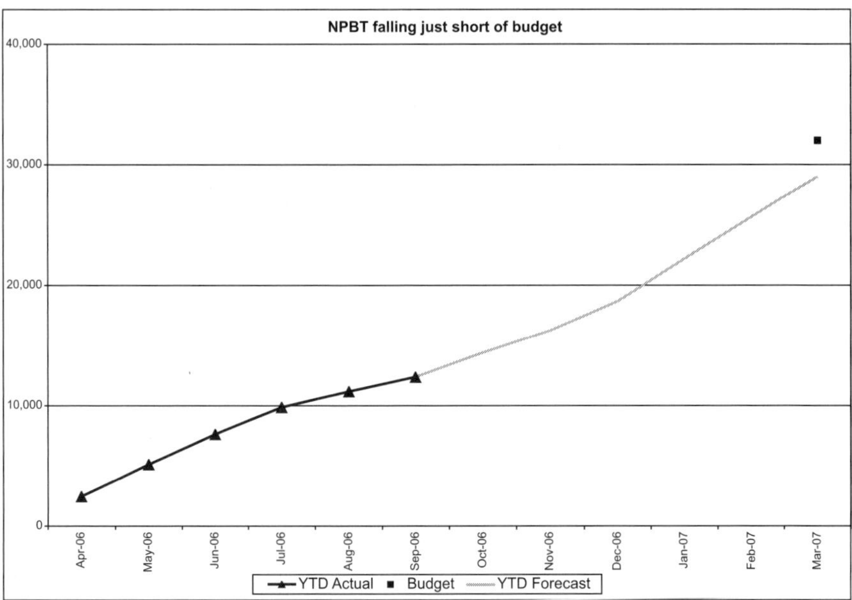

Return on capital employed: The old stalwart of reporting. The difference now is that it is no longer a key performance indicator (KPI) but a key result indicator (KRI). This graph needs to be a 12- to 15-month trend graph.

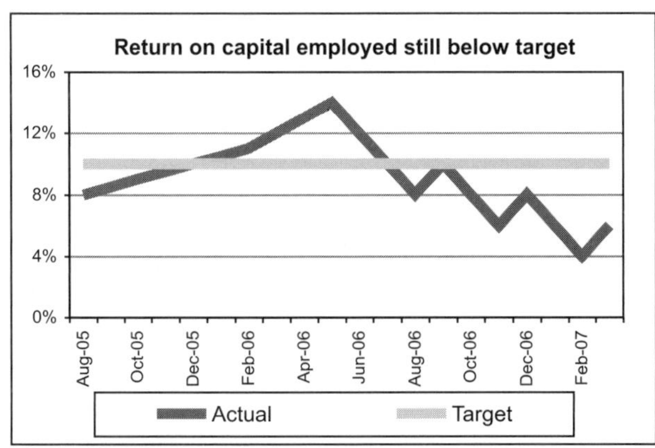

Cash flow: This graph goes back at least 12 months and should be projected out at least six months forward.

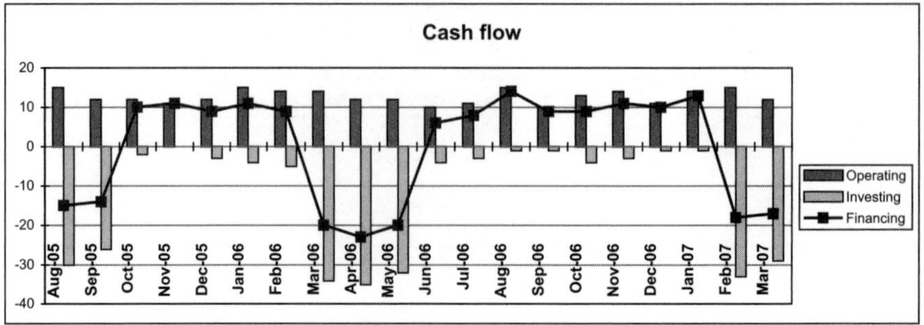

Note

1. To see how the process is accomplished see David Parmenter's *Key Performance Indicators: Developing, Implementing, and Using Winning KPIs* (Hoboken, NJ: John Wiley & Sons, 2007).

CHAPTER 5

Timely Annual Planning Process: Ten Working Days or Less!

Having an annual planning process that takes ten or less working days sounds impossible, yet it is achieved by organizations. It takes good organization and recognition that the annual planning process is not adding value; instead it is undermining an efficient allocation of resources, encouraging dysfunctional budget holder behavior, negating the value of monthly variance reporting, and consuming huge resources from the Board, senior management team (SMT), budget holders, their assistants and, of course, the finance team. When was the last time you were thanked for the annual planning process? At best you have a situation where budget holders have been antagonized, at worst budget holders who now flatly refuse to cooperate!

The future for your organization is quarterly rolling planning, which is covered in Chapter 14. However, it will take upward of nine months to implement and your annual planning cycle may be just around the corner. This chapter will help develop better practices that will be carried over into quarterly rolling planning and forecasting.

SELL CHANGE THROUGH EMOTIONAL DRIVERS

It is important to sell to management why a quick annual plan is a good annual plan. This is not particularly difficult because I have yet to find a manager who enjoys the process or finds it rewarding and worthwhile. The difficulty is that while they will concur with the concept, getting them to change old and embedded bad practices requires a culture change.

To start the process off we need to sell the change using emotional drivers rather than selling by logic as already discussed in the introduction.

The following are some of the emotional drivers you would use to sell the need to streamline the annual planning process to the SMT:

- The monthly budgets from the AP create meaningless month-end reports (e.g., "it is a timing difference")
- Lost months! Lost weekends with family! Producing the annual plan
- Huge cost associated with the annual plan—estimate on the high side, as costs motive the SMT and the Board
- Time spent by the Board and SMT second guessing the next year—it is more efficient on a rolling quarterly basis
- It is a best practice to implement quarterly rolling forecasting and planning (e.g., 80% of major U.S. companies expect to be doing quarterly rolling forecasts, etc.)

The emotional drivers to create change in an annual planning process within the finance team include:

- In the weeks before the annual planning process commences are you already depressed about the evenings you will be spending at work and the family time you will be missing?
- Are you frustrated by going down the same annual planning process just like a laboratory rat?
- Are you and your team held prisoner for three months by the annual planning process, which creates yardsticks that are out of date before the ink dries?

- Are you anxious about the reliability of the spreadsheets that are generating your budgets?
- Do your in-house clients get frustrated about your unavailability during this period?
- Are you dismayed at the lack of value the annual process adds?
- Are you frustrated with the same "it's a timing difference" commentary derived from the inappropriateness of the monthly budgets?

Exhibit 5.1 shows the key processes and who is involved in the ten working day annual planning process.

NEVER BUDGET AT ACCOUNT CODE LEVEL: APPLY PARETO'S 80/20 RULE

As accountants we never needed to set budgets at account code level. We simply did it because we did last year, without thinking. Do you need a budget at account code level if you have good trend analysis captured in the reporting tool? I think not. We therefore apply Pareto's 80/20 rule and establish a category heading that includes a number of general ledger (G/L) codes.

Some rules to follow include:

- Limit the categories in a budget holder's budget to no more than 12—have a category if it represents over 20% of the total (e.g., show revenue category if it is over 20% of total revenue). If the category is between 10% and 20%, look at it and make an assessment if separate disclosure is required; if under 10% consolidate with other categories.
- Map the G/L account codes to these categories—a planning tool can easily cope with this issue without the need to revisit the chart of accounts (see Exhibit 5.2 for an example).
- Accurate forecasting of personnel costs requires analysis of all current staff (their end date if known, their salary, the likely salary review and/or bonus), and all new staff (their starting salary, their likely start date).

Exhibit 5.1 Timeline to Generate the Annual Plan

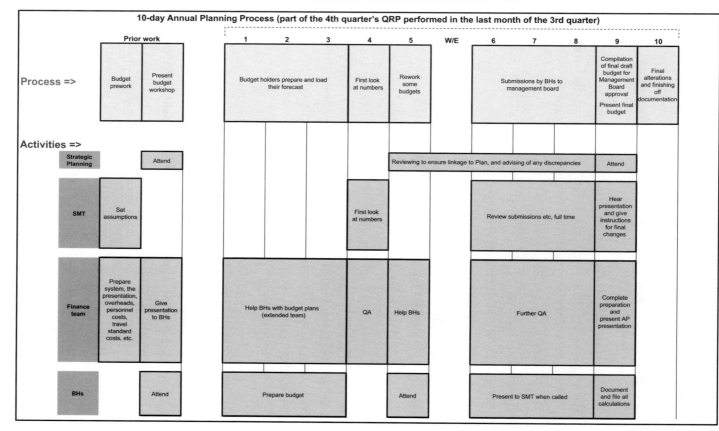

10-day Annual Planning Process (part of the 4th quarter's QRP performed in the last month of the 3rd quarter)

	Prior work		1	2	3	4	5	W/E	6	7	8	9	10
Process =>	Budget prework	Present budget workshop	Budget holders prepare and load their forecast			First look at numbers	Rework some budgets		Submissions by BHs to management board			Compilation of final draft budget for Management Board approval Present final budget	Final alterations and finishing off documentation
Activities =>													
Strategic Planning		Attend					Reviewing to ensure linkage to Plan, and advising of any discrepancies					Attend	
SMT	Set assumptions					First look at numbers			Review submissions etc, full time			Hear presentation and give instructions for final changes	
Finance team	Prepare system, the presentation, overheads, personnel costs, travel standard costs, etc.	Give presentation to BHs	Help BHs with budget plans (extended team)			QA	Help BHs		Further QA			Complete preparation and present AP presentation	
BHs		Attend	Prepare budget				Attend		Present to SMT when called			Document and file all calculations	

Exhibit 5.2 How Forecasting Model Consolidates Account Codes

Old detailed approach		Forecasting by categories		
Stationery	4,556			
Uniforms	3,325			
Cleaning	1,245			
Miscellaneous	7,654			No detail required
Consumables	2,367			
Tea and coffee	2,134			
Kitchen utensils	145			
	21,426	Consumables (category heading)	21,400	
Salaries and wages	25,567,678	Salaries and wages	27,400,000	BH first calculates S&W to the nearest $100,000
Taxes	2,488,888			
Temporary staff	2,456,532	Other employment costs	7,100,000	This number is the balancing item
Contract workers	2,342,345			
Students	234,567			
	33,090,010	Employment costs (category heading)	34,500,000	BH then estimates costs to the nearest half million

AUTOMATE CALCULATION OF CATEGORIES WHERE TREND DATA IS THE BEST PREDICTOR

A number of the 12 to 15 categories can be pre-populated because the budget holder will only look at past data and may even misinterpret this. Face it, you are best equipped to do this. The obvious categories to populate are:

- Communication costs
- Accommodation costs
- Consumables
- Fleet costs
- Depreciation
- Miscellaneous costs

ACCURATE REVENUE FORECASTING: TALKING WITH THE RIGHT PEOPLE AT YOUR MAIN CUSTOMERS

Many organizations liaise with customers to get demand forecasts only to find them as error prone as the forecasts done in-house. The reason is that you have asked the wrong people. You need to get permission to meet with the staff who are responsible for ordering your products and services.

> *One participant told me that they decided to contact their major customers to help with demand forecasting. Naturally, they were holding discussions with the major customers' HQ staff. On reflection they found it better but still error prone so they went back to the customer and asked "How come these forecasts you supplied are so error prone?" "If you want accurate numbers you needed to speak to the procurement managers for our projects" was the reply. "Can we speak to them?" "Of course, here are the contact details of the people you need to meet around the country." A series of meetings were then held around the country. They found that these managers could provide very accurate information and were even prepared to provide it in an electronic friendly format. The sales forecast accuracy then increased sevenfold.*
>
> —CFO in the timber sector

The lesson to learn is when you want to forecast revenue more accurately by delving into your main customer's business, ask them "who should we speak to in order to get a better understanding of your likely demand for our products in the next three months?"

IF USING EXCEL, SIMPLIFY THE MODEL TO MAKE IT ROBUST

Forecasting requires a good robust tool, not a spreadsheet built by some innovative accountant that now no one can understand. However, you may not have the time to replace the Excel model. A new planning tool will take at least six months for researching, acquiring, and implementing for organizations over, say, 500 full-time employees. In this case you can:

- Improve the revenue predictions by focusing in on some major customers
- Budget at category rather than account code level
- Pre-populate those categories you can
- Forecast the annual plan using quarterly figures (hiding two of the monthly columns for each quarter)
- Consolidating via the G/L instead of the spreadsheet (if you can add the category headings easily into the G/L)

HOLD A BRIEFING WORKSHOP

Never issue budget instructions because you already know that they are never read. Follow the lesson of a leading accounting team who always hold a briefing workshop that is compulsory to attend. With technology today you can also hold the workshop simultaneously as a webcast so budget holders in remote locations can attend, albeit electronically. (For an example, attend a webcast on www.bettermanagement.com to see what I mean.)

Hold a workshop budget preparation covering the way to complete the input form, explaining why they do not need to forecast monthly numbers, only quarterly; the three-day window; the daily update to the CEO; the fact that late returns will be career limiting; stressing that the bigger items should have much more detail; and why you have automated some of the categories, the help they will receive, and so forth.

Make sure at the workshop the CEO makes it clear that everybody has to cooperate to achieve a quick time frame. It would be most useful if the CEO states they will be monitoring compliance in the critical days and making it clear that "late forecasting" will be a career limiting activity.

EXPAND YOUR ANNUAL PLANNING TEAM

Many budget holders will need one-to-one support. Yet I have shown in Exhibit 5.1 that we are to do this all in three working days. We thus need to expand the support team. Some suggestions to expand your team are:

- Get all qualified accountants involved, even those not working in the finance team (e.g., this involves the CFO too)
- Ask the auditors to loan some auditor seniors from their local offices to cover those remote locations—the audit seniors will be grateful for being involved in an interesting task (those who have been an auditor will know what I mean)
- Bring in some temp staff with budget experience
- For smaller budget holders the senior accounts payable staff would be ideal

Thus all budget holders, wherever they are located, who need help can be supported during the three-day window for data entry.

BOLT DOWN YOUR STRATEGY BEFOREHAND

Leading organizations always have a strategic workshop out of town prior to the annual planning fortnight. The session is to look forward. Normally Board members will be involved because their strategic vision is a valuable asset. These retreats are run by an experienced external facilitator. The key strategic assumptions are thus set before the annual planning round starts; also the Board can set out what they are expecting to see.

AVOID PHASING THE ANNUAL BUDGET

Quarterly data for the next year is perfectly adequate. You want to have the ability to phase the monthly budgets closer to the event. This is explained in the quarterly rolling planning chapter, Chapter 14.

PROVIDE AUTOMATED CALCULATIONS FOR TRAVEL

A key area of wasted time is the budget holder calculating the travel and accommodation costs. Set a simple calculator with standard costs (e.g., four people going to Sydney for three nights and airfares, accommodation, transfers, overnight allowances all calculated using standard estimates).

HAVE TREND GRAPHS FOR EVERY CATEGORY FORECASTED

Better quality can be achieved through analysis of the trends. There is no place to hide surplus funding when a budget holder has to explain why the future trend is so different from the past trend. The graph shown in Exhibit 5.3, if made available for all the categories budget holders are required to forecast, will increase forecast accuracy.

SET A BUDGET COMMITTEE WHO SIT IN A "LOCK-UP"

Most organizations have a budget committee comprising CEO, CFO and two general managers. You need to persuade this budget committee that a three-day lock-up is more efficient than the current scenario.

Exhibit 5.3 Forecast Expenditure Graph

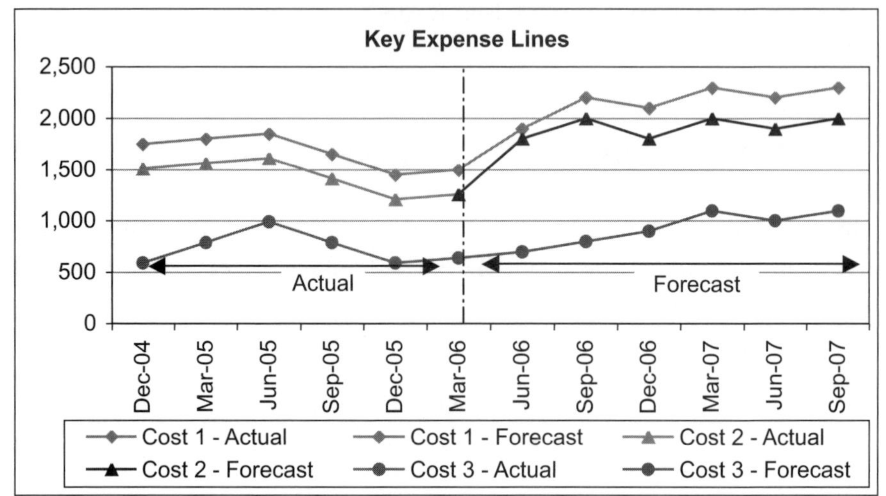

During the lock-up each budget holder has a set time to:

- Discuss their financial and non-financial goals for the next year.
- Justify their annual plan forecast.
- Raise extra funding issues.
- Raise key issues (e.g., the revenue forecast is contingent upon the release to market and commissioning of products X and Y).

See Appendix C for a checklist on "Streamlining an Annual Planning Process." This will help with the quality assurance process.

CHAPTER 6

Managing the Most Important Resource: The Accounting Team

There are many ways to better manage your accounting staff. Some of the major ones are discussed in this chapter.

HOLD AN OFF-SITE MEETING FOR THE ACCOUNTING TEAM AT LEAST TWICE A YEAR

Some teams hold a half-day off-site meeting every month after they have completed their quick month-end. Exhibit 6.1 shows the agenda items of a typical off-site meeting. One of the meetings will set the annual goals of the team. The CFO will prepare the first cut of the goals for the accounting team that support the organization's operating plan. During discussion these are broken down, developed, and taken on by individuals in the team. The benefits of this approach are that the team members are fully aware of each others' goals and there is a greater degree of ownership to "make it happen."

With cost-cutting exercises over the past 10 to 15 years, organized in-house courses are a rarity, and individuals are often left to their own

Exhibit 6.1 Agenda of a Team Off-Site Meeting

Agenda of the Accounting Team Meeting

Date and Time: xxxxxx

Location: xxxxxx

Suggested Attendees: All the accounting team with special guests xxxxxxxx, xxxxxxxx, xxxxxxxx

Requirements: Session secretary (Pat Carruthers), laptops × 2, data show, white boards × 2

8:30 A.M.	Welcome by CFO, a summary of progress to date, an outline of the issues, feedback from the in-house customer survey, and establishing the outcome for the workshop.
8:40 A.M.	**Setting the scene**—a talk by a member of the senior management team (SMT). Topics covered include: • Importance of the finance team • Future direction of xxxxxx • Areas where the SMT are keen to see improvements • Where the accounting team can score more goals for the SMT
9:00 A.M.	**Presentation by external party on a new methodology or tool** Topics covered could include: • Improving the use of the general ledger (revisiting the time-saving features) • Demonstration of a planning tool • Action meetings—a new approach to productive meetings • Accounts payable better practices • Team building exercises (Hermann's thinking preferences, Myers-Briggs team wheel, etc.) • Other better practices taken from this book, etc.
10:15 A.M.	Morning break
10:30 A.M.	**Workshop 1** How to implement changes to increase added value to the SMT and in-house customers (utilizing findings from survey and talk given by the SMT member).
11:00 A.M.	**Workshop 2** How to implement xxxxxxxx better practice
12:15 P.M.	Lunch at venue
1:00 P.M.	Wrap up of workshop

devices in selecting what they would consider to be a useful way to spend the training budget.

The off-site meetings, if run frequently enough, are an ideal time to have the training session. One high-performance team has a training session for every three monthly off-site team meetings. They invest considerable time planning the training workshop, which may include helping staff to revisit policies and procedures; looking at how to handle likely scenarios; what makes a supervisor excellent; client management; increasing knowledge about special processes; and so forth. We can certainly learn from the commitment that this high-performance team makes to training and the positive team spirit that these in-house workshops generate. Many accounting functions suffer from inadequate training. We are all too busy "fire fighting" so we do not have the time to acquire a 21st century fire fighting appliance.

SET UP MONTHLY ONE-ON-ONE PROGRESS MEETINGS WITH DIRECT REPORTS

Set up monthly progress meetings with your direct reports in the first week of the month and on the same day (e.g., Ted 2 P.M. first Tuesday of month, Sarah 3 P.M. first Tuesday of month, etc.) and give them performance feedback, which in most cases will be just verbal. In this meeting ask them to prepare a few PowerPoint slides rather than a written report and suggest a maximum of 30 minutes' preparation time.

These meetings will also replace the need for project report-back meetings. The content for slides would include:

- What I have done well last month
- What I have not done so well
- What I am planning to do this month
- The lessons I have learned
- The training I am going to organize

ATTRACTING THE BEST STAFF TO THE TEAM

Making the accounting team a preferred team to join will attract high-potential accounting staff. You can do this by:

- Establishing a relationship with your local universities offering prizes to the best accounting graduates, delivering guest lectures, and offering holiday jobs—this will increase the profile of the team and enable you to try before you buy!

- Writing articles in the accounting journals and delivering presentations for your local accounting branch
- Being active in the local accounting body

ADOPT BETTER RECRUITMENT PRACTICES

To have a good team it is a good idea to start with the best resources available. There are still too many staff selections made by the old and antiquated interview process, accompanied by some cursory reference checking, and the result is a too-high failure rate among new staff. A greater effort needs to be put into the selection process through the adoption of better practice recruiting techniques that include:

- Using simulation exercises and psychometric testing on the short-listed candidates
- Involving your team in the final selection process, which should include a casual walkabout the office environment
- Report writing and presentation exercises for more senior roles such as the management accountant position

One high-performance team asks the team if they know a person who would fit in the team before they advertise a position. Often this has proved successful in saving hours sifting through the great unknown.

RECOGNIZE STAFF PERFORMANCE

We all appreciate recognition, especially when we do not have to wait for it. Some participants have found some clever ways that work such as handing out of film tickets, vouchers for two at a good restaurant, and so forth, to reward accounting staff who have gone the extra mile.

Recognition is so important that all managers should count the recognitions given weekly. Reflect back, when did you last recognize the performance of your staff? As a guide you should have reason to recognize at least three times a week. Overlook this and you will be a manager that most are grateful to leave!

TEAM BALANCED SCORECARDS

Organizations that have adopted the balanced scorecard reporting have introduced team scorecards. These help the team score goals in a balanced way and increase the alignment of the individual members' work to their team and organization's goals.

Even if the organization has not adopted the balanced scorecard, the accounting team can add value by leading change in reporting team performance in a balanced way by introducing the concept for their team. Exhibit 6.2 shows a team scorecard designed in Excel. Excel is an excellent tool for designing a template and testing over a couple of months, after which it should be bedded down in a proper balanced scorecard system.

The secret for a good team scorecard is to ensure team members focus on the right things. Exhibit 6.2 will bring out the following:

- We want proactive services for our in-house customers so the finance team is being asked to organize proactive meetings, as opposed to fire fighting meetings with budget holders, to complete initiatives highlighted in the recent finance team's customer satisfaction survey and to close outstanding service requests.
- With regards to internal processes we are after efficient sales invoicing, prompt payments (thus avoiding supplier follow-up calls and maintaining those close relationships with them), progress with the finance team's major projects, and of course making sure the finance team completes what it starts.
- Regarding finances, the finance team will monitor capital expenditure (CAPEX) because the finance team can influence it and our team's expenditure profile.
- Learning and growth will help ensure we maintain training across the finance team.
- Staff satisfaction will focus on actions that improve staff satisfaction such as number of recognitions given and staff functions planned in next three months.
- Environment and community will look how we are contributing in the wider context such as number of presentations delivered to professional bodies, number of holiday jobs offered to top students, staff participating in community work, and so on.

Exhibit 6.2 Finance Team Balanced Scorecard

Balanced scorecard for the Finance function

As of 31 March 07

Customer focus

Customer focused initiatives	This month	Target
Accounting system downtime (8am-6pm)	30mins	<60mins
Last update of intranet page	12/1/06	weekly
Service requests outstanding	24	15
Service requests closed in month	8 (40%)	60%
Programme visits to budget holders	4	6
P&P updated on the intranet	0	1
Initiatives underway based on satisfaction survey	2	4

Usage of G/L by management	This month	Target
Managers accessing the G/L (#)	2	10
Managers accessing the G/L (time)	30 mins	2 hours
Suppliers on A/P	600	400

Project status

Xxxxx
Matrix
Xxxxx
Xxxxx
Xxxxx
Budget system
Balanced scorecard
Grants system
Revenue forecast
0 0.25 0.5 0.75 1
Done On-Track Behind Risk of Non-Completion

Delivery

Efficiency measures	This month	Target
Report to budget holders	2	By day 2
Report to Xxxxx	5	By day 5
Finance report to Xxxxx	10	By day 10
% of payments made by direct credit	80%	>75%
# of strategic supply relationships	1	4
# of accounts paid late	12	<20
# of customer calls in test week	15	<20
% of invoices issued on time	90%	99%
Projects completed on time on budget	44%	80%
Completions	**Current**	**Target**
Projects in progress	9	<8
Reports/documents still in draft mode	10	<5

Learning & Growth

Training needs outstanding	This month	YTD
CFO	0	2
Finance	0	5
Mngt Accounting	0	3
A/P team	0	2
A/R team	1	2
Average for all accounting staff	**n/a**	**2.5**

Post project reviews	current	target
Post project reviews undertaken to ascertain lessons learnt	0	4

Performance reviews	current	target
Staff who have had 2 performance reviews in the last year	10	23

Financial

% spent of this year's capital expenditure

0.8
0.6
0.4
0.2
0
Team #1 Team #2 Team #3 Team #4 Team #5 Team #6 Average % of Year gone

Accounting function expenditure profile

$m
4 3 2 1 0
Dec-06 Jan-07 Feb-07 Mar-07 Apr-07 May-07 Jun-07 Jul-07 Aug-07 Sep-07 Oct-07 Nov-07 Dec-07
Planned Cumulative — Forecast Cumulative — Actual Cumulative

Comments:

xxxxxx x xxxxxxxx x xxxxxxxxxxxx xxxxxxxxx xxxxxxxxxxx xxxxxxxx x xxxxxxxxxxxxx x x xxxxxxxxx x x xxxxxxxxxxx xx xxxxxxxxx x xxxxxx xx xxxxxxxxx

Xxxxxxxx Xxxxxxxx xxxxxxx xxxxxx x xxxxxxxx x xxxxxxxxxxxx xxxxxxxxx xxxxxxxxxxx xxxxxxxx x xxxxxxxxxxxxxxxxxxxx x x xxxxxxxxx x x xxxxxxxxxxx xx xxxxxxxxx x xxxxxx xx xxxxxxxxx

Xxxxxxxx Xxxxxxxx xxxxxxx xxxxxx x xxxxxxxx x xxxxxxxxxxxx xxxxxxxxx xxxxxxxxxxx xxxxxxxx x xxxxxxxxxxxxxxxxxxxx x x xxxxxxxxx x x xxxxxxxxxxx xx xxxxxxxxx x xxxxxx xx xxxxxxxxx

BETTER PRACTICE TRAINING

Some better practices that have been used to improve the effectiveness of training include:

- Providing in-house tailored courses so staff can easily achieve five days of training a year, some of which can be held as part of the off-site meetings mentioned earlier

- Supporting tertiary education, especially MBA programs
- Including interpersonal skills in-house courses
- Ensuring the management accountants attend consultancy skills courses
- Running satisfaction surveys on in-house customers and implementing training to close any noted gaps

OUTDOOR PURSUIT ADVENTURE

I recently met a coach of a national team who had taken his team to three consecutive world cup finals and won. One of his team building exercises was to ensure that the team went on an outdoor pursuit adventure where there were basic accommodation amenities. He ensured there was no television because he wanted the team to always be together learning more about each other.

I have also met a senior partner in an accounting firm who recalled that one weekend a group of staff got together and went on an overnight hike. It turned out to be more of an adventure than most had anticipated. The team dynamics after the hike were truly amazing. Those who went became known as the "A framers" and to this day they still have reunions, with members flying in from abroad.

TEAM BUILDING LESSONS FROM A WORLD CLASS COACH

The same coach of the world champion team gave me some tips about building a team and they included:

- Find out what makes each of your team members tick—this requires a number of meetings outside the work environment.
- Always remember an emotional outburst may create emotional damage, which takes a long time to heal.
- Remember selling the message to your team is important.
- Focus on shared leadership—be a facilitator rather than a leader.

- Team building is vital—take your team away to outdoor pursuit centers.
- Ask your team members individually "what do you want from me?"
- Be accepting of mistakes and analyze the decision making that led to the mistake; both the coach and the team player will learn something.

CFO AND ALL STAFF REPORTING DIRECTLY TO THEM MUST FIND A MENTOR IMMEDIATELY

In this day and age, only the foolish venture forward without having a mentor supporting them from "behind the scenes." A mentor is normally someone older than you, wiser, with more grey hairs who knows something about what you are doing. In other words, it could be a retired CEO of the business, a retired Board member who has known you for a while, a professional mentor, or someone in the sector where there is no conflict of interest.

A good mentor will save your career a number of times. With the advent of e-mail, a career-limiting event is only a "click on the send button" away! The mentor is someone who you ask, "Please look at this; I am thinking of copying in the CEO." To which the mentor replies, "Let's have a coffee first before it is sent," after which, when asked about the e-mail, you reply "What e-mail!"

Mentors are also well connected and will often further your career during discussions on the 19th hole. They often only receive as payment a good meal once a quarter, while others will do it for a living.

When looking for a mentor, start at the top and work down. Even the most successful people are happy, to set time aside, to mentor up-and-coming "younger guns." Asking someone to become your mentor is one of the greatest compliments you can give them.

CHAPTER 7

Quick Annual Reporting: Within 15 Working Days Post Year-End

The annual reporting activity is part of the "trifecta" of lost opportunities, the other two being month-end reporting and the annual planning process. While annual reporting is an important legal requirement, it does not create any value within your organization and thus seldom is it a task where your team has received any form of gratitude. Accounting functions therefore need to find ways to extract value from the process while at the same time bringing it down into a tight time frame.

Before you can have a quick year-end you need to speed up month-end reporting so staff are disciplined to a tight month-end. Your goal should be reporting numbers and comments by day 3. See Chapter 2 on quick month-end monthly reporting.

COSTS OF A SLOW YEAR-END

The costs of a slow year-end include:

- Months where the accounting team are simply doing annual and monthly reporting—thus little added value is created by the finance team in that time
- Too much time goes into the annual report as we lose sight of Pareto's 80/20 rule
- Little or no client servicing during this time and thus bad habits are picked up by budget holders

Accounting teams are often "hijacked" by the annual reporting process.

—CFO with blue chip international experience

Given the amount of time this activity takes, the 80/20 rule still applies. Most organizations look at the annual report financials as being special" numbers that they have reworked many times. There is absolutely no reason in 99% of the cases why the "first cut" of year-end for internal reporting should not be the same as the last cut for external reporting. Most adjustments are trivial and result in printing delays. The annual report comes out so late virtually nobody reads it anyway!

—CFO with blue chip international experience

Exhibit 7.1 shows how to calculate the costs of an annual accounts process. The times are estimates and show what a 300-to-500 full-time employee (FTE) public company may be investing in their annual report preparation. It does not include investor relations and so forth. The senior management team (SMT) has lower productive weeks in a year because you have to take out, in addition to holidays, training, and sick leave, the time they spend travelling and in general meetings.

There are many ways in which we can improve the way we do year-end, and they can all be grouped around three words:

1. **Organization.** Establishing an audit coordinator, the working paper files, the deadlines, and so forth.
2. **Communication.** Communicating with both the auditors and staff.

Exhibit 7.1 Cost of the Annual Accounts Process

	Accounting team	BHs	SMT
Liaison with auditors throughout audit	3 to 5		1 to 2
Planning audit	1 to 3		
Interim audit assistance	4 to 6	20 to 40	
Preparing annual accounts	2 to 5		
Preparing audit schedules	2 to 5		
Extra work finalizing year-end numbers	20 to 30		
Final audit visit assistance	10 to 20	20 to 40	
Finalizing annual report	10 to 20		5 to 8
Total weeks of effort	52 to 94	40 to 80	6 to 10
Average salary cost	$80,000	$55,000	$200,000
Average productive weeks	42	42	32
	Low	High	
Average personnel cost	$190,000	$350,000	
Printing costs	45,000	75,000	
Audit fees	45,000	65,000	
Estimated cost	$280,000	$490,000	

3. **Pre year-end work.** Bring forward many year-end routines earlier, such as cutting off at month 10 or 11 and rolling forward. This also includes preparing a comprehensive auditors' file, saving the audit team considerable audit time.

COST THE ANNUAL ACCOUNTS PROCESS

In order to create a change in the way the senior management team (SMT), Board, and management address the annual accounts you need to establish the full cost of the annual accounts process including all Board, management, and staff time, and all those external costs (e.g., audit fees, printing costs, public relations (PR), and legal fees).

QUICK YEAR-END IS A GOOD YEAR-END

Exhibit 7.2 shows a rating scale for the time frame to have an audited and signed annual report (time from year-end date).

Many top U.S. companies report very quickly to the stock exchange; in my days as an auditor IBM was well known for its speed of reporting.

Exhibit 7.2 Year-End Reporting Time Frames
(From the Year-End to Signed Annual Report)

Exceptional	Outstanding	Above Average	Average
Less than 10 working days	10–15 working days	16–20 working days	21–30 working days

If your organization reports very quickly at year-end, ignore this section; otherwise read and implement because you and your organization are wasting too much time in this area.

There are a number of benefits, including:

- Better value from the interim and final audit visits
- Improved data quality through improved processing
- Reduced costs in both audit and staffs' time
- More time for finance staff for critical activities such as analysis, decision making, and forecasting
- Improved investor relations

HELP GET THE AUDITORS ORGANIZED

An audit can very easily get disorganized. The audit firm will more than likely have a change in either the audit senior or audit staff, and their first-year staff will know little about what they are trying to audit, no matter what training they have had.

So, help the audit—it is in your interests by:

- Allocating appropriate facilities for the audit room (phones, desks, security)
- Providing an induction session for new audit staff, because up to 40% of junior audit time is wasted in an unknown environment
- Preparing a financial statement file and handing it over on day one of the final visit (this file will contain papers supporting all numbers in the financial statements, including completed audit lead schedules ready for their files, 12 months of monthly re-ports, etc.)

- Advising staff to assist the auditors and having a specific person in every section who should be contacted in first instance should the auditors need information
- Holding meetings at key times with the auditors (e.g., the planning meeting, the interim meeting, and meetings to discuss the final results). The steps in each of these stages are set out and analyzed in detail in the annual accounts checklist in Appendix D.

APPOINT AN AUDIT COORDINATOR

The first step to improving communication between staff and the audit team is to have a full-time audit coordinator. This person should be a staff member, not necessarily in finance, who knows most people in the company and knows where everything is; in other words, "an oracle."

You may find the ideal person is someone in accounts payable or someone who has recently retired. The important point is that they should have no other duties during the audit visits (both interim and final visits) other than helping the audit team. Give them a nice room and say "when not helping the audit team you can simply put your feet up." Do not get tempted to give them additional duties. Their tasks include:

- Providing an induction session for new audit staff
- Gathering any vouchers and so forth that the auditors need
- Responding to information requests the auditors have made that are still outstanding
- Setting up designated contact points in every function (e.g., who to speak to in the marketing department)
- Organizing meetings with the designated person in the section they need to visit
- Arranging meetings at key times between CFO and the auditors

COMPLETE DRAFTING OF THE ANNUAL REPORT BEFORE YEAR-END!

It is desirable to complete the annual report, other than the final year's result, by the middle of month 12. This will require coordination with the PR consultant who drafts the written commentary in the annual accounts, and discussions with the Chairperson of the Board and with the CEO. Your last month's numbers will not greatly impact the commentary.

Also remember that nobody reads the annual report. If you are a publicly listed company, the stock broker analysts rely on the more in-depth briefing you give them, mainstream shareholders do not understand them, and the accounting profession just skim them.

LIMIT WHEN CHANGES CAN BE MADE

It is important to be disciplined over cut-offs and when journal vouchers can be processed. One company I know only allows three opportunities to adjust the year-end numbers, and one of them is for the final tax numbers. The stages are as follows:

Stage 1 is at the close of the second working day

Stage 2 on the sixth working day

Stage 3 is for tax entries only

HAVE A MONTH 10 OR 11 HARD CLOSE

The larger and more complex the organization is, the greater the need for a hard close on month 10 results. All other organizations should go for a hard close at month 11. Effectively month 11 becomes the year-end with all major assets being verified such as debtors, stock, and fixed assets. If a debtor's circularization is to be performed, this will need to be performed on month 9 or 10 balances, thus allowing enough time for responses. Once the auditors have confirmed that the stock, fixed assets, and debtors' balances are a "true and fair view," the auditors need only to confirm the movements of these balances in the remaining month or two.

EFFECTIVE STOCK TAKES

Stock takes should never be conducted at any month-end let alone the year-end. There is no need because your stock records should be able to be verified at any point in time. It is a better practice to conduct rolling stock counts rather than one major count that closes all production. A well-organized stock take includes:

- Trained stock takers working in pairs, each from a different department, to enhance independence and thoroughness
- The highlighting obsolescence stocks. These can be targeted in the preceding months to reduce the write down at year-end
- Rolling stock takes throughout the year (e.g., a jewelry company with a chain of stores counts watches one month, rings the next month, etc.); the stock takes occur in quiet times during the month
- Ensuring that the stock area is tidied and organized before the counting to ensure a more accurate count (e.g., same stock items are together)
- Visible tags are added to counted items
- Once the count has been done a good celebration is in order; this will ensure willing helpers next time

ESTIMATING "ADDED VALUE" IN WORK-IN-PROGRESS (WIP) AND FINISHED GOODS

Auditors can get lost in auditing the added value in WIP and finished goods very easily. On one audit it took me a couple of weeks of elapsed time tracing the WIP through its stages, using random samples.

In the second year it was suggested that I look at how many weeks of production there were in WIP. This was easy to confirm, then how much direct and indirect overhead could and should be absorbed. The audit of WIP took two days!

Thus, help your auditors see the "woods for the trees" and provide working papers to support complex valuations such as WIP.

EFFECTIVE FIXED ASSETS VERIFICATION

The key to effective fixed asset verification is a correct fixed asset register (FAR). Many organizations see the fixed asset register as a necessary evil, thus little focus is given to really driving it properly. The rare few grab the opportunity and turn the FAR into a valuable system by:

- Using bar codes on all assets so asset verification is a paperless exercise with a scanner
- Setting higher capitalization levels than those stated by the tax authorities, radically reducing the volume in the FAR—it being recognized that a tax adjustment can be performed easily if necessary
- Recording the maintenance for key plant and their expected lives so useful graphics can be shown to management and the Board
- Reducing the number of fixed asset categories, because every extra coding only serves to create more chance for miscoding—remember we are to apply Pareto's 80/20 rule!
- Performing rolling fixed asset checks rather than doing it all at one time (e.g., verify equipment in the factory this month, computer equipment next month, etc.)

Following these steps will mean that the auditors will be able to successfully test the FAR and then rely on it for the correct asset cost and depreciation (amortization).

IMPORTANCE OF INTERNAL AUDITORS

Internal auditors can significantly reduce the external auditors' work. Many organizations contract out this function to an independent firm. An in-house internal audit team will pay for themselves many times over by:

- Helping the use of efficient and effective procedures
- Providing a great training ground for new graduate staff
- Focusing on re-engineering exercises and other revenue generating or cost saving activities (e.g., in a one-week exercise most internal auditors would be able to save 5% off future telecommunication costs)
- Providing the external auditors with all their main working papers filled out—they will know how to do this because they will have attended the external auditor's staff training courses

EXTRACT MORE VALUE FROM THE MANAGEMENT LETTER

It is important that you insist that the auditors put a bit more care and attention into the management letters and that they are delivered within two weeks of the interim and final visits. Prompt management letters mean that management can get on and rectify a problem immediately.

A minor comment about a procedural failure can easily be taken out of context by the Board. All errors that they want to comment on should be stated in context (e.g., we found 20 invoices with the wrong prices, we understand this was because xxxxxxxx. Management has rectified the situation and we tested a further sample of xxxx and found no further errors. We note that of all the other price tests we performed there were no other errors. We do not believe this has led to a loss of profits greater than $xxxx.)

Also we want the auditors to comment on our strengths (e.g., we would like to comment that the new month report formats are the best we have seen, they are clear, concise, and cost effective in terms of production time, well done!).

> *During the audit we commented to the auditors that we had found a better way of carrying out a process. They turned around this knowledge and noted the current process as a weakness in the management letter when in fact it had not created a problem. I blew up the audit partner and they apologized and removed the comment.*
>
> —CFO with blue chip international experience

DERIVE MORE VALUE FROM THE INTERIM AUDIT VISIT

In conjunction with the external auditors look at making more use out of the interim audit. You may have implemented a new expense system so ask the auditors to spend some time testing compliance. Ask them to cover more branches, ensuring nearly all branches are covered every two years. This will cost more but will be worthwhile. Always remember it is perception that rules the roost; staff in remote branches will begin to conform to company policies if they know auditors are to arrive and they always test out the compliance of the key systems along with all the new systems.

It is a good practice to ensure that the first interim visits occur in the first half of the year so that the staff are "kept on their mettle."

RESTRICT ACCESS OF CONFIDENTIAL INFORMATION TO THE AUDIT PARTNER

It is important to inform staff and the audit team about what is restricted access (e.g., it may be that only the audit partner is able to sight the SMT's payroll). I remember the days when the audit staff would fight over who was to look at payroll—just remember it is human nature to be nosy. Make it clear to the audit manager what role they should play with this more sensitive information.

RUN A WORKSHOP TO "POST-IT" RE-ENGINEER YEAR-END REPORTING

Reengineering can be a complex and expensive task or a relatively easy one; the choice is yours. Many organizations start off by bringing in consultants to process map the existing procedures. This is a futile exercise, because why spend a lot of money documenting a process you are about to radically alter and when it is done only the consultants will understand the resulting data-flow diagrams!

As previously discussed in Chapter 2 and bears repeating here, the answer is to "Post-it" re-engineer your year-end procedures in a workshop (see Exhibit 7.3 for an outline of the workshop).

"Post-it" re-engineering processes is quite simple; all it requires is:

- Each team listing all their processes on to the "Post-it" stickers allocated to them (as set out in Exhibit 2.4) prior to the workshop and documented as set out in Exhibit 2.5.
- In a workshop environment the teams gather together and start off by explaining what better year-end procedures are.

  "Post-its" are placed in time order under column headings week − 2, day − 1, week + 1, week + 2, and so on using a white board (the "Post-its" do not stick well to walls!).

Exhibit 7.3 Outline of "Post-it" Re-engineering Annual Reporting Workshop

Agenda and Outline of the Quick Year-End Workshop

Date and Time: xxxxxx

Location: xxxxxx

Suggested Attendees: All those involved in year-end including accounts payable, accounts receivable, fixed assets, financial and management accountants, representatives from teams interface with year-end routines, e.g., someone from IT, payroll, PR, etc.)

Learning Outcomes:

Attendees after this workshop will be able to:

- Discuss and explain to management why their organization should have quicker year-end reporting
- Use better practices to streamline their current bottlenecks
- Use a step-by-step implementation framework
- Describe better practice year-end routines
- Recall all agreements made at the workshop (these will be documented)

9:00 A.M.	Welcome by Financial Controller
9:10 A.M.	**Setting the scene**—a review of better practices among accounting teams that are delivering swift annual reporting, topics covered include: • What is quick year-end reporting? • Benefits of quick annual reporting to management and the finance team • Better practice year-end procedures—stories • Current performance gap between xxxxxxxxx and better practice • Precision versus timeliness **Senior management, PR expert involved in annual report, representative from the legal team, and a selection of budget holders (who are locally based) will be invited to attend this session "setting the scene"**
9:50 A.M.	**Agreement on the current key bottlenecks of year-end reporting presented by Financial Controller** • Current cost estimate of year-end reporting • Human cost of the annual accounts process (weekends and late nights worked) • What we are doing well • We need to work within existing systems • Goal is "signed annual accounts by 15 working days"

(continues)

Exhibit 7.3 *(Continued)*

10:05 A.M.	**Workshop 1 to analyze the year-end procedures using "Post-its"** (yellow—accounts payable, green—accounts receivable, red—production, purple—annual report, blue—finance accounting team, CAPEX—pink, management accounting team—light yellow, etc.)
10:30 A.M.	Morning break
10:45 A.M.	**Workshop 1 continues**
11:20 A.M.	Feedback and pulling it together, participants will document agreed changes and individuals will be encouraged to take responsibility for implementing the steps
12:00 P.M.	**Workshop 2 to set out the appropriate implementation steps to implement quick annual reporting.** Each team prepares a short presentation of the key steps they are committed to making (teams will use PowerPoint on laptops).
12:30 P.M.	Lunch
1:15 P.M.	**Workshop 2 continues**
2:00 P.M.	Each team presents reports to the group what changes they are going to implement and when. They can also raise any issues they still have. **Those senior management team and budget holders who attended the first session will be invited to attend this session**
2:30 P.M.	Wrap up of workshop by Financial Controller
2:45 P.M.	Finish

- Movie voucher is given to each attendee who identifies a process that can be removed as not necessary (they were done because they were done last year)—each one removed is like finding gold because it means less work, fewer steps.
- Reorganize the key processes and bottlenecks based on better practice (e.g., accounts payable close-off occurring on noon last working day and now reschedule tasks that can be done earlier). You will find it hard to justify any task needing to be done after day 3!

Rules for "Post-it" stickers include:

- One procedure per "Post-it"

- State when it is done—time scale is week − 2 (week minus two), week − 1 (last week before year-end), week + 1 (first week after year-end), week + 2, etc.
- Write in big letters (must be seen from 15 feet)

SOME CASE STUDIES

A large U.S. company has its results available by the fourth working day. They have a month 10 close with full stock take at end of month 10. The auditors then audit the ten months and then the remaining two months. They ensure comprehensive coordination and communication exists between the company and the auditors.

One government agency had their annual accounts completed by working day 15, signed by directors on working day 18, and signed off by the auditors on the 20th working day. This pace was required because of a major refinancing deal.

One finance company completed their annual accounts in 24 working days; they had only three opportunities or stages for adjustment:

Stage 1 is at the close of the second working day

Stage 2 on the sixth working day

Stage 3 is for tax entries only

Within these deadlines they complete three reporting packs to their overseas parent.

One public sector hospital ensures a smooth year-end by providing the external auditors with comprehensive end-of-year files. The finance staff complete lead schedules; provide copies of key documentation; provide analytical review comments; and copies of every month's accounts. The audit is completed within two weeks by an audit team of three people. The finance team raised 20 key accounting issues prior to year-end and sought the auditor's judgment. They also ensured the management letter is more constructive, including both positive comments as well as areas for improvement.

CHAPTER 8

Managing Debtors

There are many workshops on debt management and collection practices and this section assumes that your accounts receivable (AR) staff have attended these. This chapter concentrates on the practices that may not be covered by these courses.

OPERATIONAL IMPROVEMENTS TO ACCOUNTS RECEIVABLE

Some better practices you may wish to adopt are:

- Have the right mental attitude to credit control (e.g., don't feel guilty asking for money . . . . it's yours and you are entitled to it); and when asking for your money be hard on the issue but soft on the person.
- Provide immediate notice of overdue debt to the sales team.
- Establish clear credit practices and communicate these credit practices to staff and customers.
- Be professional when accepting new accounts and especially larger ones (e.g., perform the credit checks that a bank would when lending the same amount).
- Continuously review credit limits, especially for major customers if tough times are coming or if operating in a volatile sector.

- Monitor sales invoicing promptness and accuracy.
- Charge penalties on overdue accounts.
- Consider accepting credit cards for smaller high-risk customers.

People will take as much credit as you give—and that doesn't mean what your credit policy allows, it means what you let them take.

A lot of bad practice has grown around the giving and taking of credit. Conventional wisdom says that the less credit you give, and the more you take, the better off you are. However this ignores the real overhead cost created by tracking and reconciling "overdues" and outstandings. It also makes your suppliers dislike you. They won't support you when you need them if you constantly pay late. Credit is best minimized on both sides. Demand quick payment and provide incentives. Pay your bills right away. Your administration costs will fall!

—CFO with blue chip international experience

REPORTING ON YOUR ACCOUNTS RECEIVABLE

The graph shown in Exhibit 8.1 will reduce much of the need for a larger debtor report. This graph focuses on the debtors' aging trend. You need to go back at least 12 months, preferably 15 to 18 months, to catch the impact of last year's seasonal fluctuations.

AVOIDING ACCOUNTS RECEIVABLE MONTH-END PROCESSING BOTTLENECKS

Once again electronic interfaces with key customers and electronic cash receipting are the keys to moving out of the processing battle at month-ends within AR. Some better practices are:

- Cut off AR at noon last working day, with the afternoon sales being dated as the first day of the new month—you will need to ensure that customers still pay invoices according to your terms.
- Change the sales invoice cycle for all "monthly sales invoices" to customers (e.g., May 26th to June 25th).

Exhibit 8.1 Aged Debtors Over Time

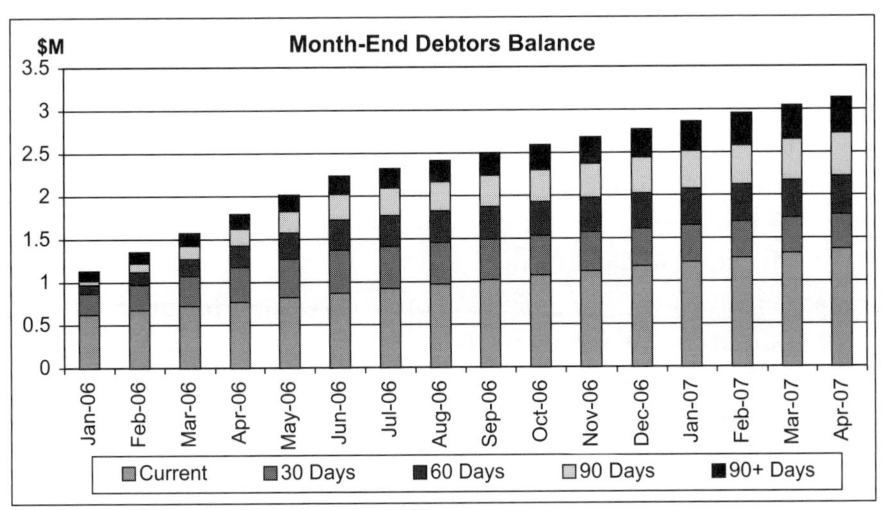

- Consider invoicing all transactions to 25th of the month, with a second invoice for the remaining period of month.
- Send electronic invoices to your major customers, including their general ledger codes—the easier you make it for them the better for both parties.
- If you need details from sub-contractors in order to invoice, look to streamline processes in a meeting between your customer and your main sub-contractors to ensure a prompt and accurate billing process.
- If you have a lot of sub-contractors consider offering them a free accounting system that has an automatic link to yours for all invoices relevant to you.

INCREASING THE USE OF DIRECT DEBITING OF CUSTOMERS' ACCOUNTS

My father walks into town to pay many of his accounts by check. It is good exercise and an excuse to get out of the house. However, this activity is very costly to the receipting supplier, typically some utility. Many companies have tried in vain to get customers to allow direct debiting access to their bank account. There are many hurdles to cross including the perception that their bank account is now at the mercy of another company. Some better practice ways to sell direct debiting are:

- Offer a cash draw each month financed by the cash flow savings from receiving prompt payment. One telecommunications company offers three $10,000 prizes each month. All those who pay by direct debit have three chances to win $10,000 every month. My father would sign up for this.
- On your next price increase offer to waive it for all those who sign up to a direct debit (DD).
- Offer a DD discount each month on the total invoice, splitting the benefit you gain between you and the customer. You can make this appear more attractive by offering a large discount on a small fixed-price component of the transaction (e.g., one energy retailer gave a 20% discount on the fixed charges, which was only $6 per customer for every month where a DD authority was present).

DEBTORS COLLECTION BEFORE YEAR-END

While debtors should be a focus year round and in some cases involve the CFO and CEO in direct contact with their counterparts, there needs to be an added drive from month 9 onward to clean up everything over 60 days (e.g., a phone call from your CEO to the other CEO could save thousands of dollars in legal fees and possibly the whole debt, because you have collected the debt before the company has gone into receivership).

Remember if it takes 10 hours of CFO time to collect $50,000 from a high-risk account, that is a very good return on time—$5,000 per hour!

CHAPTER 9

Marketing the Accounting Function

Accounting functions can never do enough marketing. Lack of marketing is the main reason why accounting functions are not appreciated fully by management, and why many accounting team implementations take longer and are less successful than anticipated. If accountants were good marketers, many may well have chosen a different career path! It is important to recognize these shortcomings and to fill the gap with expert advice—either find yourself a marketing mentor, touch base with your in-house public relations (PR) expert, or acquire some PR external advice—you will not regret it.

Some ways you can improve the marketing of your team are:

- Have informative intranet pages including success stories and the photos and short-form CVs of all of the accounting team members; see Exhibit 9.1 for an example of a team's intranet page(s)
- Walk about more—encourage the management and financial accountants, AP staff, and so forth to spend more time on proactive visits
- Ensure someone from the finance team is attending corporate functions
- Contribute to your organization's newsletter

- Spend time adding value to the senior management team by increasing their understanding of their business
- Run "cuppa for a cause" events where the finance team organize a morning tea to raise funds for a local charity and budget holders donate a dollar or so and enjoy some hospitality at the finance team's office
- Use breaks for networking with budget holders and other stakeholders
- Make the quarterly rolling planning cycle a good way to learn about what your customers need from you
- Invite new staff from major subsidiaries or departments to call in when they are next in the head office

FITTING INTO THE WIDER TEAM

Why is it that many hard working corporate accountants, who are dedicated to the organization, are ostracized by their fellow colleagues? Here are some of the reasons:

- They are workaholics that make all others feel inferior
- They undertake tasks in such detail that they make work for all the others
- They are always complaining of being overworked, albeit most of their excess workload is self-inflicted
- Seldom do they take time out to network
- They treat every activity as if their life depended on it
- They are too intense, often boring one with unnecessary detail

If you are one of these people there is time to change before it is too late. I suggest the following:

- Limit your working hours to no more than 50 hours a week so you have to change your habits
- Ensure to network with your peers and in-house clients, over a coffee in an outside location, at least twice a week for the next 12 weeks

Exhibit 9.1 Finance Team's Intranet Site Example

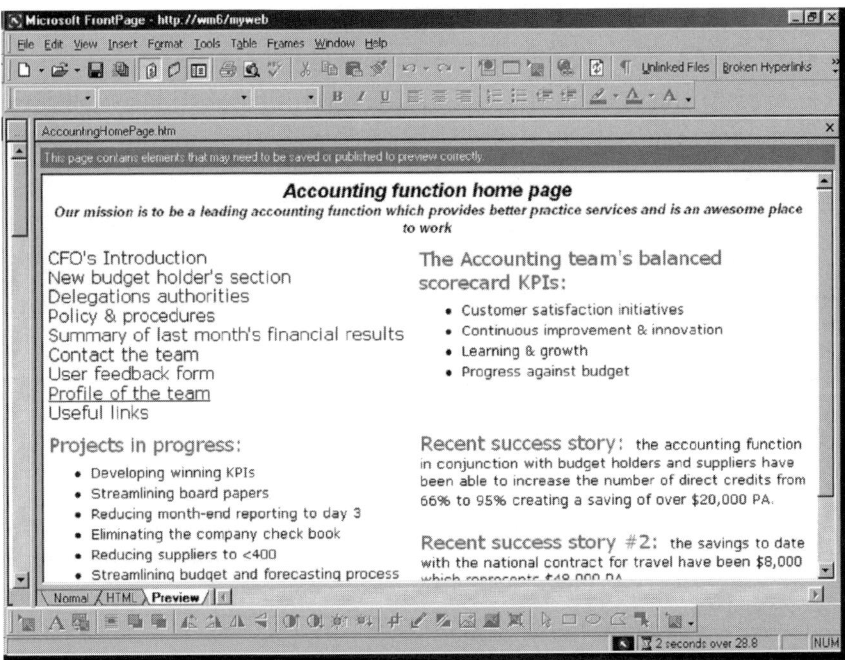

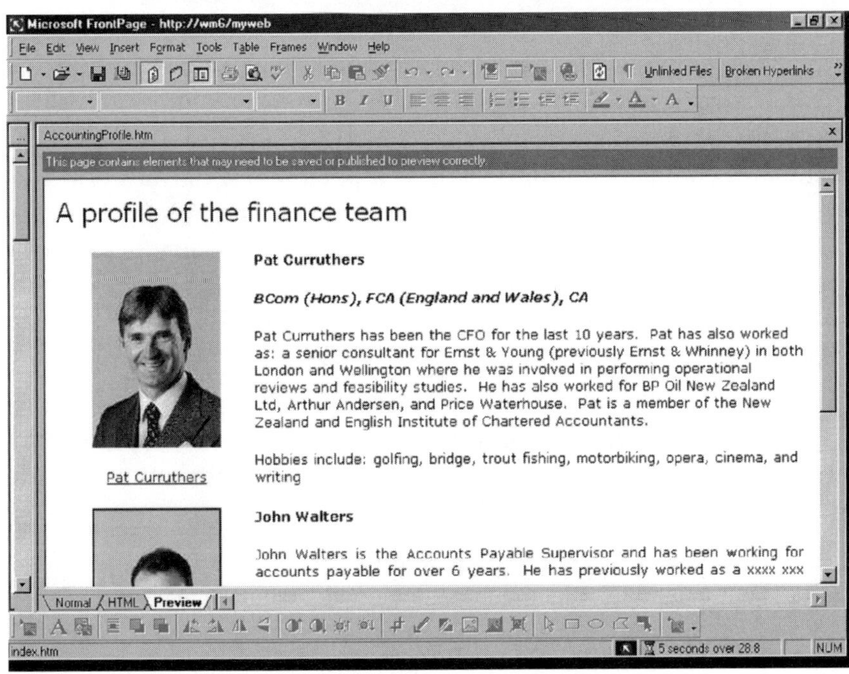

- Before embarking on a major project speak to your mentor as you may well be on the wrong track
- Have a makeover so you look and feel like a million dollars
- Ensure you talk positively to others (popular people are seldom the fountains of negative thoughts—learn to keep these to yourself)
- Avoid writing long reports, as nothing was ever changed by a report; it was the follow-up action that made the change
- No matter how much pressure, learn to smile every time someone comes to your desk (this needs plenty of practice)
- Remember to always try and see the bigger picture—nobody, to my knowledge, has ever died because a corporate accountant's work was late; fortunately or unfortunately our work is not that important
- Learn to give recognition more freely

BECOME KNOWN FOR BEING ONE WHO GIVES RECOGNITION FREELY

I have for a long time been aware of the significance of recognition, but only recently have I been aware that it is a fundamental foundation of all our relationships. The ability to appreciate and recognize all those we come in contact with defines us as a person and defines how successful, in the broadest terms we can be. Giving recognition, freely, makes us a person who people like to work for and with and one we naturally gravitate towards.

Many of us will need to count the recognitions we give, until it becomes a natural part of our make up. The checklist on the following page will help you achieve this behavioral change.

For some of us the simple task of recognizing all the types of support we receive will be unnatural. If you are having difficulty trying to recognize contribution think of GAS:

- G for **guidance** that has been helpful
- A for **actions** done that make your life easier
- S for **support** and commitment

	Suggested Frequency	Week 1	Week 2	Week 3	Week 4	Week 5, etc.
Our staff	Weekly					
Our work colleagues	Weekly					
Our boss	Weekly					
Our mentor	Quarterly					
Our suppliers	Quarterly					
Our budget holders	Quarterly					

Some participants have found some clever ways that work such as handing out of film tickets, vouchers for two at a good restaurant, etc., to reward accounting staff who have gone the extra mile.

Do not underestimate the power of the signed memo or letter recognizing superior performance. I have included a few recognition templates in Appendix I for your convenience.

CHAPTER 10

Client Management: Improving Relationships with Budget Holders

The accounting function needs to focus much more on client management. Too much time is spent sitting behind a desk, instead of scoring goals in front of managers and the senior management team (SMT). Corporate accountants need to be business advisors first.

Some ways you can improve your client management with budget holders are:

- Give them new insights into their operation, e.g., you could save $xxx if you did this.
- Include trend information (rolling 12- or 24-month graphs) and key performance indicators (KPIs) in the reporting.
- Talk through the monthly results with them—they might not understand the reports!
- Provide training sessions for budget holder's staff.
- Help budget holders with their new re-forecast—you can expand your support team temporarily for this purpose.

- Help budget holders with bringing forward projects
- Run a satisfaction survey on your in-house customers and implement the recommendations
- Provide a reward for the first correct budget holder monthly return (e.g., cinema tickets, etc.)

PERFORM AN IN-HOUSE CUSTOMER SATISFACTION SURVEY

Initially once a year and then twice a year run a statistically based sample survey on your in-house customers. Send them the survey set out in Appendix J. The key features are:

- Ask two open-ended questions that will generate most of the benefit of the survey, such as "what are the three things we do well" and "what are the three things we can improve on"—never ask about the problems because half of them will not be fixable
- Categorize all responses to these questions in a database and sort out by positive comments and suggestions for improvement (see Exhibit 10.1)
- Use a 5-point scale (5 = Very satisfied, 4 = Satisfied, 3 = Neither satisfied nor dissatisfied, 2 = Dissatisfied, 1 = Very dissatisfied, X = Not applicable, cannot rate)
- Separate out accounting system problems from the services your team provides by asking a series of system-related questions
- Send them by e-mail or use a web-based survey package
- Never ask questions you will not act upon; in other words, make the questionnaire simple and able to be completed in ten minutes

One CFO who has experience with running satisfaction surveys wanted to improve results. So he went around to every budget holder and member of the senior management team and asked "What would the finance team need to do to get at least a very good rating from you on services our team provides?" Surprise, surprise, the team listened, actioned the suggestions, and in the next survey they got the best result out of all teams.

—CFO from the electricity sector

Exhibit 10.1 Extract from a Commentary Section Showing Identification of Comments

Judgment on Comment	Comment
Customer focus	**Staff prepared to go the extra mile** **Helpful (trying to be)** **Good PA** **Good ability to respond to circumstances and needs that change rapidly** **Fairness and courtesy to all** **Staff willingness and very positive attitude** **Supportive well-trained support staff** **Client focus and we give all parties more than reasonable time and attention** **If there are upsets, there is usually immediate attention by senior staff** **Pleasant and efficient staff**
Communication	**Initiatives to improve communication within the xxxxxxxx have been positively received and changes (for the better) have been made** **Good communications** **Good liaison with the xxxxx and xxxxx** My staff were not told that they were not needed for the meeting in xxxxxxx when it was cancelled. Much time was wasted!
Database	Improvements of the database are overdue Computer database inadequacies are causing major problems for us

CHAPTER 11

Working Smarter Not Harder

I have been fortunate to have witnessed a number of amazing teams. Set out in this chapter are some of their practices along with some of my thoughts on working smarter, not harder.

DEBRIEFING OF FINANCE STAFF AT THE END OF THE DAY

Finance staff debriefings are a rare sight these days and if they are scheduled, they are often the first meeting to be deferred or cancelled. This is often because the debriefings are not handled in the appropriate way, and thus staff attending may consider them a waste of time. It can be different; one high-performance team has an open-ended debriefing every evening in the last 15 minutes of the working day. Normally it only takes the allotted 15 minutes but it can be extended should the team require it. In their debriefing sessions they cover the following issues:

- How best to help a particular in-house client who is having difficulties
- Ways to improve operations
- Plans for the next day and next week

- Finishing off communication, which due to the pressures of the day was not completed
- "Popping the balloon" on those difficult issues that may have grown out of proportion during the day

Another point worth noting is that this high-performance team could not operate if it chose to have meetings during its key service delivery time. Yet that is the very thing we all tend to do.

BANNING MORNING MEETINGS FOR THE FINANCE STAFF

A good start is to avoid having meetings in your productive time (e.g., the mornings). I fail to see why CFOs feel the urge to have a meeting at 9 A.M. on a Monday morning with their direct reports. This meeting is often followed with more meetings as the debrief is passed down the chain in the finance team. Why not have this meeting at 4.30 P.M. on a Friday? It certainly will be a quick meeting!

Ask anybody about their productivity and you will find frustration about how time has been taken away in nonproductive activities. Would it not be better to schedule meetings toward the tail end of the day and leave the morning for service delivery? Exhibit 11.1 provides an example of how a manager's diary often looks and could look.

The main change is bigger and more productive chunks of service delivery time, the delaying of e-mail duties to after the morning break, and meeting times rescheduled to the afternoons. The moving of meetings to the afternoon also allows us to be more relaxed, having scored some goals in the morning. Having rescheduled the meetings we now need to make the meetings more productive.

IMPLEMENTING "ACTION MEETINGS" METHODS

Most managers have at some time received training in managing meetings, yet the level of frustration with meetings remains the same. The problem has been that the training has not looked at all the core reasons

Exhibit 11.1 Before and After Working Day Diary Example

The working day

	Typical Manager's Diary	Suggested
8 am	Admin	Service Delivery
9 am		Time
10 am	Meetings	Admin
11 am	Service Delivery	Service Delivery
Noon	Meetings	Time
1 pm	Break	Break
2 pm	Meetings	Meetings
3 pm		Meetings
4 pm	Service Delivery	Follow Up
5 pm	Meetings	Meetings
6 pm	Follow Up	Service Delivery
evening	Service Delivery Time	Time

for failure. Even the legendary John Cleese's "meetings bloody meetings" serves to entertain rather than tackle these issues.

Two management consultants, Mike Osborne and Dave McIntosh, have developed a methodology that is breathtaking in its simplicity yet profound in its impact.

Action Meetings (see www.actionmeetings.com) has attacked the core of dysfunctional meetings and the common features of unclear agendas, lack of engagement, rambling discussions, a total lack of understanding of "the space" the fellow attendees are in, and worst of all, poorly defined action points and follow-through.

Some of the key features of "action meetings" are:

- Getting people properly into and out of the meeting—the introduction of a first word and last word where attendees briefly say what state they are in. The first words could range from "I am very time challenged and this meeting is last thing I need" to "keen to make progress with this assignment and to hear Bill's view on the XYZ development." The last words could include "This meeting once again promised little and delivered nothing" to "I look forward to receiving Pat's report and working with the project team." The key to the first and last words is that attendees can say anything about how they feel at that point in time, and their comment is just that and is to remain unanswered.

Exhibit 11.2 What Meeting Outcomes Could Include Example

- Project XYZ progress examined and **understood**
- Monthly results **understood**
- Next steps for project XYZ **agreed** and **assigned**
- This month's key initiatives **agreed**
- Responsibilities on the acquisition of ABC Limited **assigned**

- An effective agenda constructed as outcomes—the introduction of precise wordings about meeting outcomes (see Exhibit 11.2). Outcomes provide focus and the ability to easily check whether an item has in fact been completed. One major benefit of establishing "meeting outcomes" worded in this way is that requested attendees can and should extract themselves from attending if they do not think they can add value or assist in achieving the outcomes.
- Meetings are participant-owned, not chairperson-owned—all attendees are trained in the new methodology and thus meetings are owned and policed by all the participants and so are less reliant on the capability of the chairperson.

HANDLING E-MAILS

Many of us either fortunately or unfortunately are not heart or brain surgeons. Our work is not critical to life. Many things we end up doing have little or no relevance to where we or our organizations are heading.

The handling of e-mails is a major case in point. Prior to the invention of e-mail, we would handle the mail at 10:30 A.M. when it arrived from the mail room. We thus started the day with scoring a goal, undertaking a service delivery activity. Now the first thing we do is open up the e-mail and suddenly one hour has evaporated. Some of us even get interrupted when every e-mail arrives.

One suggestion is to not open e-mail until after your morning break and then only look at e-mails at two more intervals during the day. If something is very important you will get a phone call. This technique will help you get more 1.5 hour blocks of concentrated time in your day.

CONTINUOUS INNOVATION IN THE FINANCE TEAM

For one high-performance team, innovation is discussed every day during the end-of-day debrief. This practice will benefit those finance teams that adopt it. Innovation needs to be on every meeting's agenda; it needs to be pushed so that the finance team knows what is expected, otherwise we are simply standing still. In many organizations the staff, including the finance team, has the perception that innovation is not required. In many finance teams you can find someone who is "building his yacht in his back yard" after work yet is performing the same unproductive tasks day after day like a laboratory rat hunting for its cheese.

How is it that organizations can take an individual who is innovative at home and turn him or her into an automaton? There are many aspects of the corporate culture that need to change—more delegation, more risk taking, less witch-hunting, and more celebration of success—then you truly can have continuous innovation.

GETTING THE INDUCTION PROCESS RIGHT

All good organizations put a lot of time and effort into a good induction process, which is committed to, not only by the team leader but by all other staff. Far too often the induction process gets left to an item on the agenda. When new staff members arrive, they get the sense that they are a burden.

An induction, in the finance team, should include:

- Detailed handover with person leaving, or failing that, someone familiar with routines
- Meeting in a relaxed atmosphere (e.g., over coffee) with some of the general managers or middle managers depending on seniority of the new recruit
- Specified meeting times with the manager (e.g., 3 P.M. Wednesday, 3 P.M. Friday) to pick up any loose ends
- A selection of easy tasks where goals can be scored easily
- Vetting of meetings so the new employee gets to go to meetings that are functioning well

- Meeting with helpdesk and IT support staff to cover intranet, systems, e-mail, hours of operation, remote access, security, and so forth
- Meeting with Human Resources scheduled for three months after joining date
- Visit to any production facilities
- Phone number and e-mail address of last person who did the job

CREATING A SERVICE CULTURE IN THE FINANCE TEAM

Instilling a focus on customer satisfaction in the finance team is difficult. It requires commitment, training and good recruitment practices. I was speaking to the bursar on a plane where the service level was exceptional. I asked "can you train for this level of service" to which she replied "no you have to recruit for it."

For those finance teams who work for organizations who are legendary at service delivery things will be easier as you have most likely recruited for it or at least attracted recruits who are service orientated. Make being service orientated a priority, organize some training, have an in-house workshop to discuss what this means in day-to-day activities, and ensure the CFO and all the corporate accountants lead by example.

One feature I have noted when you walk through the door at a high-performance team is that you are greeted with a smile and eye contact by all staff who you meet. Often finance teams are a less than welcoming place; you arrive and everybody is head down and the greeting is, at best, a reluctant one! At one high-performance team I have met, making eye contact is part of their training and part of their job, so it should be for every finance team.

HAVING FUN IN THE WORKPLACE

The finance team needs to be seen as a team that works hard and has fun doing this.

Some initiatives you can make to improve the working environment in the finance team include:

- Buy ten movie tickets (a discounted ten pack) and give two tickets to members of staff who have gone beyond the call of duty. Besides the initial shock shown by the grateful recipients you will find this simple recognition will create a small shift toward a more positive culture.
- Hold a finance team meeting in a café once a month and treat the staff to coffee and muffins.
- Set up a regime where birthdays are honored and celebrated. The staff person is actively encouraged to take that day off (out of their holiday allowance) and then celebrate it the next day in the office, with the birthday staff member being expected to bring in the cake and receiving a small gift from the team (to save time, do not bother with a collection—pay for it out of the finance budget).
- Take the finance team to a lunch-time visit to the movies with the staff investing their lunch hour in the process. This is great for staff with young children where a visit to the movies is a distant memory!
- For the end of the year finance team function give the finance staff options; for example, my staff elected to go to the movies once a week for five weeks rather than have an end of year function.
- During finance team meetings ensure that you find at least three team members to thank or to recognize their achievements, some of which may have occurred outside work.

CHAPTER 12

Maximize the Use of the General Ledger

Most likely you are only using 30% to 40% of your general ledger's (G/L) features or capability. Some better practices to maximize value out of your existing G/L include:

- You can make "a silk purse out of a pig's ear" if a reporting tool (e.g., Crystal, PowerPlay) and a planning tool are linked to your G/L
- Train your budget holders on how to use the G/L
- Delegate the responsibility of maintaining their part of the G/L to budget holders
- Invest only in a G/L upgrade if you already have invested in a procurement system and a planning tool
- Get your G/L consultant in to see where you can better use your G/L's built-in features

One company has a G/L consultant visit three to four times a year to review what they are doing. The consultant reminds them of short-cuts, or good features they have forgotten.

INTRODUCE A REPORTING APPLICATION TO SIT OVER THE G/L

The advancement of reporting tools has meant that the use of the G/L is merely to act as a collecting area for financial data for the month. A better practice today is to have a reporting tool collect this data from the G/L overnight or in some cases weekly, so that the budget holders can drill into their revenues and costs during the month. Management accountants will also use this reporting tool when analyzing costs because it contains prior months' figures in a continuous stream, enabling them to do cross-year financial comparisons seamlessly.

TIDY UP THE CHART OF ACCOUNTS

Show me a company with fewer than 100 expense account codes in the general ledger (G/L) and I will show you a management accountant who has seen the light. However, I have seen many charts of accounts with more than 300 expense account codes in the G/L, with up to 30 accounts for repairs and maintenance!

Far too often the job is given to a management accountant who looked skyward as a youngster yearning to become a rocket scientist. They thus live out this dream when they have an Excel spreadsheet in their hands or the chart of accounts. Common sense goes out the window, the CFO's eyes just glaze over at the chart of accounts progress meetings, the objective to reduce the account codes by over 40% gets lost, and slowly but surely, just like the budget instructions, the chart of accounts takes on a life of its own.

Some rules to stop this from happening are:

- Do not break down costs into a separate account code unless they represent 1% or greater of total expenses. You will find this will limit the number of account codes covering your operating costs to below 60.
- Do not break revenue in separate account codes unless revenues represent over 3% or greater of total revenue. You will find this will limit the number of account codes covering your revenue to below 20.

- The CFO should ensure they have a stiff coffee before the chart of accounts meeting and keep their strategic vision in the forefront.
- Think about your project codes; it is only worth separating out those projects that really matter. The others can be grouped under the budget holder's name called "Pat Carruthers' other projects."

PART TWO

Areas to Focus on Once Core Gains Have Been Achieved

Once the core gains have been achieved, these are additional goals well worth attaining:

Goal	Reason
1. Commence the selling process to throw out your annual planning and associated monthly budget cycle.	This is an important sale—ensure you use public relations (PR) advice to maximize the sale. Remember you need to use the emotional drivers rather than logic and reason.
2. Commence the process to purchase a planning and forecasting tool and commence quarterly rolling forecasting.	This project has a six-month time frame and thus you need to start now.
3. Plan to cease using monthly budgets from the annual planning cycle; instead use the forecast from the most recent quarterly rolling forecast.	This assumes goal 1 has been scored and goal 2 is on its way.

(continues)

Goal	Reason
4. Commence the investigation into your organization's winning key performance indicators (KPIs).	Again this is a big sale—once the senior management team (SMT) is on board and the KPI project team established, it should be a 16-week process.
5. Implement winning KPIs throughout the organization.	KPIs are the only thing that links day-to-day activities to the organization's strategic objectives. Enough said!
6. Place a ban on Excel spreadsheets in all daily, weekly and monthly routines within the finance team.	This will improve the reliability of these routines.
7. More emphasis placed on daily and weekly reporting.	Reporting as soon as the barn door is left open will, over time, help management to learn to shut it immediately!
8. Better use of the organization's intranet.	The finance team can lead the way in maximizing the intranet's potential.

A checklist has been developed covering the major steps. This is set out in Appendix E.

CHAPTER 13

Throw Out Annual Planning and the Associated Monthly Budget Cycle

Let us get one thing straight—the standard annual planning process takes too long, is not focused on performance drivers, is not linked to strategic outcomes or "critical success factors," leads to dysfunctional behavior, builds silos, and is a major barrier to success. Organizations worldwide are questioning the value of the traditional annual budgeting process.

BEYOND BUDGETING

Jeremy Hope is the world's foremost thought leader on corporate accounting issues. He has stated that not only is the budget process a time-consuming, costly exercise generating little value, it also and more important, is a major limiting factor on how your organization can perform. He has many examples of how companies following the philosophies he has expounded have broken free and achieved success well beyond their expectations. Here are two quotes that challenge the very concept of budgeting:

> *So long as the budget dominates business planning a self-motivated workforce is a fantasy, no matter how many cutting-edge techniques a company embraces.*
>
> *Modern companies reject centralization, inflexible planning, and command and control. So why do they cling to a process that reinforces those things?*
>
> *The same companies that vow to respond quickly to market shifts cling to budgeting—a process that slows the response to market developments until it's too late.*
>
> —Jeremy Hope and Robin Fraser, "Who Needs Budgets?," *Harvard Business Review,* April 2003

We will now look at why the budget process as it currently stands is a "no brainer." A survey performed in 1998 found:

- The average time for a budget process was four months
- 66% of CFOs stated their budget was influenced more by politics than strategy
- Nearly 90% of CFOs were dissatisfied with their budget process
- 60% of CFOs acknowledged that there was no link from the budgets to strategy

This level of dissatisfaction is similarly among Boards, CEOs, general managers, and budget holders. For many organizations the incessant game playing extends the budget round and limits the need for teams to stretch or seek breakthrough solutions.

There is an answer: Throw the annual budgeting cycle out—it takes too long, is not linked to strategy, strategic outcomes, or critical success factors.

By 2010 very few progressive organizations will be annual-planning as we know it today.

I was presenting beyond budgeting and KPIs in New Zealand and was introducing myself to the Managing Director of a large road contracting company, when he politely informed me that he was mainly interested to hear the KPI part of the workshop because the beyond budgeting session would be of little interest as they are already doing it. In fact the group has never had an annual planning process. He said if the group could predict when it was going to be sunny and when it was going to rain, annual planning would be useful.

The business encompasses concrete, transport (local and rural), fuel distribution, and road construction. The group has approximately 1,000 staff and a constant profit growth, the envy of many larger organizations.

They monitor key ratios and have different league tables depending on size of operations so the companies, in the group, can compare with each other. The ratios they monitor include:

- Return per kilometer (km)-revenue and cost per km
- Margin per liter
- Delivery cost per liter
- Concrete cost per cubic meter
- Cubic meter delivered by pay hour

Monthly reports are short and based on major cost categories (not at detail account code level). They do not waste time showing a consolidated result each month; this is done at year-end only.

There is much delegation to the branches who manage staff levels with given limits, set staff salaries, and chose which suppliers to use (providing there is not a national contract in place).

All readers are encouraged to read *Beyond Budgeting* by Jeremy Hope and Robin Fraser.[1] It is also worthwhile to read Hope's articles and his other books. He has an uncanny ability to always be at least five years ahead regarding what better corporate accounting practices should be. His work also embraces remuneration and performance management.

REPORTING WITHOUT A BUDGET

A major mistake in all annual planning cycles has been the monthly apportionment of the plan. If you still need to perform an annual planning process you can at least remove the need to establish the 12 monthly budgets during the annual planning process. Instead report against more recent monthly targets derived from the quarterly rolling forecasting process (see Exhibit 13.1). This change has a major impact

Exhibit 13.1 Business Unit Reporting Against Latest Forecast Instead of a Budget Example

Operating Statement for the period ending 31 March 20XX

Month $000s Act	Forecast	Var			Full Year $000s Forecast	Annual Plan	Var		YTD (75% of year) Act	% of forecast
				Revenue						
155	155	0		Appropriation	2,055	2,055	0		1,541	75%
3	5	(2)	×	3rd-Party Revenue	36	45	(9)	×	27	75%
158	160	(2)	⇔	**Total Revenue**	2,091	2,100	(9)	⇔	1,568	75%
				Expenses						
78	74	(4)	⇔	Wages & Salaries	930	900	(30)	⇔	558	60%
18	17	(1)		Project Expenditure	215	230	15	⇔	134	62%
20	22	2	⇔	Travel & Accommodation	240	180	(60)	×	171	71%
5	4	(1)		Staff Development	60	120	60	✓	36	61%
25	25	0		Premises & Related Costs	300	350	50	✓	182	61%
20	18	(2)		Other Operating Costs	235	320	85	✓	414	176%
165	160	(5)	⇔	**Total Expenses**	1,980	2,100	120	⇔	1,495	76%
(7)	0	7		**Surplus/(Deficit)**	111	0	111		73	

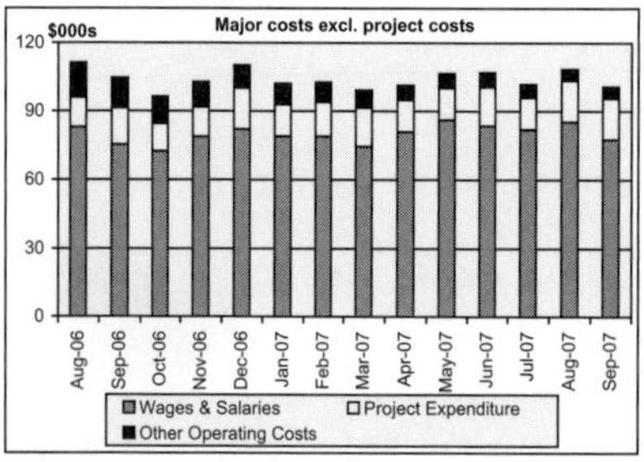

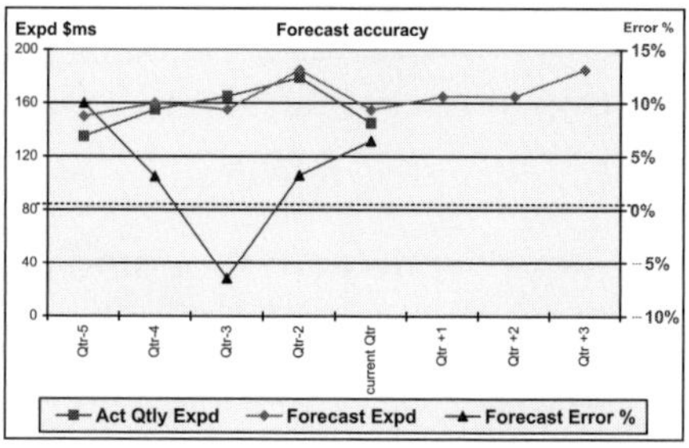

Highlights:

1. Xxxxxxxxxxxxxxxxxxxxxxxxxxxxxxxxxxxxxxxx xxxxxxxxxxxxxxxxxxxxxxxxxxxxxxxxxxxxxxxxxxxxxxxxxxxxxxxxxxxxxxxxxxxxx xxxxxxxxxxxxxx xxxxxxxx xxxxxxx xxxxxxxxxxx xxxxxxxxxxxxxxxxxxxxxxxxxxxxxx
2. Xxxxxxxxxxxxxxxxxxxxxxxxxxxxxxxxxxxxxxxx xxxxxxxxxxxxxxxxxxxxxxxxxxxxxxxxxxxxxxxxxxxxxxxxxxxxxxxxxxxxxxxxxxxxx xxxxxxxxxxxxxx xxxxxxxx xxxxxxx xxxxxxxxxxx xxxxxxxxxxxxxxxxxxxxxxxxxxxxxx
3. Xxxxxxxxxxxxxxxxxxxxxxxxxxxxxxxxxxxxxxxx xxxxxxxxxxxxxxxxxxxxxxxxxxxxxxxxxxxxxxxxxxxxxxxxxxxxxxxxxxxxxxxxxxxxx xxxxxxxxxxxxxx xxxxxxxx xxxxxxx xxxxxxxxxxx xxxxxxxxxxxxxxxxxxxxxxxxxxxxxx
4. Xxxxxxxxxxxxxxxxxxxxxxxxxxxxxxxxxxxxxxxx xxxxxxxxxxxxxxxxxxxxxxxxxxxxxxxxxxxxxxxxxxxxxxxxxxxxxxxxxxxxxxxxxxxxx xxxxxxxxxxxxxx xxxxxxxx xxxxxxx xxxxxxxxxxx xxxxxxxxxxxxxxxxxxxxxxxxxxxxxx

on reporting. We no longer will be reporting against a monthly budget that was set, in some cases, 17 months before the month being reviewed.

The report in Exhibit 13.1 compares last month's actual against the most recent forecast for that month. The year-to-date (YTD) actual is no longer compared against a YTD budget. Instead YTD progress is evaluated alongside progress against the year-end forecast or against YTD last year. Trend graphs will be used as discussed in Chapter 3. The forecast year-end numbers are now more prominent and moved to where the YTD numbers are traditionally placed. Commentary is much more targeted because there is little scope for the "explain it all away" timing difference comment as the forecast is updated quarterly.

In Exhibit 13.1 by comparing YTD expenditure against the full year forecast we have found an error. The YTD expenditure for other operating costs is higher than the full year forecast. This error is now spotted and the full year forecast would be awarded.

Note

1. Jeremy Hope and Robin Fraser, *Beyond Budgeting: How Managers Can Break Free from the Annual Performance Trap* (Boston, MA: Harvard Business School Press, 2003).

CHAPTER 14

Quarterly Rolling Planning: An Evolvement from Quarterly Rolling Forecasting

Quarterly rolling planning (QRP) is a process that will revolutionize any organization whether public or private sector! It removes the four main barriers to success that an annual planning process erects: An annual funding regime where budget holders are encouraged to be dysfunctional, a reporting regime based around monthly targets that have no relevance, a three-month period where management are not particularly productive, and a remuneration system based on an annual target. The only thing certain about an annual target is that it is certainly wrong; it is either too soft or too hard for the operating conditions.

The critical building block is the quarterly rolling forecast (QRF). This chapter explains why the QRF is the most important management tool of this decade and why the rolling forecasts of the past are different than the 21st century QRF.

- QRFs normally going out six quarters are a bottom-up process, with the forecast of the next quarter being the reporting benchmarks
- QRPs takes QRF a step further—budget holders are now funded quarterly in advance from the approved forecast

The quarterly forecasting planning process is where management sets out the plans for the next 18 months. Each quarter, before approving these estimates, management sees the bigger picture six quarters out. All subsequent forecasts while firming up the short-term numbers for the next three months also update the annual forecast. Budget holders are encouraged to spend half the time on getting the detail of the next three months right because these will become targets, on agreement, and the rest of the time on the next five quarters. Each quarter forecast is never a cold start because they have reviewed the forthcoming quarter a number of times. Provided you have appropriate forecasting software, management can do their forecasts very quickly; one airline even does this in three days! The overall time spent in the four quarterly forecasts should be no more than five weeks.

Most organizations can use the cycle set out in Exhibit 14.1 if their year-end falls on a calendar quarter end. Some organizations may wish to stagger the cycle; say, May, August, November, and February. Each forecast will now be explained using a June year-end organization.

- **December.** We forecast out to the June year-end, with monthly numbers, the remaining period in quarterly breaks. Budget holders obtain approval to spend January to March numbers subject to their forecast still going through the annual plan goal posts. The budget holders at the same time forecast next year's numbers for the first time. Budget holders are aware of the expected numbers and the first cut is reasonably close. This is a precursor to the annual plan. This forecast is stored in the forecasting and reporting tool. This update process should only take one elapsed week.
- **March.** We reforecast to year-end and the first quarter of next year with monthly numbers, the remaining period in quarterly breaks. Budget holders obtain approval to spend April to June numbers.

Exhibit 14.1 Rolling Forecast for an Organization (June Year-End)

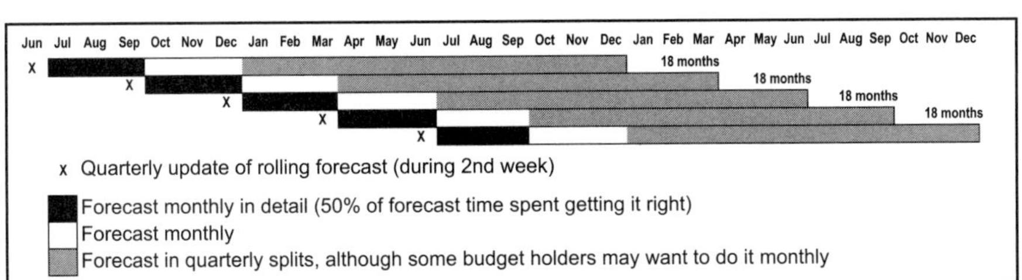

The budget holders at the same time revisit the December forecast (the last forecast) of next year's numbers and fine-tune them for the annual plan. Budget holders know that they will not be getting an annual lump sum funding for their annual plan. The number they supply for the annual plan is for guidance only.

This March forecast is stored in a new field in the forecasting and reporting tool called "March XX forecast." This is the second look at the next year so the managers have a better understanding. On an ongoing basis you would only need a two-week period to complete this process.

- **June.** We can reforecast the end of June numbers and should have found that the frantic activity that is normally associated with the "spend it or lose it" mentality is not so evident. Budget holders are now also required to forecast the first six months of next year monthly and then on to December in the following year in quarterly numbers. Budget holders obtain approval to spend July to September numbers provided their forecast once again passes through the annual goal posts. This is stored in a new field in the forecasting and reporting tool called "June XX forecast." This update process should only take one elapsed week.
- **September.** We reforecast the next six months in monthly numbers, and quarterly to March, 18 months forward. Budget holders obtain approval to spend October to December numbers. This is stored in a new field in the forecasting and reporting tool called "September XX forecast." This update process should only take one elapsed week.

You will find that the four cycles take about five weeks, once management is fully conversant with the new forecasting system and processes.

The key points of a rolling forecast are:

- Budget holders provide an annual plan through the bottom-up quarterly rolling forecasting regime but are not assigned those funds; this is done on a quarter-by-quarter funding basis.
- Monthly reporting is more meaningful because it measures performance against the most recent forecast and not a monthly split of the original annual plan.
- Each subsequent forecast is still expected to put the ball through the posts at the end of the field (year-end annual plan), the difference being the ball carries on to the next pitch (into next year) (e.g., budget holders always looking forward 18 months).
- Forecasting is carried out on an appropriate planning tool that can handle a bottom-up forecast once a quarter—Excel is not an appropriate tool for a key company system.

LINKAGE TO CHAPTER 5 (TIMELY ANNUAL PLANNING PROCESS)

If you have implemented the practices set out in Chapter 5 you are already part of the way to implementing the better practices for QRP. For the sake of completeness some of the better practices discussed in Chapter 5 are repeated once again in this chapter.

FLAWED LOGIC OF THE MONTHLY BUDGET

As accountants we never needed to break the annual plan down into 12 monthly breaks before the year had started. We could have been more flexible. Instead we created a reporting yardstick that undermined our value to the organization. Every month management throughout the organization writes variance analysis, which could be done by me in my office because I can write as well as anybody else "this variance is due to a timing difference."

A sports analogy can be used to explain the folly of the monthly budget (see Exhibit 14.2). Imagine a game where you have to get a ball from your end of the field to the other and place it between two goal posts. The annual plan is the establishment of goal posts at the end of the pitch; the budget process is where we set 12 × 10 meter lines to report against. The problem is that the 10 meter lines (the monthly budgets) are wrong as soon as the game has started. When there is stoppage, a player feigning injury on cue, so management can come on the pitch and ask "Why are you here? You should have been over there." The reply from the team is "the ball is over here"; this reporting back progress is the same as our monthly variance commentary.

SELLING QUARTERLY ROLLING PLANNING THROUGH THE "EMOTIONAL DRIVERS"

As mentioned in Chapter 1, nothing was ever sold by logic!! You sell through emotional drivers. This project needs a public relations (PR) machine behind it. No presentation, e-mail, memo, or paper should go out unless it has been vetted by your PR expert. All your presentations should be road-tested in front of the PR expert. Your PR strategy should include selling to staff, budget holders, senior management team (SMT), and the Board.

Exhibit 14.2 Annual Plan Analogy

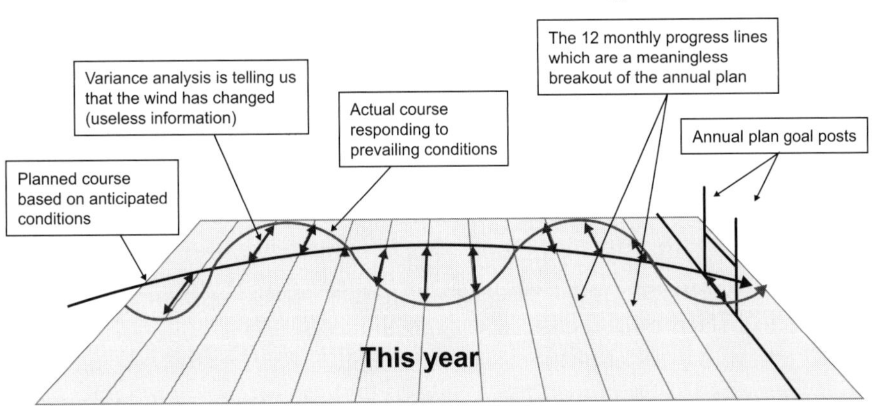

Some of the emotional drivers around the annual planning process that you would use if selling the acquisition of a planning tool include:

- Meaningless month-end reports (e.g., "it is a timing difference")
- Lost evenings/weekends producing meaningless variances comments
- Lost months! The lost weekends with family! Producing the annual plan
- The huge costs associated with annual plan preparation (e.g., estimate on the high side as costs are an emotional driver for Boards)
- Time spent by the Board and SMT second-guessing the next year —it is more efficient on a rolling quarterly basis
- Best practice to implement quarterly rolling forecasting and planning (e.g., 80% of major U.S. companies expect to be doing QRFs, etc.)

The project team needs to focus on the marketing of a new concept as much as it does on the training. Budget holders will need to understand how this process is going to help them manage their business. Providing success stories throughout the implementation is therefore a must.

RECOGNIZE THAT QUARTERLY ROLLING PLANNING INVOLVES ALL BUDGET HOLDERS

Most forecasting models, built in Excel, tend to have restricted consultation with budget holders and are carried out by people in HQ who are remote from the "work-face." This is done for practical reasons—it would be a disaster to unleash the Excel model once a quarter because it takes weeks to get completed once a year! These forecasts do not have any buy-in from budget holders, cannot be used to create meaningful targets for the months in the next quarter, and are often a skewed view of the future business operations simply reiterating the misconceptions that head office management wish to believe.

Having all budget holders involved requires an investment in training and good coordination. The benefits include buy-in to the numbers, a forecast that more closely resembles reality, and a positive learning curve, as budget holders get better at a repetitive task.

NEVER FORECAST AT ACCOUNT CODE LEVEL: APPLY PARETO'S 80/20 RULE

As accountants we never needed to set targets at account code level. We simply did it because we did last year, without thinking as well. Do you need a target or budget at account code level if you have good trend analysis captured in the reporting tool? Probably not. You should apply Pareto's 80/20 rule and establish a category heading that includes a number of G/L codes.

Rules that can be used include:

- Limit the categories that budget holders need to forecast to no more than 12.
- Select the categories that can be automated, and provide these numbers.
- Separate out a forecasting line if the category is over 20% of total (e.g., show revenue line if revenue category is over 20% of total revenue). If category is between 10% and 20% look at it and make an assessment if separate disclosure is required. If under 10% consolidate with another category.
- Allow the budget holders to have some flexibility in the categories to best reflect their operation. Planning tools can easily cope with this complexity by the mapping of general ledger (G/L) codes to categories (try doing this in an Excel spreadsheet! If you can you should work for NASA).
- Accurate forecasting of personnel costs requires analysis of all current staff (their end date if known, their salary, the likely salary review, and/or bonus), all new staff (their starting salary, their likely start date).

In one workshop I ran for a service sector organization the group came up with the decision that there would be a maximum of *15 categories,* of which 7 would be automated. These are set out in the following table.

Budget Holder's Forecast Only These Categories	The Categories That Can Be Automated
Revenue (three to four categories)	Operational equipment repairs and maintenance
Salaries and wages ordinary time	Office equipment, computer and consumables
Other personnel expenditure	Communications costs
Health and welfare	Fleet costs
Training and conferences including travel	Building maintenance
Operational equipment—that is not capitalized	Miscellaneous costs
Property costs	Depreciation
Promotional activities	

HAVE TREND GRAPHS FOR EVERY CATEGORY FORECASTED

Better quality can be achieved through analysis of the trends (see Exhibit 14.3). There is no place to hide funding when a budget holder is accountable for the past and future trends. The graph shown in Exhibit 14.3, if made available for all the categories budget holders are required to forecast, will increase forecast accuracy. Budget holders will want to ensure their forecasts make sense against the historic trend.

ACCURATE REVENUE FORECASTING WILL INVOLVE TALKING WITH THE RIGHT PEOPLE AT YOUR MAIN CUSTOMERS

Many organizations liaise with customers to get demand forecasts only to find them as error prone as the ones done in-house. The reason is that you have asked the wrong people.

One participant told me that they decided to contact their major customers to help with demand forecasting. Naturally, they were holding

Exhibit 14.3 Forecast Revenue Graph

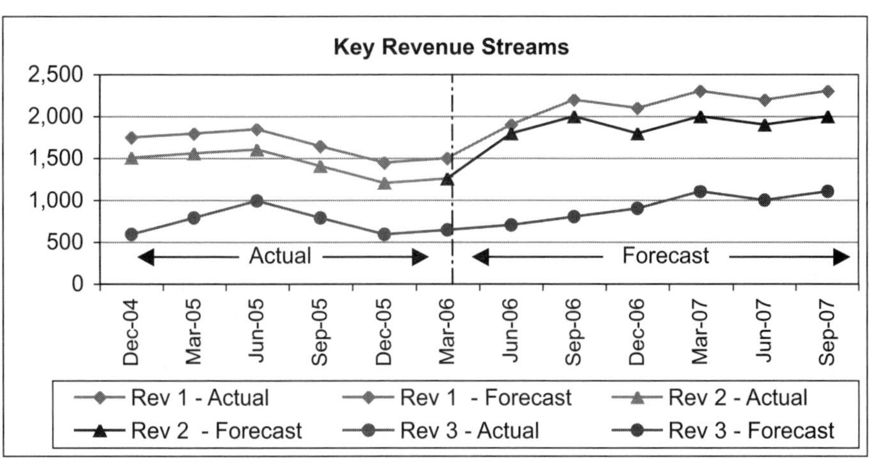

discussions with the major customers' headquarters staff. On reflection they found it better but still error prone so they went back to the customer "How come these forecasts you supplied are so error prone?" "If you want accurate numbers you needed to speak to the procurement managers for our projects" was the reply. "Can we speak to them?" "Of course, here are the contact details of the people you need to meet around the country." A series of meetings were then held around the country. They found that these managers could provide very accurate information and were even prepared to provide it in an electronic friendly format. The sales forecast accuracy increased seven-fold due to focusing on getting the demand right for the main customers.

The lesson to learn is when you want to forecast revenue more accurately by delving into your main customer's business, ask them *"who should we speak to in order to get a better understanding of your likely demand for our products in the next three months?"*

QRP CREATES THE ANNUAL PLAN GOAL POSTS QUICKLY

The QRP process will allow you to have a quick annual planning process, because budget holders will become more experienced at forecasting (they are doing it four times a year), they have already looked at the next year a number of times, and they realize that there is no use demanding more than you need because the real funding is sorted out on a quarter-by-quarter basis where slush funds cannot be hidden.

Organizations that have truly adopted the beyond budgeting principles will also throw out the annual plan target. Why should one view of year-end be any better than a subsequent, more current view? The March quarter forecast is no longer called the annual plan, but simply the March quarter forecast. The Board will want to monitor the extent there is forecast creep and this can be easily shown in a graph.

QRP CREATES A QUARTER-BY-QUARTER FUNDING MECHANISM

The key to a better allocation of resources is to fund budget holders on a rolling quarter-by-quarter basis. In this process management asks, "Yes, we know you need $1 million for the twelve months and we can fund it, but how much do you need for the next three months?" At first the budget holder will reply, "I need $250,000 this quarter," to which is replied, "How is this? Your last five quarterly expenditures have ranged between $180,000 and $225,000. You are two team members short and your recruiting is not yet underway. Be realistic; you will only need a maximum of $225,000 for the next quarter."

It will come as no surprise that when a budget holder is funded only three months ahead the funding estimates are much more precise and there is little or nowhere to hide those slush funds.

Reusing the sporting game analogy, the "ground staff" are only asked to draw the lines on the first quarter of the pitch. The game plan for the first quarter has only just been set minutes before the game started and is therefore very relevant to the prevailing conditions and the opposition team. The team becomes very accountable about progress (see Exhibit 14.4).

This quarter-by-quarter process means that the approval of the annual plan numbers by the SMT and the Board will be quicker because the SMT and Board are not approving the funding. This is done on a quarter-by-quarter basis as the conditions and environment dictate.

Exhibit 14.4 Quarterly Rolling Planning Analogy

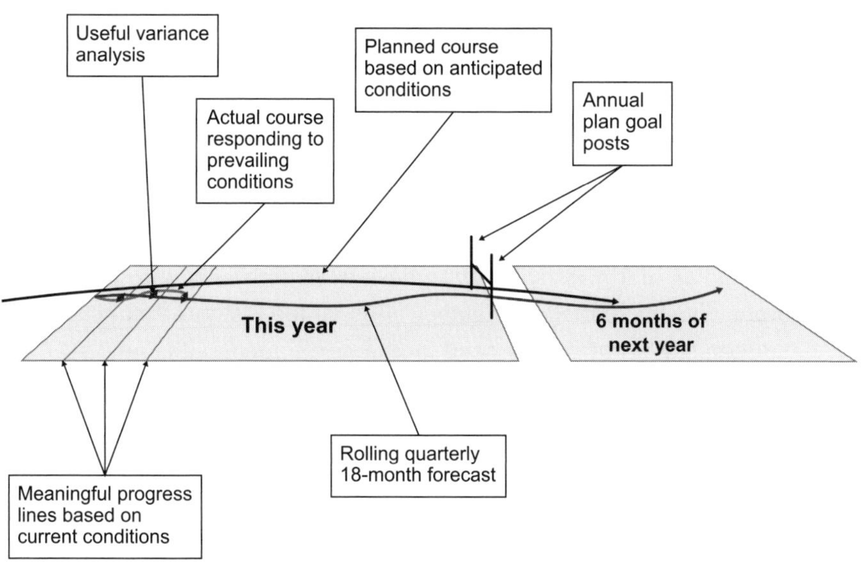

Some organizations are recognizing the folly of giving a budget holder the right to spend an annual sum, while at the same time saying if you get it wrong there will be no more money. By forcing budget holders to second-guess their needs in this inflexible regime you enforce a defensive behavior, a stockpiling mentality. In other words, you guarantee dysfunctional behavior from day one! The quarterly rolling planning process thus highlights "free funds," which can be reallocated for new projects earlier on in the financial year.

The released funds can fund new initiatives that the budget holder could not have anticipated at the time of the budget round. This will get around the common budget holder dilemma of "I cannot undertake that initiative, though we should, because I did not include it in my budget." In the new regime the budget holder would say "I will put it in my next update and if funds are available I am sure I will get the go ahead."

This more flexible environment, as long as it is communicated clearly and frequently to budget holders, will have good buy-in. The logic of quarterly rolling funding can be shown in a "birthday cake" analogy.

> **Quarterly rolling funding process** has a lot in common with the handling of a 9-year-old's birthday cake. A clever parent says to Johnny, "Here is the first slice. If you finish that slice, and are not going 'green around the gills' and want more, I will give you a second slice." Instead, what we do in the annual planning process is divide the cake up and portion all of it to the budget holders. Like 9-year-olds, budget holders lick the edges of their cake so even if they do not need all of it nobody else can have it. Why not, like the clever parent, give the manager what they need for the first three months, and then say "what do you need for the next three months" and so on. Each time we can apportion the amount that is appropriate for the conditions at that time.

QRP IS BASED ON A PLANNING APPLICATION—NOT EXCEL

Forecasting requires a good robust tool, not a spreadsheet built by some innovative accountant that now no one can understand. Often the main hurdle is the finance team's reluctance to divorce itself from Excel. It has been a long and comfortable marriage, albeit one that has limited the finance team's performance.

Acquiring a planning tool is the first main step forward, and one that needs to be pursued not only for the organization but also for the finance team members' future careers. It will soon be a prerequisite to have planning tool experience, and conversely career limiting to be an Excel guru.

See Appendix F for how a QRF can be laid out in a planning tool.

New planning tools are being sold all the time and these "search strings" will help unearth many applications:

- "Planning tools" + "name of your country," e.g., USA
- "Quarterly rolling forecasting" + "applications" + "name of your country"
- "Forecasting tools" + "rolling" + "name of your country"

A forecasting tool needs to be based on the key drivers of the business (e.g., for a credit card company the average spend and the number of credit cards) and thus be able to quickly inform management of the impact should there be a major change with any of these drivers. In addition the model should be able to answer the likely questions that the SMT will want answered quickly. In-depth interviews with the SMT coupled with some brainstorming will quickly identify the likely questions. These questions might include:

- What if we contract in size (e.g., stop production of one line, sell a business)?
- What if we grow through acquisition?
- What if we lose a major customer?
- What if there is a major change to key economic indicators (e.g., interest rates, inflation)?
- What if a major overseas competitor sets up in our region?
- What are the plant capacity ramifications from gaining a large increase in business (e.g., folding of a major local competitor)?

A FAST LIGHT TOUCH (AN ELAPSED WEEK)

QRFs should be performed within five working days (see Exhibit 14.5), with the one exception that the fourth quarter forecast, which creates the annual plan (see Exhibit 14.6), will have one extra week for additional negotiations and quality assurance. QRFs can be quick because:

- Consolidation is instantaneous with a planning tool.
- You have run a workshop on budget preparation with budget holders so they know what to do.
- The model is based around Pareto's 80/20 principle.
- Training has been given to budget holders so they can enter directly into the planning tool.
- The quarterly repetition aids efficiency.
- Forecasting is at a high level, at category not account code level (e.g., only 12 to 15 categories per budget holder).

- Repeat costs can all be standardized for the whole year (e g., Dublin to London return flight € 250, and overnight in London € 280).

Exhibits 14.5 and 14.6 show that this process will only take seven working days for three of the four quarters and up to ten working days for the quarter where you are setting the annual plan goal posts.

Make sure you have the CEO's support for a quick time frame and encourage the CEO to get involved in making "late forecasting" career limiting.

Jeremy Hope in his book *Reinventing the CFO*[1] states that there is no reason why the forecast process could not be done in a day in a financial services organization, where there is no physical supply chain and inventories to manage. For more complex businesses, Jeremy Hope believes these forecasts can be done in several days. Note that this means a quicker forecasting timeframe than I am suggesting.

Every quarter you will need to prepare the best view using this "fast light touch" process. See Appendix H for a checklist on "Performing a Quarterly Rolling Forecast." This will help with the quality assurance process.

QRP IS A ROLLING 18 MONTHS, NOT 12-, 13-, OR 15-MONTH PROCESS

I advocate an 18-month rolling forecast regime, because it has some substantial benefits that include:

- You see the full next year half way through the current one (e.g., the third quarter forecast can set the goal posts for next year's annual plan)
- The QRF is consistent each time it is performed, as opposed to organizations that always look ahead for two financial years (the QRFs will vary between 15 and 24 months)
- Your annual goals are never set with a cold start

QRP IS A QUARTERLY PROCESS, NOT MONTHLY

Only businesses that are in a very dynamic environment would need to forecast monthly. One has to remember that for every event that goes

Exhibit 14.5 Timeline for the First Three Quarterly Forecasts within a Financial Year

7-day quarterly rolling forecasting/planning process

	Prior work	Prior work	1–2	3	4–5	W/E	6	7
Process =>	Forecast pre-work	Deliver forecast workshop	Budget holders prepare and load their forecast	First look at numbers	Submissions by BHs to management board (does the forecast still go through the goal posts)		Re-run of forecast and presentation to CEO	Final alterations and finishing off documentation
Activities =>								
Strategic Planning		Attend			Reviewing to ensure linkage to strategic plan, and advising of any discrepancies		Attend	
SMT	Set assumptions			First look at numbers	Review submissions etc., full time		Hear presentation and give instructions for final changes	
Finance team	Prepare system, the presentation, overheads, personnel costs, travel standard costs, etc.	Give presentation to BHs	Help BHs with forecast (extended team)	QA	Further QA		Complete preparation and present forecast presentation	Finish off documentation
BHs		Attend	Prepare forecast		Present forecast and business plan where there is a major change		Present to SMT when called	Document and file all calculations

Exhibit 14.6 Timeline for the Fourth Quarter Forecast (Which Generates the Annual Plan)

10-day Annual Planning Process (part of the 4th quarter's QRP performed in the last month of the 3rd quarter)

	Prior work		1	2	3	4	5	W/E	6	7	8	9	10
Process =>	Budget pre-work	Present budget workshop	Budget holders prepare and load their forecast			First look at numbers	Rework some budgets		Submissions by BHs to management board			Compilation of final draft budget for Management Board approval	Final alterations and finishing off documentation
Activities =>													
Strategic Planning		Attend					Reviewing to ensure linkage to Plan, and advising of any discrepancies					Attend	
SMT	Set assumptions					First look at numbers			Review submissions etc., full time			Hear presentation and give instructions for final changes	
Finance team	Prepare system, the presentation, overheads, personnel costs, travel standard costs, etc.	Give presentation to BHs	Help BHs with budget plans (extended team)			QA	Help BHs		Further QA			Complete preparation and present AP presentation	
BHs		Attend	Prepare budget				Attend		Present to SMT when called			Document and file all calculations	

your way, there will be another event in the future negating the positive impact (e.g., it is not worthwhile changing your year-end forecast due to the loss or gain of a large customer). These changes are better picked up on a quarterly basis; this will help ensure less oscillation of your year-end numbers.

For those organizations that are in a dynamic environment, you do not need to get all budget holders to participate in a monthly reforecast; you may be able to limit this monthly reforecast work to sales and production with the major reforecast still being quarterly.

One organization every month forecasts in the last week of the month that month's result and the next three months. They find this process most useful. I would recommend that you only embark on this level of forecasting when the process is well bedded down, can be completed in hours not days, and creates more value than it costs to do. Certainly not worth contemplating in the first year of operating a QRP process.

BARRIERS TO IMPLEMENTING QRP AND HOW TO OVERCOME THEM

Exhibit 14.7 provides some ways to overcome the common barriers accountants face in implementing QRP.

IMPLEMENTING A QRP PROCESS

This is a major implementation and you should acquire a white paper from www.waymark.co.nz, on implementing quarterly rolling planning, listen to the David Parmenter webcast on www.bettermanagement.com. One of the first steps is to undertake a one-day focus group workshop as set forth in Exhibit 14.8. See Appendix I for a draft invitation which would be sent out by the CEO to selected staff.

The workshop is important for a number of reasons:

- There are many pitfalls in such a project and many have failed to deliver.
- A wide ownership is required and a focus group can have a huge impact in achieving this ownership.

- The foundation stones need to be understood and put in place early on in the project.
- The focus group will give valuable input in how the implementation should best be done to maximize its impact.

Exhibit 14.7 Ways to Surmount the Main Issues

Common Barriers	Suggested Actions
Lack of budget holder skills	• Find those staff who thrive with new technology and train them first • Set up new forecasting regime in one unit, a quarter ahead, to iron out the bugs and to promote the efficiencies • Train all significant budget holders including one-to-one training • Set up from the outset a quarterly follow-up training course
"Stop and start" annual planning syndrome	• Big sell to management (historic evidence including costs, better practices, benefits to them) • Get commitment for a quick bottom-up forecasts • Work closely with the Executive Assistants regarding meeting schedules so SMT and budget holders are all present during the forecasting weeks
"Inaccurate and late data	• Provide more one-to-one support • Workshop the forecast process with all major budget holders (with laptop and data show) • Provide incentives for prompt forecast returns (e.g., movie vouchers) • Provide a daily progress report to CEO with names of all budget holders who have not yet completed their forecast
Lack of management ownership	• Take SMT to some better practice forecasting sites • Deliver more interesting information from the forecast process (e.g., trend graphs, key performance indicators)

Exhibit 14.7 *(Continued)*

Common Barriers	Suggested Actions
Lack of management ownership *(continued)*	• Obtain and circulate articles on QRP • Market better practice stories constantly • Ensure budget holders are directly involved in the forecasting process (e.g., not delegating tasks)
"Lack of faith" in the reliability of the forecast	• Establish in-depth quality assurance (QA) procedures • Have good working papers to support forecasts • Provide reasonability checks • Audit the forecast application prior to use • Migrate away from Excel to a planning tool
Lack of understanding of the application	• Have forecasting/budget models reviewed and audited prior to use • At least four staff with an in-depth knowledge of the design of the QRF • Full documentation of logic • Keep to Pareto's 80/20 (e.g., personnel costs should have much more detail) • Key drivers should be easily identifiable
Lack of linkage to strategic decisions	• Brainstorm with the SMT the likely questions they might want answered urgently • Ensure you can accommodate the key drivers of the business in the model design
Competency of the forecasting team	• Select for: self starter, innovation, good communicator, finisher, big picture thinker, team player, prepared to work overtime and broad experience of organization • Look for experience with problem solving, interviewing, process re-engineering, forecasting • Train to cover any shortfalls • Appoint an external facilitator to mentor the project team

Exhibit 14.8 Agenda for a One-Day Focus Group Workshop

<table>
<tr><td colspan="2">

Date and Time: xxxxxx

Location: xxxxxx

Suggested Attendees: Budget committee, selection of business unit heads, all management accountants, and a selection of budget holders involved in forecasting.

Learning Outcomes:

After this workshop attendees will be able to:

- Discuss and explain to management why Xxxxxxx should adopt QRP
- Use better practices to streamline current forecasting bottlenecks
- Describe better practice month-end routines
- Recall all agreements made at the workshop (these will be documented)

Pre Work: Teams to document forecasting procedures on "Post-it" stickers. One procedure per "Post-it." Each team to have a different color "Post-it."

Requirements: Event secretary, two laptops, data show, two white boards

</td></tr>
<tr><td>8:30 A.M.</td><td>Welcome by CFO, a summary of progress to date at Xxxxxxx, an outline of the issues and establishing the outcome for the workshop.</td></tr>
<tr><td>8:40 A.M.</td><td>

Setting the scene—why clever organizations are not involved in the annual planning cycle—a review of better practices among public and private sector organizations. Topics covered include:

- Why annual planning is flawed and the rise of the *Beyond Budgeting* movement
- Why quarterly rolling planning can and should work at Xxxxxxx
- Benefits of QRP to the Board, SMT, finance team, and budget holders
- Better practice stories
- Current performance gap between Xxxxxxx and better practice
- Some of the building blocks are already in place at Xxxxxxx
- Some better practice features within Xxxxxxx's forecasting process
- How the annual plan drops out of the bottom-up quarterly rolling forecasting regime
- Impact of assigning funds on a quarter-by-quarter basis
- Impact on monthly reporting
- How each subsequent forecast works
- Involvement of SMT in a forecasting process

This session would be attended by a wider audience. After the questions and answers these people would leave.

</td></tr>
</table>

Exhibit 14.7 *(Continued)*

9:40 A.M.	**Workshop 1: Analyzing the current pitfalls of Xxxxxxx's forecasting.** Separate teams look at the key pitfalls and how they can be overcome.
10:15 A.M.	Morning break.
10:30 A.M.	**Workshop 2: Mechanics of rolling forecasting.** Workshop where separate teams look at the key components: • Who should be involved in a bottom-up forecasting process • Potential pitfalls • Reporting needs • When can it be implemented • Training requirements • What cost categories should be forecast (higher than G/L account code) • Project structure
11:00 A.M.	**Workshop 3: Workshop on "Post-it" re-engineering of Xxxxxxx's forecasting process.** During the workshop we analyze the bottlenecks of the forecasting process. In this workshop we use "Post-its" to schedule the steps (e.g., yellow—budget holder activities, red—forecasting team activities, blue—SMT activities during the forecast).
12:15 P.M.	Lunch at venue.
12:45 P.M.	Feedback from work groups on both workshops and action plan agreed (date and responsibility). Individuals will be encouraged to take responsibility for implementing the steps.
1:15 P.M.	The team prepares a short presentation of the key steps they are committed to making.
2.00 P.M.	The team presents reports to an invited audience on what changes they would like to implement and when. They can also raise any issues they still have. Suggested audience all those who attended the setting the scene morning session.
2.30 P.M.	Wrap up of workshop.

"POST-IT" RE-ENGINEERING PROCEDURES

Give each team a book of "Post-its," one color per team (e.g., Forecasting team—red, Budget holders—yellow, Marketing team—green, SMT—blue, Finance team—purple)

Ensure that there is only one procedure on one "Post-it" and that it is written in big letters (must be seen from 15 feet) (see Exhibit 14.9).

AN EFFICIENT ANNUAL PLANNING PROCESS IF ALL ELSE FAILS

If you have tried and cannot throw out the annual planning process, try again, and again. Then if all else fails consider leaving the organization because why should you waste two to three months of your life every year! Alternatively, reduce the annual planning process down to two weeks following the steps in Appendix I: Remember this is not an alternative to QRP, it is a sign of failure on your part to sell a 21st century practice.

IMPLEMENTATION ROAD MAP

This implementation plan shown in Exhibit 14.10 should help those about to start an implementation. One key feature is the time frame. A rolling forecast implementation is a six-to-eight-month process when you include the acquisition of an appropriate planning tool.

Exhibit 14.9 Completed "Post-it" Sticker Example

October 15th First cut from Budget holders

Exhibit 14.10 Example of a Timeline for Implementing a QRP Process

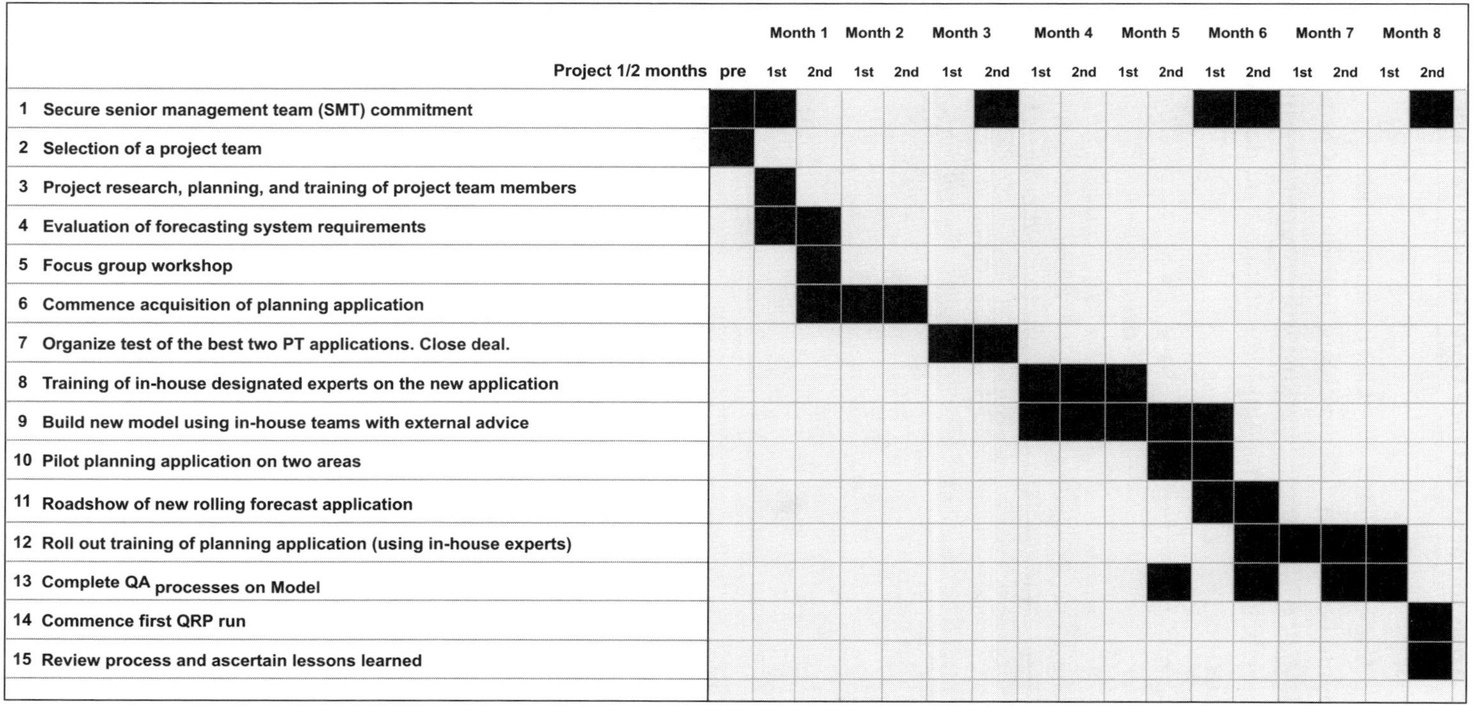

		Month 1		Month 2		Month 3		Month 4		Month 5		Month 6		Month 7		Month 8	
Project 1/2 months	pre	1st	2nd	1st	2nd	1st	2nd	1st	2nd	1st	2nd	1st	2nd	1st	2nd	1st	2nd
1 Secure senior management team (SMT) commitment	■	■					■					■	■				■
2 Selection of a project team	■																
3 Project research, planning, and training of project team members		■															
4 Evaluation of forecasting system requirements		■	■														
5 Focus group workshop			■														
6 Commence acquisition of planning application			■	■	■												
7 Organize test of the best two PT applications. Close deal.						■	■										
8 Training of in-house designated experts on the new application								■	■	■							
9 Build new model using in-house teams with external advice								■	■	■	■	■					
10 Pilot planning application on two areas											■	■					
11 Roadshow of new rolling forecast application												■	■				
12 Roll out training of planning application (using in-house experts)													■	■	■	■	
13 Complete QA processes on Model											■		■		■	■	
14 Commence first QRP run																	■
15 Review process and ascertain lessons learned																	■

See Appendix G for a checklist on implementing a QRF. This checklist should be treated as an evolving tool and thus be tailored to better suit your needs. Using a checklist will ensure that while you are "juggling the balls" during the implementation, you do not drop the ones that matter.

Note

1. Jeremy Hope, *Reinventing the CFO: How Financial Mangers Can Transform Their Roles and Add Greater Value* (Boston, MA: Harvard Business School Press, 2006).

CHAPTER 15

Cost Apportionment: Do Not Do It Monthly!

Traditionally we have spent much time apportioning head office costs to business units to ensure they have a net profit bottom-line. However, few ask the budget holders and business unit managers whether they look at these apportioned head office costs. I have never found any business unit manager who showed much interest other than to complain about the cost of IT, accounting, and so on.

In fact these cost apportionments, besides slowing down reporting, often lead management to complain about strategic costs that cannot be reviewed for a few years due to locked-in agreements (e.g., the accounting system).

Pareto's 80/20 principle reminds us that the time processing levels upon levels of apportionments to arrive at some arbitrary full costing is not creating management information that leads to decision making. Corporate accountants can often arrive at full costing approximations through a more simplistic route.

Some better practices are:

- Keep head office costs where they are because budget holders see them as uncontrollables in any case
- Use "product costing" as periodic one-off exercises to understand a full costing situation

- Develop a full costing model, if you really need one, in an appropriate planning application that has been designed with the big picture in mind

If you have on-charged head office costs and it is creating the right environment, then continue with the process. There are a number of case studies where on-charging head office costs do work well. They, however, are the exception rather than the rule.

Control of overhead office costs can be best achieved through:

- Engage in major process re-engineering to simplify head office processes
- Analyze head office costs by activities rather than account codes, for example, where are the head office IT costs spent—delivering new projects, correcting errors, providing one-to-one training, provision of equipment, etc.—and compare these over time and against third-party benchmarks
- Set targets in the future where you expect to see head office costs. These can be expressed as acceptable ratios to sales. Naturally you will have researched the lowest cost operators as benchmarks (e.g., by 2010 we want finance cost to be between x% and y% of revenue). This sets a general direction for the head office teams and helps curb empire building.

CHAPTER 16

Ban Excel from Core Monthly Routines

Excel has no place in reporting, forecasting, budgeting, and other core financial routines. Excel was never intended for the uses we put it to. In fact, many of us, if we worked for NASA, would be using Excel for the space program, and believe me when I say this, would probably make a good go of it. I, however, would not like to be the astronaut, in "outer space," when I find out that there is a 90% chance of a logic error for every 150 rows in the workbook.

Excel is a great tool for an expense claim at the airport, doing one-off graphs for a report, or designing and testing a template. It is not and never should have been a building block for your company's key financial systems. There are better alternatives as shown in Exhibit 16.1.

As a forecasting tool Excel fails on a number of counts:

- It has no proper version control; we have all burnt the midnight oil pulling our hair out wondering whether all spreadsheets are the correct versions!
- For every 150 lines there is a 90% chance of a logic error (from a recent study).
- Its lack of robustness (show me a CFO who can be confident of the number an Excel forecast churns out!).

Exhibit 16.1 Excel Replacements

Current Use for Excel	**Replacement**
Reporting—downloading from the general ledger (G/L) to get better quality reports	Reporting package
Cash flow forecasting	Planning application
Rolling accrual forecasting	Planning application
Budgeting	Planning application
Consolidations	Reporting package or your G/L
Balanced scorecards	Balanced scorecard package

- It cannot accommodate changes to assumptions quickly (e.g., could you respond to the CEO asking "What is the financial impact if we stopped production of computer printers? Please tell me the answer by close of play today.").
- It is used by accounting staff, who are not programmers, to design core financial systems. The staff has not been trained in documentation, quality assurance, and so forth, which you might expect from a designer of a core company system.

Jeremy Hope of *Beyond Budgeting* fame and more recently author of the groundbreaking book on "Reinventing the CFO" points out that Sarbanes-Oxley may be the sword that finally removes the spreadsheet in key financial monthly routines. "For in theory at least, every change to a formula or even a change to the number of rows needs to be documented."[1]

Note

1. Jeremy Hope, *Reinventing the CFO: How Financial Managers Can Transform Their Roles and Add Greater Value* (Boston, MA: Harvard Business School Press, 2006).

CHAPTER 17

More Emphasis on Daily and Weekly Reporting

Why is the monthly reporting so important? For leading organizations, decision-based information is based around daily/weekly information on progress within the organization's critical success factors (CSFs). In these organizations the month-end has become less important and consequently the management papers reduced to 15 pages or less.

In one company the senior management team (SMT) have a 9 o'clock news report every morning followed by further weekly information. At the monthly management meeting to discuss the results, even the Human Resources manager is able to enter the sweepstakes guessing the month-end result. Talking about the monthly numbers is a small part of the meeting, with most of the time spent discussing the current month's activities. This meeting occurs in the first week of the following month.

As a corporate accountant, you have arrived when your management team intuitively knows whether the month is a good or bad month during that month, enabling them to do something about it.

Corporate accountants should look at providing the following daily and weekly reporting:

- Yesterday's sales reported by 9 A.M. the following day

- Transactions with key customers reported on a weekly basis
- Weekly reporting on late projects and late reports
- Reporting some weekly information of key direct costs
- Progress with the key performance indicators (KPIs) on a daily/weekly basis (see Chapter 18).

YESTERDAY'S SALES REPORT

If the CEO and SMT receive a report on the daily sales they will better understand how the organization is performing. Exhibit 17.1 shows the sort of detail they will be interested in.

Exhibit 17.1 Yesterday's Sales Report

Daily Sales Report

	$000s			
	Yesterday's sales	Daily average Last 30 days	Daily average Last 90 days	
Revenue by Key Product				
Product 1	450	430	400	✓
Product 2	400	380	560	✗
Product 3	375	355	425	✗
Other products	275	195	175	✓
Total Revenue	1,500	1,360	1,560	✗
Revenue by Branch				
Branch 1	580	560	700	✗
Branch 2	440	420	400	
Branch 3	220	200	180	
Branch 4	180	160	140	
Other branches	80	20	140	✗
Total Revenue	1,500	1,360	1,560	✗
Revenue by Key Customer				
Customer 1	180	160	140	
Customer 2	140	120	100	
Customer 3	160	140	120	
Customer 4	190	170	150	
Other customers	1,230	1,170	1,450	✗
Total Revenue	1,500	1,360	1,560	✗

Highlights:
1. Xxxxxxxxxxxxxxxxxxxxxxxxxxxxxxxxxxxxxxxx
xxxxxxxxxxxxxxxxxxxxxxxxxxxxxxxxxxxxxxxxxxxxxxxxxxxxxxxxxxxxxxxxxxxxxxx xxxxxxxxxxxxxxx xxxxxxxxx xxxxxxx
xxxxxxxxxxxx xxxxxxxxxxxxxxxxxxxxxxxxxxxxxxxx
2. Xxxxxxxxxxxxxxxxxxxxxxxxxxxxxxxxxxxxxxxx
xxxxxxxxxxxxxxxxxxxxxxxxxxxxxxxxxxxxxxxxxxxxxxxxxxxxxxxxxxxxxxxxxxxxxxx xxxxxxxxxxxxxxx xxxxxxxxx xxxxxxx
xxxxxxxxxxxx xxxxxxxxxxxxxxxxxxxxxxxxxxxxxxxx
3. Xxxxxxxxxxxxxxxxxxxxxxxxxxxxxxxxxxxxxxxx
xxxxxxxxxxxxxxxxxxxxxxxxxxxxxxxxxxxxxxxxxxxxxxxxxxxxxxxxxxxxxxxxxxxxxxx xxxxxxxxxxxxxxx xxxxxxxxx xxxxxxx
xxxxxxxxxxxx xxxxxxxxxxxxxxxxxxxxxxxxxxxxxxxx
4. Xxxxxxxxxxxxxxxxxxxxxxxxxxxxxxxxxxxxxxxx
xxxxxxxxxxxxxxxxxxxxxxxxxxxxxxxxxxxxxxxxxxxxxxxxxxxxxxxxxxxxxxxxxxxxxxx xxxxxxxxxxxxxxx xxxxxxxxx xxxxxxx
xxxxxxxxxxxx xxxxxxxxxxxxxxxxxxxxxxxxxxxxxxxx

WEEKLY KEY CUSTOMERS' SALES

In a similar vein it is important for the SMT to monitor how products are being purchased by the key customers. This is especially important after a launch of a new product, or after your competitors' launch a new competing product. Exhibit 17.2 shows the sort of detail they will be interested in.

Exhibit 17.2 Weekly Sales to Key Customers

Weekly sales with key customers

	$000s			
	Last week's sales	**Daily average Last 30 days**	**Daily average Last 90 days**	
Customer #1				
Product 1	450	430	400	✓
Product 2	400	380	560	✗
Product 3	340	320	310	
Product 4	375	355	425	✗
Other products	185	125	5	✓
Total Revenue	1,750	1,610	1,700	✓
Customer #2				
Product 1	380	410	450	✗
Product 2	380	410	450	✗
Product 3	120	150	190	✗
Product 4	180	210	190	
Other products	140	220	220	✗
Total Revenue	1,200	1,400	1,500	✗
Customer #3				
Product 1	220	200	160	✓
Product 2	190	170	140	✓
Product 3	160	140	120	
Product 4	190	170	150	
Other products	1,140	1,120	1,130	
Total Revenue	1,500	1,400	1,300	✓

Highlights:
1. Xxxxxxxxxxxxxxxxxxxxxxxxxxxxxxxxxxxxxxxxx
xxxxxxxxxxxxxxxxxxxxxxxxxxxxxxxxxxxxxxxxxxxxxxxxxxxxxxxxxxxxxxxxxxxxxxxx xxxxxxxxxxxxxxx xxxxxxxxx xxxxxxx
xxxxxxxxxxxx xxxxxxxxxxxxxxxxxxxxxxxxxxxxxxxxx
2. Xxxxxxxxxxxxxxxxxxxxxxxxxxxxxxxxxxxxxxxxx
xxxxxxxxxxxxxxxxxxxxxxxxxxxxxxxxxxxxxxxxxxxxxxxxxxxxxxxxxxxxxxxxxxxxxxxx xxxxxxxxxxxxxxx xxxxxxxxx xxxxxxx
xxxxxxxxxxxx xxxxxxxxxxxxxxxxxxxxxxxxxxxxxxxxx
3. Xxxxxxxxxxxxxxxxxxxxxxxxxxxxxxxxxxxxxxxxx
xxxxxxxxxxxxxxxxxxxxxxxxxxxxxxxxxxxxxxxxxxxxxxxxxxxxxxxxxxxxxxxxxxxxxxxx xxxxxxxxxxxxxxx xxxxxxxxx xxxxxxx
xxxxxxxxxxxx xxxxxxxxxxxxxxxxxxxxxxxxxxxxxxxxx
4. Xxxxxxxxxxxxxxxxxxxxxxxxxxxxxxxxxxxxxxxxx
xxxxxxxxxxxxxxxxxxxxxxxxxxxxxxxxxxxxxxxxxxxxxxxxxxxxxxxxxxxxxxxxxxxxxxxx xxxxxxxxxxxxxxx xxxxxxxxx xxxxxxx
xxxxxxxxxxxx xxxxxxxxxxxxxxxxxxxxxxxxxxxxxxxxx

WEEKLY REPORTING ON LATE PROJECTS AND LATE REPORTS

Many managers are innovative people who love to get on with a project but often fail to tie up the loose ends or finish it. I am always encountering projects that are stuck in limbo and so will only be of value to the organization when someone refocuses and completes them. Set out in Exhibits 17.3 and 17.4 are two report formats that should be tabled weekly to the senior and middle management to enable them to focus on completion. Exhibit 17.3 has a dual focus, on the project manager and the project. Exhibit 17.4 is a "shame and name" list, or as an attendee reworded, "managers requiring further training." The list focuses management on those reports that are well past their deadline. The version number helps management realize the cost of revisions. The manager's in-tray column focuses on the guilty manager and helps encourage action.

Exhibit 17.3 Overdue Projects Report

Manager	**Number of Projects Currently Outstanding**	**Number of Outstanding Projects Last Month**	**Total Projects Currently Being Managed**
Pat Carruthers	5	3	10
Robin Smith	3	3	12
Kim Bush	7	0	8
XXXXXXX	3	2	5
List of Major Projects That Are Past Their Deadline	**Original Deadline**	**Project Manager (Sponsor)**	**Completion Timeframe**
Xxxxxxxxxxxx	1/06/0X	AB (YZ)	☺
Annual report	1/07/0X	DE (RS)	☺
Strategic plan publication	1/08/0X	AB (RS)	☹
Balanced scorecard report	1/09/0X	DE (YZ)	☺
Outcomes 2010	1/12/0X	AB (YZ)	☹

Exhibit 17.3 *(Continued)*

Completion Timeframe			
Will be completed within five working days	Will be completed this month	Will be completed this quarter	Risk of non-completion at year-end

Exhibit 17.4 Weekly List of Overdue Reports

Past Deadline Reports Week Beginning 20/xx/xx				
Report Title	**Date: First Draft**	**Manager's in Tray**	**Version #**	**Original Deadline**
Annual report	1/2/xx	DP	>10	15/9/xx
20xx/20x1 Annual budget	15/9/xx	DP	>20	15/3/xx
xxxxxxxxxxxxxxxxxx	1/9/xx	DP	>10	30/7/xx
xxxxxxxxxxxxxxxxxx	30/8/xx	DP	5	15/4/xx
xxxxxxxxxxxxxxxxxxxxxxxxx	15/2/xx	DP	4	30/1/xx
xxxxxxxxxxxxxxxxxx	30/3/xx	PC	>10	1/2/xx
xxxxxxxxxxxxxxxxxxxxxxxxx	1/8/xx	PC	1	15/5/xx
xxxxxxxxxxxxxxxxxxxx	15/2/xx	PC	1	30/1/xx
xxxxxxxxxxxxxxxx	1/9/xx	PC	3	1/2/xx
xxxxxxxxxxxxxxxx	15/3/xx	PC	7	1/3/xx
xxxxxxxxxxxxxxxxxxxx	1/9/xx	MM	7	30/7/xx
xxxxxxxxxxxxxxxxxx	15/3/xx	MM	1	15/1/xx
Actions to be taken: XXXXXX XXXX XXXXXX XXXX XXXXXX XXXX XXXXX XXXXXX XXXXX XXXXX XXXXXX XXXX XXXXXX XXXX XXXXXX XXXX XXXXX XXXXXX XXXXX XXXXX				

CHAPTER 18

Reporting Your Winning Key Performance Indicators

Many companies are working with the wrong measures, many of which are incorrectly termed key performance indicators (KPIs). Very few organizations really monitor their true KPIs. The reason is very few organizations, business leaders, writers, accountants, or consultants have explored what a KPI actually is. There are three types of performance measures:

1. Key result indicators (KRIs) tell how you have done in a perspective.
2. Performance indicators (PIs) tell you what to do.
3. KPIs tell you what to do to increase performance dramatically.

Many performance measures used by organizations are thus an inappropriate mix of these three types.

I use an onion analogy to describe the relationship of these three measures as shown in Exhibit 18.1. The outside skin describes the overall condition of the onion, how much sun, water, and nutrients it has received, and how it has been handled from harvest to grocery shelf. However, as we peel the layers off the onion at home we find out more information. The layers represent the various performance indicators and the core represents the key performance indicators.

10/80/10 RULE

Kaplan and Norton recommend no more than 20 KPIs, and Jeremy Hope (of *Beyond Budgeting* fame) suggests less than 10. To aid those involved in performance measurement I have developed the 10/80/10 rule. This means an organization should have about 10 KRIs, up to 80 PIs, and 10 KPIs. Very seldom do there need to be more measures than these numbers, and in many cases less can be used.

So what are KRIs? KRIs are measures that have often been mistaken for KPIs including:

- Customer satisfaction
- Net profit before tax
- Profitability of customers

Exhibit 18.1 Three Types of Performance Measures

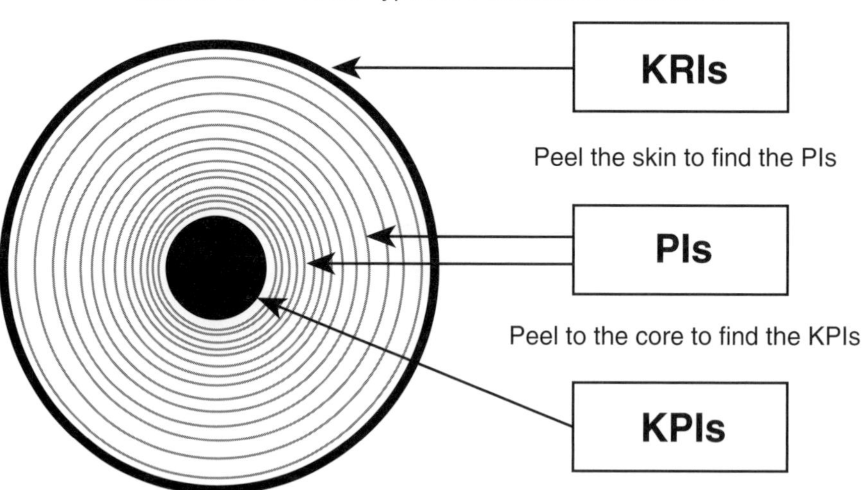

- Employee satisfaction
- Return on capital employed

The common characteristic of these measures is that they are the result of many actions. They give a clear picture of whether you are traveling in the right direction. They do not, however, tell you what you need to do to improve these results. Thus KRIs provide information that is ideal for the Board (i.e., to those not involved in day-to-day management).

A car's speedometer provides a useful analogy. The Board will simply want to know the speed the car is traveling at. However, management needs to know more information since the traveling speed is a combination of what gear the car is in and what revs the engine is doing. Management might even be concentrating on completely different measures, such as how economically the car is performing (miles per gallon), or how hot the engine is running. These are two completely different gauges, and are performance indicators or may even be KPIs.

KRIs cover a longer period of time than KPIs—they are reviewed on monthly/quarterly cycles, not on a daily/weekly basis.

Separating KRIs has a profound impact on reporting, resulting in a separation of performance measures into those impacting governance and those impacting management. In other words, an organization should have a governance report (ideally in a dashboard format), made up of up to ten measures providing high-level KRIs for the Board and a Balanced Scorecard (BSC) comprising up to 20 measures (a mix of KPIs and PIs) for management.

In between KRIs and the true KPIs are numerous performance indicators. These complement the KPIs and are shown with them on the organization's, divisions', departments', and teams' scorecards.

PIs that lie beneath KRIs could include:

Profitability of the top 10% of customers
Net profit on key product lines
Percentage increase in sales with top 10% of customers
Number of employees participating in the suggestion scheme

KPIs represent a set of measures focusing on those aspects of organizational performance that are the most critical for the current and future success of the organization. They have specific characteristics.

LATE PLANES KPI

My favorite KPI story is about a senior BA official, who set about turning British Airways (BA) around in the 1980s by reportedly concentrating on one KPI. He was notified, wherever he was in the world, if a BA plane was delayed. The senior BA manager at the relevant airport knew that if a plane was delayed beyond a certain "threshold," they would receive a personal call from the BA official. It was not long before BA planes had a reputation for leaving on time. This KPI affected all six of the BSC perspectives.

I add staff satisfaction and environment and community to the standard four balanced scorecard perspectives of financial, customer satisfaction, internal process, and learning and growth as shown in Exhibit 18.2.

The late planes KPI also linked to many critical success factors (CSFs) for the airline. It linked to the "delivery in full and on time" CSF, namely the "timely arrival and departure of airplanes." The importance of the CSF "timely arrival and departure of airplanes" can be seen by its impact on all the six perspectives of a modified BSC (see Exhibit 18.3).

UNDER WEIGHT TRUCKS KPI

A CEO of a distribution company realized that a CSF for their business was trucks leaving as close as to capacity as possible. Large trucks capable of carrying more than 40 tons were being sent out with small loads as dispatch managers were focusing on "deliver in full on time" to customers.

Each day by 9 A.M., the CEO received a report of those trailers that had been sent out under weight. The CEO rang the dispatch manager and asked whether any action had taken place to see if the customer could have accepted that delivery on a different date that enabled better utilization of the trucks. In most cases the customer could have received it earlier or later, fitting in with a past or future truck going in that direction. The impact on profitability was significant.

Just as with the airline example, the staff did their utmost to avoid a career-limiting phone call.

Exhibit 18.2 Six-Perspective Balanced Scorecard

FINANCIAL	CUSTOMER	ENVIRONMENT/ COMMUNITY
Utilization of assets Optimization of working capital Focus on top 10% of customers, etc.	Seamless service Increased customer satisfaction, etc.	Supporting local business Green Globe 21 Community leadership
INTERNAL PROCESS	**EMPLOYEE SATISFACTION**	**LEARNING AND GROWTH**
Delivery in full on time Effective relationship with key stakeholders Optimizing technology	Positive company culture Retention of key staff Increased recognition	Empowerment Increasing expertise Adaptability, etc.

SELLING KPIs THROUGH THE "EMOTIONAL DRIVERS"

As mentioned in the beginning of the book, nothing was ever sold by logic! You sell through emotional drivers. This project needs a public

Exhibit 18.3 Late Planes Impact on the Six Balanced Scorecard Perspectives

Late planes:

1. Increased cost in many ways: including additional airport surcharges, and the cost of accommodating passengers overnight as a result of late planes being stopped from flying out due to the noise restrictions "curfew," which comes into force, late at night, in many airports around the world;
2. Increased customers' dissatisfaction, and alienation of those people meeting passengers at their destination (possible future customers);
3. Contributed more to ozone depletion (environmental impact) as additional fuel was used as a result of the pilot using full boost to make up time;
4. Had a negative impact on staff development as staff would replicate bad habits that had created late planes;
5. Adversely affected supplier relationships and servicing schedules resulting in poor service quality;
6. Increased employee dissatisfaction as they had to deal both with frustrated customers and the extra stress each late plane created.

relations (PR) machine behind it. No presentation, e-mail, memo, or paper should go out unless it has been vetted by your PR expert. All your presentations should be road-tested in front of the PR expert. Your PR strategy should include selling to staff, budget holders, senior management team (SMT), and the Board.

The potential emotional drivers for your SMT may include:

- A lack of linkage of daily activities to strategy
- Endless performance management meetings that are not improving the performance, yet adversely affecting job satisfaction
- Many lost weekends with family, producing performance reports that are meaningless
- A lack of linkage between the CEO and key staff in the organization
- A lack of focus by management and staff because the CSFs have not been identified and/or communicated
- Staff not sharing the same vision as the management team due more to ignorance than disagreement

The KPI project team needs to focus on the marketing of the concept as much as it does on the training. Budget holders will need to understand how this process is going to help them manage their business.

CHARACTERISTICS OF A KPI

The main characteristics of a KPI are:

- Non-financial measures (not expressed in dollars, yen, pounds, euro, etc.)
- Measured frequently (e.g., daily or 24/7)
- Acted upon by CEO and SMT
- All staff understand the measure and what corrective action is required
- Responsibility can be tied down to the individual or team
- Significant impact (e.g., it impacts most of the core CSFs and more than one BSC perspective)

- Has a positive impact (e.g., affects all other performance measures in a positive way)

When you put a dollar sign on a measure you have already converted it into a result indicator (e.g., daily sales is a result of activities that have taken place to create the sales). The KPI lies deeper down. It may be the number of visits to/contacts with the key customers who make up most of the profitable business.

KPIs should be monitored 24/7, daily, and a few maybe weekly. A monthly, quarterly, or annual measure cannot be a KPI because it cannot be *key* to your business as you are monitoring them well after the "horse has bolted." KPIs are therefore "current" or future-oriented measures as opposed to past measures (e.g., number of key customer visits planned in next month, or a list by key customer of the date of next planned visit). When you look at most organizational measures, they are very much past indicators measuring events of the last month or quarter. These indicators cannot be and never were a KPI.

All good KPIs that I have come across, that have made a difference, had the CEO's constant attention, with daily calls to the relevant staff. Having a "career-limiting" discussion with the CEO is not something staff want to repeat, and in the airlines case, innovative and productive processes were put in place to prevent a reoccurrence.

A KPI should tell you about what action needs to take place. The British Airways "late plane" KPI communicated immediately to everybody that there needed to be a focus on recovering the lost time. Cleaners, caterers, ground crew, flight attendants, and liaison officers with traffic controllers would all work some magic to save a minute here, a minute there while maintaining or improving service standards.

A KPI is deep enough in the organization that it can be tied down to an individual. In other words, the CEO can ring someone and ask "why." Return on capital employed has never been a KPI because it cannot be tied down to a manager; it is a result of many activities under different managers.

A good KPI will affect most of the core CSFs and more than one BSC perspective. In other words, when the CEO, management, and staff focus on the KPI, the organization scores goals in all directions.

A good KPI has a flow on effect. An improvement in a key measure within the CSF of "maximizing key customers' satisfaction" would have a positive impact on many other measures. Timely arrival and departure of planes gives rise to improved service by ground staff because there is less "fire fighting" to distract them from a quality and caring customer contact.

IMPORTANCE OF DAILY CEO FOLLOW-UP

If the KPIs you currently have are not creating change, throw them out because there is a good chance that they may be wrong. They are probably measures that were thrown together without the in-depth research and investigation KPIs truly deserve. CEOs will know intuitively that you have struck gold when six weeks of intense monitoring and a follow-up action creates significant change. What I mean is the CEO follows up every, yes every shortfall, with a personal phone call.

Branch managers, store supervisors, or a sales rep after their first phone call from the CEO about nonperformance will move heaven and earth to avoid another "career-limiting" phone call from the CEO. Performance will change quickly! It, however, should be balanced with publicly congratulating high-performance teams. Do not fall down the hole an airline has. As one flight attendant said to me, "our bosses monitor performance, real time; you are contacted immediately if there is a problem but you never hear from them when we deliver timely planes day-in day-out."

The SMT and the CEO have to be committed to developing and driving KPIs in the organization. Many KPI initiatives fail because of this lack of commitment. For a CEO to spend time, each day, monitoring and following up the KPIs with staff is a major culture change for many CEOs and thus one which requires a major "sell."

REPORTING KPIs 24/7 OR DAILY TO MANAGEMENT

Reporting KPIs to management needs to be timely. As mentioned KPIs need to be reported 24/7, daily or at the outside weekly; other performance measures can be reported less frequently monthly and quarterly.

The main KPIs are reported 24/7 or daily via the intranet. Exhibit 18.4 shows how they should be reported giving the SMT contact details, the problem, and some history so a meaningful phone call be made.

Exhibit 18.4 Screen Layout for a Daily KPI Report

Late Planes Over 2 Hours

Time:

	Statistics of Last Stop							Contact Details			No. of Late Planes Over 1 Hour		
Flight Number	**How Late**	**Expected Arrival Time**	**Arrived Late**	**Left Late**	**Time Added**	**Region Manager Name**	**Current Time at Location**	**Work**	**Mobile**	**Home**	**Last 30 Days**	**30-Day Average of Last 3 Months**	**30-Day Average of Last 6 Months**
BA1243	02:15	21:45	01:45	02:15	00:30	Pat Carruthers	18:45	xxxxx	xxxxx	xxxxx	5	4	4
BA1244	02:15	21:45	01:45	02:15	00:30	xxxxxxxxx	19:45	xxxxx	xxxxx	xxxxx	6	4	4
BA1245	02:15	21:45	01:45	02:15	00:30	xxxxxxxxx	20:45	xxxxx	xxxxx	xxxxx	7	4	4
BA1246	02:15	21:45	01:45	02:15	00:30	xxxxxxxxx	21:45	xxxxx	xxxxx	xxxxx	8	4	4
BA1247	02:15	21:45	01:45	02:15	00:30	xxxxxxxxx	22:45	xxxxx	xxxxx	xxxxx	9	4	4
BA1248	02:15	21:45	01:45	02:15	00:30	xxxxxxxxx	23:45	xxxxx	xxxxx	xxxxx	10	4	4
BA1249	02:15	21:45	01:45	02:15	00:30	xxxxxxxxx	23:45	xxxxx	xxxxx	xxxxx	11	4	4

Total: 7 planes

Another benefit of providing senior management with daily/weekly information is that the month-end reporting process becomes less important. In other words, if organizations report their KPIs on a 24/7 or daily basis, management knows intuitively whether the organization is having a good or bad month.

REPORTING WEEKLY KPIs AND PERFORMANCE INDICATORS TO MANAGEMENT

Some KPIs need only be reported weekly. Set out in Exhibit 18.5 is an example of how they could be presented. Note that while all the KPIs will be graphed over time, going back at least 15 months, only the three KPIs showing a decline would be graphed. The other two KPI graphs would be maintained and used when necessary.

REPORTING MONTHLY PIs TO MANAGEMENT

There are endless ways these can be shown—through icons, gauges, traffic lights, and so on. It is best to visit the www.waymark.co.nz site for good examples or search the web using these search strings: "balanced scorecard" + formats + templates. Exhibit 18.6 shows an example.

REPORTING TO STAFF: THEIR TEAM'S PROGRESS

Set out in Exhibit 18.7 is an example of a team scorecard using Excel. Excel is a useful tool for designing and piloting a template until a more robust and integrated solution is found.

REPORTING TO STAFF: THE ORGANIZATION'S PROGRESS

It is a good idea to have some form of monthly icon report for staff, a report that if left on a bus would not be damaging to the organization

Exhibit 18.5 Weekly KPI Report Example

Top five KPIs
Weekly report xx xxxx 20xx

Top 5 indicators	Target	Result	Rating
Xxxxxxx xxxxx xxxxx (see graph below)			☹
Xxxxxxx xxxxx xxxxx (see graph below)			☹
Xxxxxxx xxxxxxx xxxxxxx.			☺
Xxxxxxx xxxxx xxxxx (see graph below)			☹
Xxxxxxx xxxxxxx xxxxxxx..			😐

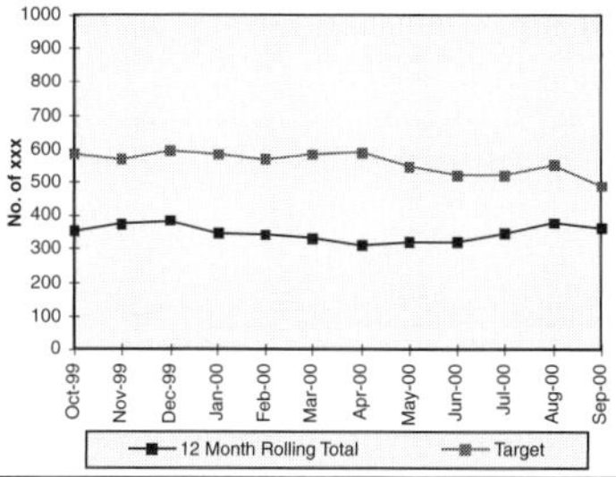

Issues:

Actions to be taken:

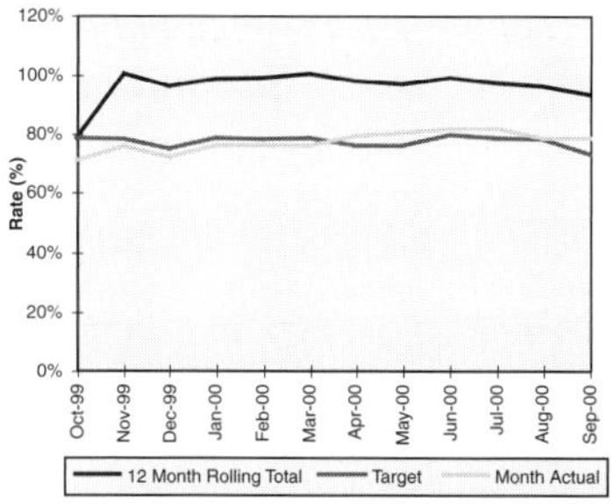

Issues:

Actions to be taken:

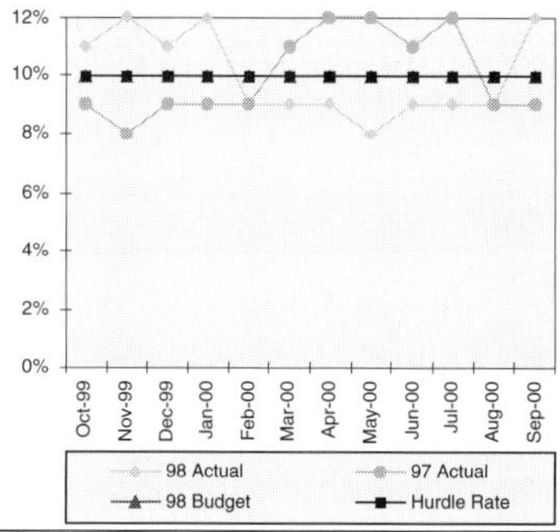

Issues:

Actions to be taken:

Exhibit 18.6 Scorecard Example

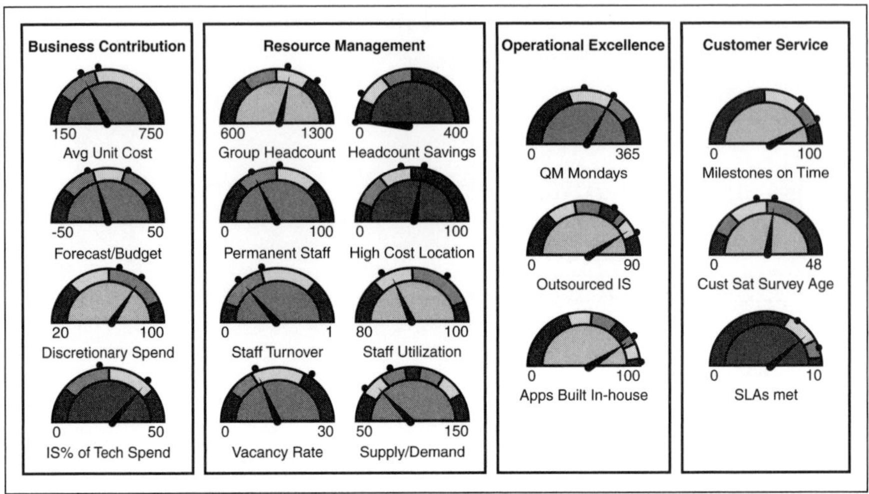

Source: www.ergometrics.com.

if it found its way to a competitor. Icon reports, as shown in Exhibit 18.8, are ideal because they tell you what is good, what is adequate, and what needs to be improved without disclosing sensitive data. This is a particularly good example because it shows icons and reminds staff about the strategies.

IDENTIFYING ORGANIZATION-WIDE CRITICAL SUCCESS FACTORS IS AN IMPORTANT STEP

Many performance measurement initiatives fail because accountants do not undertake the research into what are the organization's CSFs. The relationship between CSFs (also referred to as key result areas) and KPIs is critical as illustrated in Exhibit 18.9. Once you have found the CSFs, it is very easy to locate the KPIs!

CSFs identify the issues that determine organizational health and vitality. When you first investigate CSFs you may come up with 30 or so issues that can be argued are critical for the continued health of the organization. The second phase of thinning them down is quite easy because the more important CSFs have a broader influence, cutting across

Exhibit 18.7 Team Scorecard Built in Excel

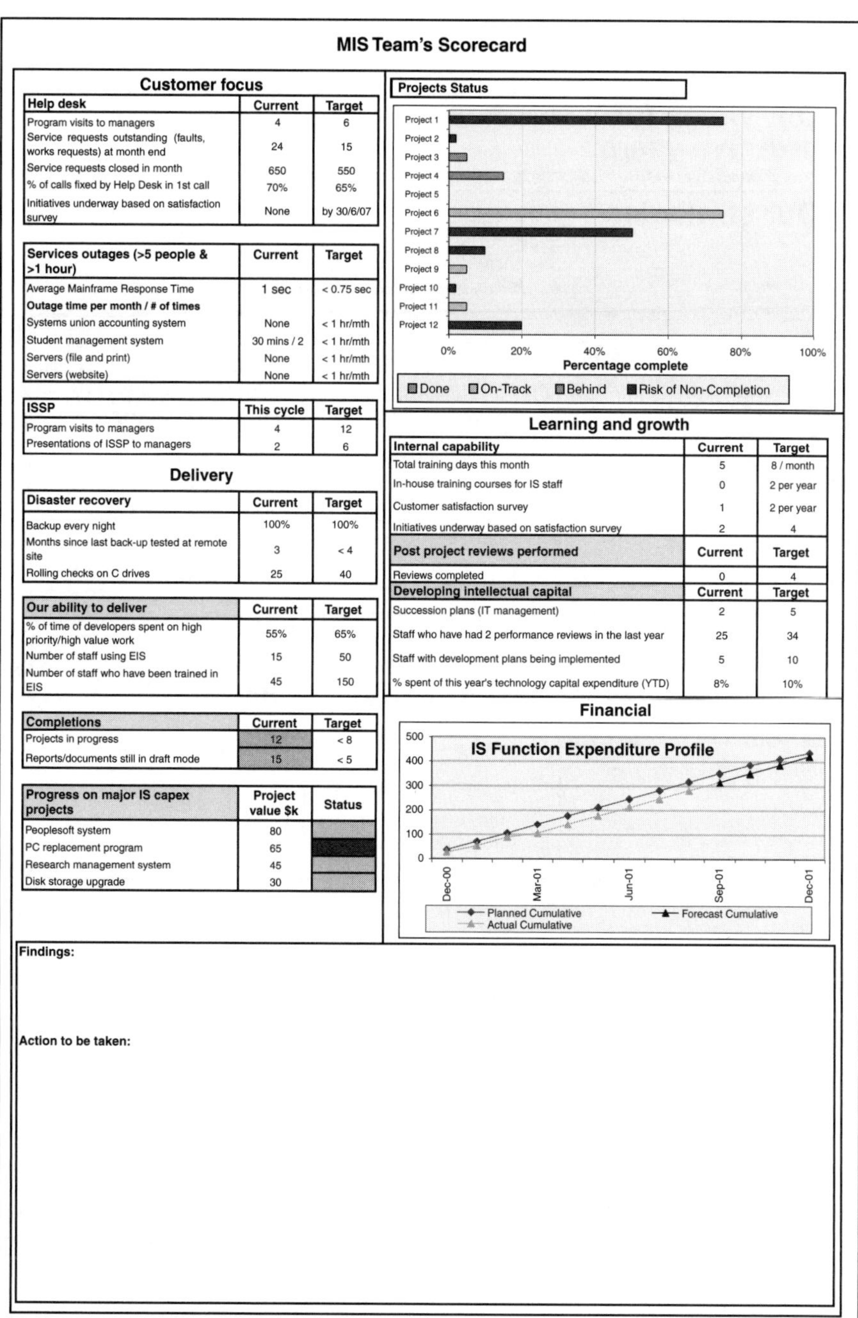

MIS Team's Scorecard

Customer focus

Help desk	Current	Target
Program visits to managers	4	6
Service requests outstanding (faults, works requests) at month end	24	15
Service requests closed in month	650	550
% of calls fixed by Help Desk in 1st call	70%	65%
Initiatives underway based on satisfaction survey	None	by 30/6/07

Services outages (>5 people & >1 hour)	Current	Target
Average Mainframe Response Time	1 sec	< 0.75 sec
Outage time per month / # of times		
Systems union accounting system	None	< 1 hr/mth
Student management system	30 mins / 2	< 1 hr/mth
Servers (file and print)	None	< 1 hr/mth
Servers (website)	None	< 1 hr/mth

ISSP	This cycle	Target
Program visits to managers	4	12
Presentations of ISSP to managers	2	6

Delivery

Disaster recovery	Current	Target
Backup every night	100%	100%
Months since last back-up tested at remote site	3	< 4
Rolling checks on C drives	25	40

Our ability to deliver	Current	Target
% of time of developers spent on high priority/high value work	55%	65%
Number of staff using EIS	15	50
Number of staff who have been trained in EIS	45	150

Completions	Current	Target
Projects in progress	12	< 8
Reports/documents still in draft mode	15	< 5

Progress on major IS capex projects	Project value $k	Status
Peoplesoft system	80	
PC replacement program	65	
Research management system	45	
Disk storage upgrade	30	

Projects Status

Learning and growth

Internal capability	Current	Target
Total training days this month	5	8 / month
In-house training courses for IS staff	0	2 per year
Customer satisfaction survey	1	2 per year
Initiatives underway based on satisfaction survey	2	4
Post project reviews performed	**Current**	**Target**
Reviews completed	0	4
Developing intellectual capital	**Current**	**Target**
Succession plans (IT management)	2	5
Staff who have had 2 performance reviews in the last year	25	34
Staff with development plans being implemented	5	10
% spent of this year's technology capital expenditure (YTD)	8%	10%

Financial

Findings:

Action to be taken:

Exhibit 18.8 Icon Report to Staff Example

Our mission	To provide energy at the right price at the right time
Our vision for next five years	To be the preferred energy provider in the xxx
Our strategies	1. Acquiring profitable customers 2. Increase cost efficiencies 3. Innovation through our people 4. Using best business practices

Our perspectives and progress

FINANCIAL	CUSTOMER FOCUS	ENVIRONMENT/ COMMUNITY
☺ Utilization of assets 😐 Optimization of working capital, EBIT, growth, etc.	😐 Increasing customer satisfaction ☺ Gaining profitable customers, etc.	☺ Supporting local businesses ☹ Linking with future employees ☺ Community leadership, etc.
INTERNAL	**EMPLOYEE SATISFACTION**	**LEARNING AND GROWTH**
☺ Delivery in full on time ☺ Optimizing technology ☹ Work accidents, etc.	☺ Positive company culture 😐 Retention of key staff ☹ Increased staff recognition, etc.	☺ Increasing empowerment ☺ Increasing staff adaptability 😐 Coaching increasing, etc.

a number of BSC perspectives (e.g., the timely arrival and departure of planes impacts nearly all the BSC perspectives of an airline). Better practice suggests that you need to have between *five and eight* CSFs.

FINDING YOUR WINNING KPIs

Once the KPI project has located the most useful performance measures, the next stage is to find those that are likely to be KPIs. This is when you apply the seven KPI characteristics across the likely measures. By applying the first two KPI characteristics, "checking to see that they

Exhibit 18.9 Importance of CSFs

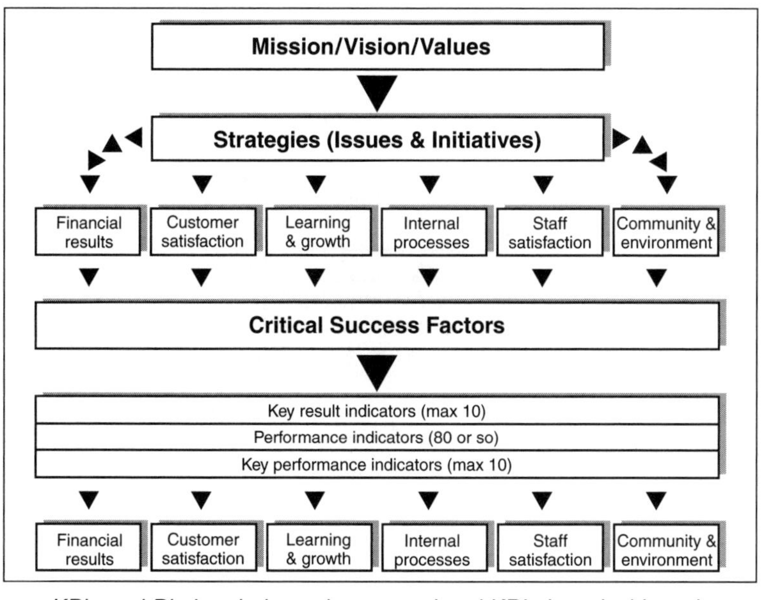

KPIs and PIs in a balanced scorecard and KRIs in a dashboard.

are nonfinancial" and secondly "that they would need to be measured frequently" will eliminate many measures, from the selection process.

Once you have found the measures that appear to have all the KPI characteristics you now need to test whether the behavioral impact will be positive. There have been many examples where measures fail this test. One hospital started to measure waiting time in the emergency department in a thrust to reduce these times. Times were reduced but to the horror of management, patients were being held in ambulances until the emergency department was ready to receive them, thus creating a problem with ambulance availability!

HOW KPIs AND FINANCIAL REPORTING FIT TOGETHER

Exhibit 18.10 shows how the components of performance management fit together. The reporting framework has to accommodate the requirements of different levels in the organization and the reporting frequency that supports timely decision making.

Exhibit 18.10 Performance Management Reporting Framework

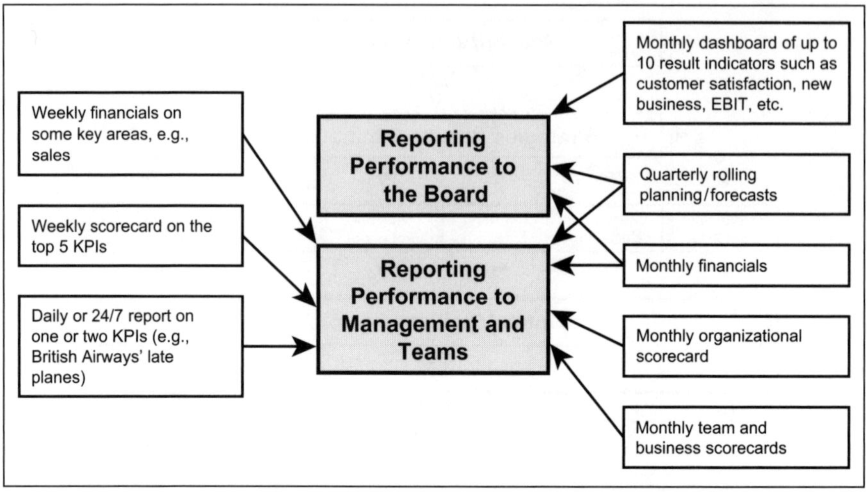

CHAPTER 19

Where to Invest in Your Accounting Systems for Maximum Benefit

Far too much money is reinvested in upgrading the general ledger. In a modern company the general ledger (G/L) does only the basic task of holding the financial numbers for the year. Monthly reporting, latest forecast numbers, budget numbers, and even the drill-down facility available to budget holders often reside outside the G/L package, so why reinvest?

Worst still, many CFOs are party to a huge investment in systems that serve to lock in analysis at the micro level, e.g., activity-based costing applications. Jeremy Hope of *Beyond Budgeting* fame points out in his recent book[1] that many such systems are dubious. I concur because they are often designed by the people who always wanted to be a "NASA scientist" and who have never run a finance function in their life.

The finance team has better investment opportunities, which will turn the accounting function into a paperless office. The order of priority should be:

- Implement a planning and forecasting tool and migrate all forecasting and budgeting processes onto it

- Upgrade accounts payable systems (e.g., scanning equipment, electronic ordering and receipting)
- Acquire a reporting tool and migrate all reporting onto it
- Add a drill down front end to the G/L if it is not already part of your G/L (e.g., PowerPlay, Crystal reporting)
- Invest in your intranet and website so that customer statements, supplier remittances can be viewed by customers and suppliers, respectively, using password protection, 24/7
- Upgrade G/L only after you have maximized the existing G/L

Business upgrades to G/L and other core systems often simply replicate existing processes and do not take the opportunity to redesign those processes into new systems. There are many tools in modern systems that are never used!

—CFO with blue chip international experience

ACQUIRING A PLANNING AND FORECASTING TOOL

The case for the acquisition of a planning and forecasting tool has already been made. Simply get on with it now. Not to do so will be career limiting! As a corporate accountant, being an expert at Excel will show you are a technical dinosaur, one who has not embraced modern tools and one who does not understand the inherent risks in running core financial systems in a high-risk tool.

INVEST IN ACCOUNTS PAYABLE TO REDUCE TRANSACTION VOLUMES AND MAKE IT PAPERLESS

Many accounts payable (AP) processing procedures are more akin to the Charles Dickens era than the 21st century. Why do we go from an electronic transaction in the supplier's accounting system to a Charles Dickens paper-based invoice? Surely we should be able to change this easily with our major suppliers receiving electronic feeds already G/L coded!

Many U.S. multinationals have achieved this already. It requires an investment, skilled AP staff, and retraining of the budget holders. The rewards are immense. To appreciate the benefits I suggest the AP team regularly visit the website of The Accounts Payable Network (www.TheAPNetwork.com).

There have been major advancements in technology for AP teams. The return on investment in AP technology is greater than any other equivalent investment in other service departments within a business. Why then are some AP teams so under-invested? It is due partly to:

- Lack of understanding by the CFO of the technologies and their benefits
- The AP team not researching the technologies
- Poor selling of the technologies by suppliers and by the AP team

Some of the ways to work toward a paperless accounts payable function include:

- Purchase an electronic ordering system (procurement system) that automatically links with the AP system so that orders and receipting are completed electronically and invoices are matched electronically.
- Introduce scanning so that invoices can be sent electronically by e-mail for approval. You need this even if you have invested in a procurement system because invoices without orders, or invoices that are different to their corresponding order, will need originator approval.
- Load remittances electronically onto your website in a secure area so that suppliers with their password can download them. This removes the need to post remittances to suppliers. One course attendee said this was set up very easily by their IT team.
- Acquire an integrated web-based expense claim system so staff can complete their expenses wherever they are in the world.
- Introduce the purchase card to all staff with delegated authority so all small-value items can be purchased through the purchase card, thereby saving thousands of hours of processing time by both budget holders and the accounts payable teams.
- Allow your key suppliers on-line read-only access, through a password, to their AP account so they can reconcile their ledger.

Most accounting systems come with an integrated purchase order system. Some even enable the order to be sent automatically to the preferred supplier, whose price list has been reviewed via the system by the budget holder.

This is a major exercise and one that should be researched immediately. There will be an organization near your locality that has your accounting system where the purchase order system is working well. Visit them and learn how to implement it.

AQUIRE A REPORTING TOOL

Excel has no place as a reporting tool. Again it is too prone to disaster. There is no problem where the system automatically downloads to Excel with all the programming logic being resident in the system and basically bomb proof. The problem lies when the system has been built in-house, often by someone who has now left the company, with the accuracy of formatting the G/L download relying on Excel formulae reading the imported file. This is simply a disaster waiting to happen.

AQUIRE A DRILL DOWN TOOL

It is important that budget holders take ownership of their part of the G/L. To this end we need to offer them a user-friendly interface to their part of the G/L. There are a number of tools that can make a "silk purse out of a sow's ear." Companies are reporting that they have had great success by downloading transactions (daily or weekly) from the G/L into these drill down tools allowing read-only access. In fact the budget holders never look at the G/L. The drill down tool also offers trend analysis that transcends the year-end, enabling budget holders to look at the last 18- or 24-month trend in expenditure.

INVEST IN YOUR INTRANET AND WEBSITE

By allowing secure access to electronic documentation 24/7 that you currently send out by e-mail or post you will save costs and aid your customers' and suppliers' processing efficiency. Customer statements and supplier remittances can be viewed by customers and suppliers, respectively, using password protection, 24/7. Some organizations allow on-line "read only" access to their account in the accounts receivable and accounts payable ledgers to major customers and suppliers, respectively. Access security is similar to that used by banks when they allow customers access to your bank account via the Internet.

Note

1. Jeremy Hope, *Reinventing the CFO: How Financial Managers Can Transform Their Roles and Add Greater Value* (Boston, MA: Harvard Business School Press, 2006).

CHAPTER 20

Implementing a New Accounting System

If you really have to upgrade your general ledger (G/L), there are a number of better practices worth implementing:

- Do not underestimate the communication commitment—have a Web page on the intranet and tell all about the successes to date.
- Get the CEO to send out the "you must attend the training session" letter (see Appendix I).
- Celebrate every small success—the celebration alone is a great communication tool.
- Get a day or so of public relations (PR) support—ensuring that all presentations and key memos are bounced off the PR expert. You will be surprised how they can improve the sell component.
- Sell the changes to the budget holders—remember you sell by the emotional drivers, not by logic.
- Ensure you apply Pareto's 80/20 principle (e.g., only have account codes where the trend information is going to be worthwhile). Ensure the next chart of accounts is done by someone who can see the woods for the trees. Each additional account code will involve extra time including the budget holder's looking up the code and the correcting of miscoding errors. Each additional account code

will involve extra time including the budget holders looking up the code and the correcting of miscoding errors.

- Run a focus group workshop (see Exhibit 20.1) to ascertain the key issues, the problems that should be resolved, and so forth.
- Have an "accounting systems newsletter" to cover the "gems" that are found from time to time in the system, and start this in the last quarter of the G/L implementation project.
- Resist the temptation to customize the accounting system; once you have made your pick stick with it, otherwise at upgrade time you will have a nightmare on your hands—even one modification is one too many!
- If you insist on customizing the G/L make sure you have a copy of the code on all changes to the software put in a time capsule, in the company's bank (do not trust the filing systems of the information systems function or the consultants who made the changes).
- Make it clear to budget holders that the new G/L is heralding a new world where the finance team have delegated the responsibility of maintaining the G/L to budget holders (e.g., budget holders are expected to monitor their part of the G/L, there will be no spring cleaning at month-end for any miss postings, budget holders will enter accruals directly into the G/L and so on).

Exhibit 20.1 Agenda and Outline of G/L Focus Group Workshop

One-Day Focus Group Workshop on Implementing a New Accounting System—and Getting It Right the First Time

Objective:

- To ensure a key group of staff and management are fully aware of what is required to implement the new accounting system
- To fully understand the required level of involvement and the inherent hurdles this project will face

Location: xxxxx

Date and Time: xxxxx

Attendees: A focus group selected from experienced staff: covering the regions, branches, depots, head office, and covering the different roles from administrators to the senior management team (SMT)

Exhibit 20.1 *(Continued)*

Requirements:

1. Workshop administrator to help coordinate attendees
2. At least three laptops, data show, screen, three electronic whiteboards, quiet workshop space away from the office

9:00 A.M.	Introduction from CEO
9:10 A.M.	The problems with the existing accounting system and better practice accounting systems by xxxxxxxxxxxxxxx • The problems • Reasons why we are taking the system as "vanilla" (e.g., no modifications) • Case studies • Features of the new system • Why so many G/L installations fail **All SMT and major budget holders are invited to join the focus group. They leave after this session.**
10:00 A.M.	**Commence workshop 1** on brainstorming the processing bottlenecks using "Post-it" re-engineering
10:30 A.M.	Morning break
10:50 A.M.	**Re-commence workshop 1** finish off re-engineering
11:20 A.M.	**Presentation of how the selected G/L application has been implemented in better practice companies (if selection made)**
12:00 P.M.	Lunch
12:45 P.M.	**Commence workshop 3** brainstorm a new chart of accounts looking to reduce the number to less than xxx
2:00 P.M.	Feedback from groups
2:20 P.M.	Afternoon break
2:40 P.M.	Short presentation on the decision-based reporting by xxxxxxxxxxxxxxx
3:30 P.M.	**Commence workshop 4** brainstorm new report formats
4:00 P.M.	In-house team complete workshop documentation on laptops
4:30 P.M.	Presentation by the focus group to the SMT. The focus group state their opinion on the key issues to address and resources required. **SMT invited to come back to hear**
5:00 P.M.	Finish of workshop

CHAPTER 21

Better Use of the Intranet

The intranet is being used for competitive advantage. It is now too important to leave the intranet solely in the hands of the IT team. The intranet is simply the best business tool a company has. If used correctly, the intranet will enhance performance, job satisfaction, communication, and knowledge transfer between teams and individual employees. In order to extract full value, your intranet needs to be driven and supported by all teams within a company. An effective intranet becomes the hub of the company, the place where everyone goes to find the information, tools, and resources necessary to carry out their jobs.

One child, I understand, described a home page as the center of a solar system with information revolving around it. That child will go far. That is exactly what it is for your organization even if you may not have a very big solar system yet.

Exhibit 21.1 shows how the intranet is becoming the center of the organization. Some organizations are even going to the extent of placing links to most frequently visited internet sites (e.g., the traffic cams, weather cams, etc.). One organization in a crisis decided to set up "the rumor factory" where staff could ask any question and management had to answer within 24 hours. It became the must visit page which combined fact and humor!

Exhibit 21.1 Content of a Better Practice Intranet

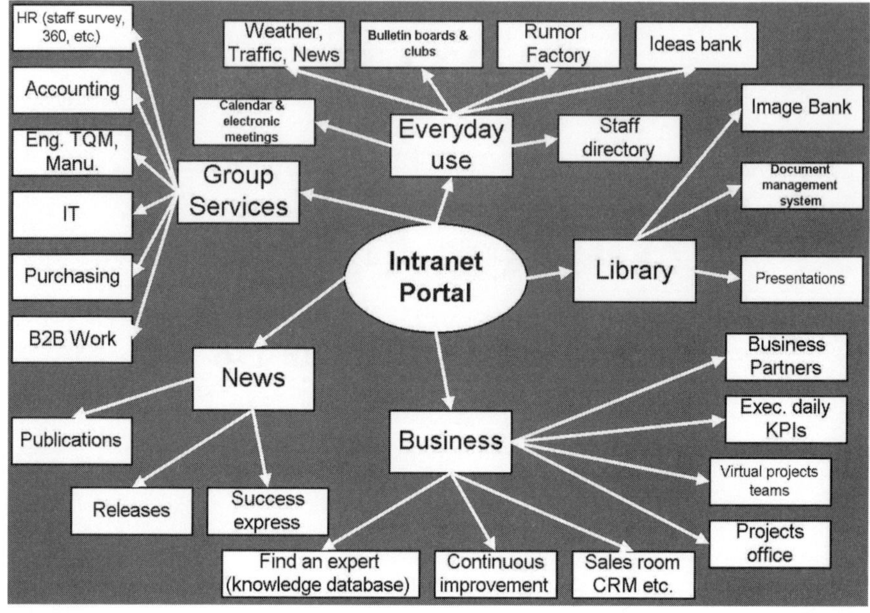

All the reports, presentations, and images are available to staff to save time. All key business systems are accessed from the intranet as well as the latest company news and press releases.

Teams and business units will have their own pages setting out their services to staff and teams in the organization.

One thing you can do immediately as a member of the finance team is to set up your finance team's home page. The content on the finance function's section page should include:

- Financial reports, at a company level, division level, and department level
- The accounting policies and procedures manual
- Financial delegations
- Accounts receivable information
- Accounts payable information
- Forecasting application so budget holders can enter budget information and it is automatically routed to their manager for approval

- Expense claim system so employees can complete and submit claims on-line, even from an airport lounge, and these can be automatically routed to their manager for approval
- On-line access to the procurement system
- The finance team's success stories

CHAPTER 22

Board Meetings Held Less Frequently Than Once a Month

When you have achieved some of the major better practices listed in this book within your organization you will have left a legacy that will remain for a long time. You will have gained selling skills and respect and will thus be in a position to tackle the thorn of the "monthly Board meeting."

Look to restructure the operations of the Board, setting bi-monthly meetings with the saved Board members' time being invested elsewhere such as:

- Sitting on subcommittees that are looking at improvements in key areas of the business
- Assisting the organization with specialist know-how by presenting on topics to management and staff
- Helping the company by opening doors to new markets

Because Board meetings are to be strategic, there is no need for monthly meetings and the enlightened companies now have bi-monthly meetings or at the most eight board meetings a year.

CHAPTER 23

Become a "Warrior Against Waste"

Jeremy Hope of *Beyond Budgeting* fame is leading a charge to transform the role of the CFO (see Exhibit 23.1 for some of the major pieces of his work that are available via the Internet or from on-line book stores). Hope has written a very informative chapter on how the CFO can become "a warrior against waste" in his book *Reinventing the CFO*.[1]

Exhibit 23.1 A List of the Ten Pieces You Need to Read

Title (Some of Which Have Been Co-Authored)	Web Source
Reinventing the CFO (book)	www.hbsp.harvard.edu search Jeremy Hope
Beyond Budgeting: How Managers Can Break Free from the Annual Performance Trap (book)	www.hbsp.harvard.edu search Jeremy Hope
Transforming the Bottom Line: Managing Performance with Numbers (book)	hbsp.harvard.edu search Jeremy Hope
Interview with Jeremy Hope: The Origins of *Beyond Budgeting* and of the *Beyond Budgeting* Round Table (BBRT)	juergendaum.com/news/01_10_2004.htm

(continues)

Exhibit 23.1 A List of the Ten Pieces You Need to Read

Title (Some of Which Have Been Co-Authored) *(Continued)*	**Web Source**
Beyond Budgeting . . . Breaking Through the Barrier to "The Third Wave"	cami.affiniscape.com/associations/3733/files/budgeting.pdf
New Ways of Setting Rewards: The *Beyond Budgeting* Model	www.hbsp.harvard.edu search Jeremy Hope
Who Needs Budgets? (HBR OnPoint Enhanced Edition)	www.hbsp.harvard.edu search Jeremy Hope
Beyond Budgeting: Pathways to the Emerging Model	www.hbsp.harvard.edu search Jeremy Hope
Competing in the Third Wave (book)	www.hbsp.harvard.edu search Jeremy Hope

If you have arrived at this point in the this book having achieved some better practices you will have time to put on your armor and become a "warrior against waste." You will find that the finance team and the budget holders will be ready and willing to fight with you against waste.

Some suggestions are:

- Use Hope's visionary words and have something symbolic with you that suggests you are a warrior against of waste. I can see mock samurai swords hanging over meetings; I can see teams developing complex rituals to prepare to take on a waste project; I can see fun emerging!
- Set up elaborate celebrations on achieving a waste project—it not only makes work fun, but it communicates to management that the finance team is adding value. Remember perception is everything.
- As CFO break your fortnight into two types of weeks: a fire fighting week and a finishing week. In the finishing week all fire fighting and routine meetings are cancelled. You are on a mission! The finishing week is for project work only.

- Always cost waste; always be able to quote a figure for processing something. The larger the cost, the better. I use $80 per transaction for accounts payable from the time taken to order, receipt, and process invoice, to payment of supplier. I could justify this figure in any large company. Remember accounting involves many judgments; it is not black and white, so make these costs estimates quickly. Half an hour with a spreadsheet would suffice to get an answer in the right "ball park."
- Hold a focus group workshop to kick-start a war against a particular waste. You will by now be experienced in running these focus group workshops! You will have run focus group workshops in the quarterly rolling planning and the key performance indicator projects.

Note

1. Jeremy Hope, *Reinventing the CFO: How Financial Managers Can Transform Their Roles and Add Greater Value* (Boston, MA: Harvard Business School Press, 2006.)

APPENDIX A

Part One Checklist on Those Areas Where the Finance Team Can Score the Easy Goals

Key Tasks to Complete	Tick Here If Covered
Accounts payable (AP)	
Is AP closed on the last working day or earlier?	❑ Yes ❑ No
Are accruals closed off before AP closure?	❑ Yes ❑ No
Have you introduced the purchase card?	❑ Yes ❑ No
Have you integrated your systems with those of your major suppliers so they can send electronic invoices with your general ledger (G/L) codes on it?	❑ Yes ❑ No
Do you have a web-based expense claim system that can be completed by staff no matter where they are in the world?	❑ Yes ❑ No
Have you introduced scanning technology for all those paper-based invoices, from your minor suppliers (all major suppliers will become electronic feeds over time)? The electronic image can then be sent to the budget holder for approval if there is no purchase invoice.	❑ Yes ❑ No

(continues)

Key Tasks to Complete	Tick Here If Covered
Accounts payable (AP) *(Continued)*	
Have all check payments been eliminated with the last one mounted on the CEO's office wall?	❑ Yes ❑ No
Are remittances loaded in a secure area of your website so that suppliers by using their password can download them?	❑ Yes ❑ No
Have you got an automated procurement system (electronic ordering) where an AP transaction is only approved once?	❑ Yes ❑ No
Have you got budget holders approving invoices (where no order, no electronic receipting, or invoice differs to order) within 24 hours?	❑ Yes ❑ No
Have you introduced consignment stock for core stock items and stationery (e.g., where the supplier is responsible for constant replenishment and they have on-line "read only" access to the relevant stock records)?	❑ Yes ❑ No
Have you sourced national contracts for stationery, travel, etc.?	❑ Yes ❑ No
Have you asked for consolidated invoices from suppliers, especially from utilities, stationery suppliers?	❑ Yes ❑ No
Have you changed invoicing cycles on all monthly accounts such as utilities, credit cards, etc. (e.g., invoice cycle including transactions from May 26 to June 25 and being received by the of June 28)?	❑ Yes ❑ No
Have you instructed major suppliers to request an order from your budget holders?	❑ Yes ❑ No
Do you return all the supplier invoices without a purchase order asking them to number the purchase order quote?	❑ Yes ❑ No
Are all large-volume small-dollar transactions going through the purchase cards (e.g., say, all under $2,000)?	❑ Yes ❑ No
Do you perform frequent direct credit payment runs?	❑ Yes ❑ No
Do you use self-generated invoices (buyer-created invoices)?	❑ Yes ❑ No
Have you sent a welcome letter to all new budget holders and given them training?	❑ Yes ❑ No
Have you introduced "shame and name" lists to focus the budget holders on compliance?	❑ Yes ❑ No
Do you reward good budget holder behavior?	❑ Yes ❑ No
Have you performed business re-engineering in AP?	❑ Yes ❑ No

Key Tasks to Complete	Tick Here If Covered
Accounts payable (AP) *(Continued)*	
Have you considered using the supplier's tax code for their account code?	❑ Yes ❑ No
Do you have an intranet site for the AP manual, AP team photos, and AP success stories?	❑ Yes ❑ No
Do you perform simulation exercises when recruiting AP staff?	❑ Yes ❑ No
Do you maintain account management within AP (e.g., Pat looks after suppliers "A" through "G")?	❑ Yes ❑ No
Timely reporting	
Have you moved as many month-end procedures as possible to the last week (e.g., cut off AP, cut off accruals in the last week instead in the new month)?	❑ Yes ❑ No
Have you pushed AP processing bottlenecks back from month-end (m/e)?	❑ Yes ❑ No
Do you cut off month-end on the same day (e.g., last Friday, last Saturday, etc.)?	❑ Yes ❑ No
Have you re-focused variance reporting to year-to-date variances?	❑ Yes ❑ No
Have you banned spring cleaning from month-end?	❑ Yes ❑ No
Do you limit budget holder commentary to one page?	❑ Yes ❑ No
Has the organization avoided major rewriting of reports as they pass up the hierarchy?	❑ Yes ❑ No
Do you issue a flash report on day 1 to the CEO?	❑ Yes ❑ No
Are your final number and commentary ready by day 3 or less?	❑ Yes ❑ No
Have you performed a "Post-it" re-engineering exercise on month-end procedures?	❑ Yes ❑ No
Decision-based reporting	
Does your reporting show a linkage between commentary, statements, notes, and graphs?	❑ Yes ❑ No
Do you limit variance reporting to major category headings?	❑ Yes ❑ No
Do all finance staff see the finished financial report?	❑ Yes ❑ No
Have you set up an icon system to highlight variances over a certain amount (whether they are within tolerance, positive, or negative)?	❑ Yes ❑ No

(continues)

Key Tasks to Complete	Tick Here If Covered
Decision-based reporting *(Continued)*	
Do you stick to a page per topic (e.g., one page profit and loss statement, one page balance sheet, one page cash flow, one page CAPEX, etc. with the accompanying notes on that page)?	❑ Yes ❑ No
Do you have a report that summaries status of projects?	❑ Yes ❑ No
Are your reports "big picture" only (e.g., short and concise)?	❑ Yes ❑ No
Can budget holders do their monthly report in less than half an hour?	❑ Yes ❑ No
Do you report on your key performance indicators daily/weekly?	❑ Yes ❑ No
Have you limited the daily, weekly, monthly routines that are in Excel?	❑ Yes ❑ No
Limiting the time invested in Board reporting	
Have you worked out the cost of preparing the Board papers each time?	❑ Yes ❑ No
Are all Board requests now scoped ("we want you to do this and do not invest more than half a day of time")?	❑ Yes ❑ No
Has the Board been approached to accept papers from the originator?	❑ Yes ❑ No
Has the Board been approached to appraise the benefit of acquiring an electronic Board paper application?	❑ Yes ❑ No
Has the Board been approached to have more timely meetings? Closer to month-end?	❑ Yes ❑ No
Has a review of Board been performed with the Chairman to eradicate unnecessary papers?	❑ Yes ❑ No
Has the Board dashboard been prepared covering the main KRIs?	❑ Yes ❑ No
Timely annual planning process: 10 working days or less	
Have you sold the change through the emotional drivers?	❑ Yes ❑ No
Have you stopped budgeting at account code level?	❑ Yes ❑ No
Are you going to hold a briefing workshop instead of issuing budget instructions?	❑ Yes ❑ No
Have you automated as many cost categories as possible (e.g., consumables, telecommunication costs, accommodation)?	❑ Yes ❑ No

Key Tasks to Complete	Tick Here If Covered
Timely annual planning process: 10 working days or less *(Continued)*	
If using Excel, have you simplified the model?	❑ Yes ❑ No
Have you assessed the cheap forecasting tools for a temporary fix?	❑ Yes ❑ No
Are your key assumptions easily identifiable in the budget model?	❑ Yes ❑ No
Have you planned to expand your team so more one-to-one help can be offered?	❑ Yes ❑ No
Have you avoided phasing the annual budget? The monthly breakdown will now come from the QRP process.	❑ Yes ❑ No
Do you have a trend graph for every cost category?	❑ Yes ❑ No
Is the Budget committee ready for the one week lock-up?	❑ Yes ❑ No
Managing the accounting team	
Do you hold half yearly team away days (e.g., covering training, accounting and interpersonal skills, revisiting corporate objectives and setting goals)?	❑ Yes ❑ No
Do your direct reports have a one-to-one meeting with you at the same time each month (e.g., Pat 2 P.M. first Tuesday)?	❑ Yes ❑ No
Have you adopted the better practice recruiting techniques?	❑ Yes ❑ No
Are you recognizing finance team's staff performance at least weekly?	❑ Yes ❑ No
Do you have an accounting function balanced scorecard?	❑ Yes ❑ No
Does your team meet "out of office" at social events?	❑ Yes ❑ No
Do you spend less than 20% of the working week in meetings?	❑ Yes ❑ No
Do you hold in-house tailored courses for the finance team? (A good benchmark is three days per year.)	❑ Yes ❑ No
Is tertiary education (e.g., MBA programs) included in your training program?	❑ Yes ❑ No
Do all the staff reporting to you have a mentor?	❑ Yes ❑ No
Do you have a mentor?	❑ Yes ❑ No
Annual reporting	
Have you costed out the annual accounts?	❑ Yes ❑ No

(continues)

Key Tasks to Complete	Tick Here If Covered
Annual reporting *(Continued)*	
Do you agree on an information needs list with the auditors?	❑ Yes ❑ No
Do you have a planning meeting with the external auditors?	❑ Yes ❑ No
Have you planned to complete final draft of the annual report before year-end? (Excluding numbers!)	❑ Yes ❑ No
Do you have a person designated as the audit coordinator?	❑ Yes ❑ No
Is the audit team provided with adequate and appropriate facilities (e.g., own room, phones)?	❑ Yes ❑ No
Do you assemble a well-structured financial statement file for the auditors?	❑ Yes ❑ No
Do you have a pre–year-end meeting to address accounting issues?	❑ Yes ❑ No
Have you agreed on a month 10 or 11 hard close?	❑ Yes ❑ No
Have you streamlined the stock taking process?	❑ Yes ❑ No
Have you worked out a quick way of verifying the "added value" in work-in-progress?	❑ Yes ❑ No
Have you discussed with the auditors ways to extract more value out of the management letter?	❑ Yes ❑ No
Have you restricted access to confidential information to the audit partner?	❑ Yes ❑ No
Accounts receivable (AR)	
Do you provide immediate notice of overdue debt to the sales team?	❑ Yes ❑ No
Have you established clear credit practices and communicated these credit practices to staff and customers?	❑ Yes ❑ No
Are you professional when accepting new accounts, and especially larger ones (e.g., are you performing the credit checks that a bank would when lending the same amount)?	❑ Yes ❑ No
Do you monitor sales invoicing promptness and accuracy?	❑ Yes ❑ No
Do you charge penalties on overdue accounts?	❑ Yes ❑ No
Do you use the banks as cash handlers?	❑ Yes ❑ No
Do you collect over 50% of debt by direct debits (DD)?	❑ Yes ❑ No

Key Tasks to Complete	Tick Here If Covered
Accounts receivable (AR) *(Continued)*	
Do you offer an ongoing rebate for DD or a monthly draw if your customer is the public (immediate vs. 20th)?	❑ Yes ❑ No
Are the senior management involved in collecting large difficult accounts?	❑ Yes ❑ No
Are you accepting credit cards for smaller high-risk customers?	❑ Yes ❑ No
Have you introduced the 15-month trend debtors graph?	❑ Yes ❑ No
Have you linked price increases with prompt payment rebates?	❑ Yes ❑ No
Do you cut off AR at noon last working day, with the last afternoon sales being dated as the first day of the new month?	❑ Yes ❑ No
Do you invoice all "monthly invoices" to customers on a 26th to 25th cycle (e.g., May 26 to June 25)?	❑ Yes ❑ No
Or do you invoice all transactions to 25th of the month, with a second invoice for the remaining period of the month?	❑ Yes ❑ No
Do you send electronic invoices to your major customers, including their G/L codes?	❑ Yes ❑ No
Have you streamlined the processes between any sub-contractors you may be using and the eventual billing to your customer to ensure a prompt and accurate billing process?	❑ Yes ❑ No
Marketing the accounting function	
Do you have an accounting function intranet page?	❑ Yes ❑ No
Is the accounting function intranet page updated at least weekly?	❑ Yes ❑ No
Do management accountants, AP, property, office services, CFO, etc. go on walkabout to internal stakeholders?	❑ Yes ❑ No
Do you attend corporate function launches, etc.?	❑ Yes ❑ No
Do you contribute to your organization's newsletter/intranet?	❑ Yes ❑ No
Are you adding value to the senior management team (SMT) (surprising them, giving them success stories)?	❑ Yes ❑ No
Do you hold "Cuppa for a cause" events (e.g., finance team holding a morning break at their workspace with guests giving a donation to a specified charity)?	❑ Yes ❑ No

(continues)

Key Tasks to Complete	Tick Here If Covered
Client management (adding value to your budget holders)	
Have you done in-house customer satisfaction surveys on the finance team?	❑ Yes ❑ No
Do you constantly give budget holders new insights into their business units' operations every time you meet them?	❑ Yes ❑ No
Have you included trend information (rolling 12- or 24-month graphs) and KPIs in the reporting on business units?	❑ Yes ❑ No
Have you provided training sessions for staff (e.g., accruals, using the G/L)?	❑ Yes ❑ No
Do you introduce a new cost saving initiative each month?	❑ Yes ❑ No
Do you help Business Unit (BU) managers with their new re-forecast?	❑ Yes ❑ No
Do you help BU managers with their projects?	❑ Yes ❑ No
Working smarter	
Do you hold a daily team debrief at the end of the day?	❑ Yes ❑ No
Do you limit the number of meetings you have in the mornings (your prime service delivery time)?	❑ Yes ❑ No
Are you using "Action Meeting" methods?	❑ Yes ❑ No
Have you stopped opening your e-mails first thing in the morning?	❑ Yes ❑ No
Is innovation talked about each day among your team?	❑ Yes ❑ No
Do you have a team mission statement (e.g., "To be awesome at what we do!")?	❑ Yes ❑ No
Are your team training sessions systematic and organized?	❑ Yes ❑ No
Do you resolve conflict effectively and efficiently between team members?	❑ Yes ❑ No
Have you invested enough in the induction process for new staff joining the finance team?	❑ Yes ❑ No
Have you created a service ethic in the accounting team culture?	❑ Yes ❑ No
Do you have fun activities in the finance team's workplace?	❑ Yes ❑ No

Key Tasks to Complete	Tick Here If Covered
Maximizing the use of the G/L	
Have you added applications like Crystal reporting, PowerPlay, or a planning tool to give budget holders better read-only access to their information during the month?	❑ Yes ❑ No
Are you constantly training your budget holders on how to use the G/L?	❑ Yes ❑ No
Have you delegated the responsibility of maintaining their part of the G/L to budget holders?	❑ Yes ❑ No
Have you brought back the G/L consultants for about a half day to see where you can better use your G/L's built-in features?	❑ Yes ❑ No
Slaughter the chart of accounts	
Have you reduced the chart of accounts to a minimal amount?	❑ Yes ❑ No
Have you costed out what each additional account code costs?	❑ Yes ❑ No

APPENDIX B

Implementation Steps to Reduce Month-End Reporting Time Frames Checklist

There are a wide range of steps that can be taken for tackling month-end processing. The following checklist allows you to see if you are utilizing all of them.

Checklist of Implementation Steps	Tick Here If Covered
All management made aware of the problem of late month-end reporting.	❑ Yes ❑ No
Buy-in obtained.	❑ Yes ❑ No
Multi-functional project team set up (reporting, marketing, operations, IT, production planning).	❑ Yes ❑ No
Quick month-end (m/e) reporting team empowered to make decisions.	❑ Yes ❑ No
Mandate from senior management team (SMT) that all service operations are to adhere to new deadlines issued by the quick month-end reporting team (QMERT).	❑ Yes ❑ No

Steps to Reduce Month-End Reporting Time Frames Checklist

Checklist of Implementation Steps	Tick Here If Covered
Identify non-value tasks and move them away from time-critical periods such as the posting of automated journals etc.	❑ Yes ❑ No
Rigorously apply the Pareto principle (80/20) focusing on the big numbers and levels of relevancy that were established.	❑ Yes ❑ No
Manual journal entry line items to be reduced by over 50% (80% has been achieved).	❑ Yes ❑ No
Eliminate all interdepartmental corrections at m/e.	❑ Yes ❑ No
Eliminate management review of budget holders' numbers because budget holders now have responsibility to resolve issues.	❑ Yes ❑ No
Business unit (BU) management report condensed into two pages, one on performance measures and one on the financial numbers.	❑ Yes ❑ No
Use estimates to avoid slowing down process.	❑ Yes ❑ No
SMT have agreed to changes to report formats communicated far in advance.	❑ Yes ❑ No
Budget holders tracked activity throughout the month eliminating the usual surprises found during the close process.	❑ Yes ❑ No
Allocations, if required, are now processed without seeing the department's spending.	❑ Yes ❑ No
Preparations for m/e close moved before period end instead of after.	❑ Yes ❑ No
Reconciling accounts in days 1 and 2 being replaced with variance analysis.	❑ Yes ❑ No
The QMERT team is issuing constant communication on achievements.	❑ Yes ❑ No
Accounts payable (AP) and accruals cut-offs before m/e.	❑ Yes ❑ No
Interview key users to determine information requirements.	❑ Yes ❑ No
Develop concise decision-based reports.	❑ Yes ❑ No
Cease issuing large computer printouts.	❑ Yes ❑ No
All key systems upgraded to be on-line in real time.	❑ Yes ❑ No
Removed duplicate data entry processes.	❑ Yes ❑ No
Removed manual reconciliations.	❑ Yes ❑ No

(continues)

Checklist of Implementation Steps	Tick Here If Covered
Budget holders trained, encouraged, and told to analyze their figures during the month and take corrective action for missed postings, etc.	❑ Yes ❑ No
Management accountants assigned to clients budget holders.	❑ Yes ❑ No
Bring management meetings to the third working day after m/e, effectively locking in the benefit of a quick month-end.	❑ Yes ❑ No
Adopt a continual focus on process improvement (e.g., every month some new change is implemented to improve processing).	❑ Yes ❑ No
Set up league tables or "shame and name" listings allowing natural competition between business units to reduce errors (nobody likes being on the bottom).	❑ Yes ❑ No
Start counting errors	❑ Yes ❑ No
Have used "Post-its" re-engineer processes.	❑ Yes ❑ No
Allow subsidiaries to keep their own accounting systems (where a migration would not be cost effective).	❑ Yes ❑ No
Closing on the same day each month (4, 4, 5 reporting periods per quarter).	❑ Yes ❑ No
Closing off capital projects one week before m/e.	❑ Yes ❑ No
In last week only essential operating entries are processed.	❑ Yes ❑ No
Accepting a level of accuracy between 5% and 10%.	❑ Yes ❑ No
Issuing a flash report by end of first working day.	❑ Yes ❑ No
Pushing processing back from m/e by avoiding having payment runs, inter-company adjustments, etc. at m/e.	❑ Yes ❑ No
Re-focus of "variance to budget" reporting to year-to-date variances, which are more stable, or better still to latest forecast for the month.	❑ Yes ❑ No
Letting the Finance report written by the management accountant go unaltered to the CEO and Board.	❑ Yes ❑ No
Ban spring cleaning at month's end.	❑ Yes ❑ No

APPENDIX C

Streamlining an Annual Planning Process Checklist

Many accountants find themselves having to maintain an annual planning process even though they would rather be doing quarterly rolling planning. This checklist is designed to help make the antiquated process quicker and at the same time plant the seed for quarterly rolling planning. This checklist assumes you have a robust planning tool.

Key Tasks	Is It Covered?
Run a workshop to analyze the annual planning pitfalls and sell the concept of quarterly funding	
1. Notify those who should attend	❑ Yes ❑ No
2. CEO to send e-mail stating permission is to be sought from CEO if not attending workshop	❑ Yes ❑ No
3. Organize outside facilitator and presenter to give the annual planning better practice stories	❑ Yes ❑ No
4. Lock in decision that: • Annual plan is not to be broken down into 12 monthly targets	❑ Yes ❑ No

(continues)

Key Tasks	Is It Covered?
Run a workshop to analyze the annual planning pitfalls and sell the concept of quarterly funding *(Continued)*	
• Annual plan does not appropriate funding to budget holders for 12 months, this is to be done on a quarter-by-quarter basis	❑ Yes ❑ No
• There is to be a ten-working day time scale and there is a ban on travel or holidays during these two weeks	❑ Yes ❑ No
• Each budget holder has one chance to discuss their annual plan with the Budget committee and the decision from the meeting is final	❑ Yes ❑ No
• There is no need to have a budget for every account code in the general ledger (G/L)	❑ Yes ❑ No
• Each budget holder is only to have up to 12–15 category headings (each category is a group of account codes)	❑ Yes ❑ No
• Each budget holder is only required to forecast a category heading that represents over 15% of total revenue or total costs, whichever is relevant	❑ Yes ❑ No
Perform pre-work	
5. Automate as many expense categories as you can (e.g., where trend analysis is as good or better than a budget holder's estimate)	❑ Yes ❑ No
6. Establish a calculator for travel and accommodation so budget holders can quickly work out their travel costs (using standard costs)	❑ Yes ❑ No
7. Download all payroll details so budget holders can quickly and accurately calculate their salaries and wages	❑ Yes ❑ No
8. Issue annual planning timetable on the intranet	❑ Yes ❑ No
9. Obtain up-to-date demand forecasts from key customers where possible	❑ Yes ❑ No
10. Set key assumptions and materiality levels	❑ Yes ❑ No
11. Prepare presentation for budget holders (slides and handouts)	❑ Yes ❑ No
12. CEO to send invitation to attend annual planning presentation	❑ Yes ❑ No
13. CEO to send e-mail stating permission is to be sought from CEO if not attending presentation	❑ Yes ❑ No

Key Tasks	Is It Covered?
Perform pre-work *(Continued)*	
14. Deliver presentation to explain to all budget holders how the annual plan is going to be done	❑ Yes ❑ No
15. Organize additional support to help with one-to-one support (using local accounting firms—their staff would have to attend the presentation)	❑ Yes ❑ No
16. Provide briefing to new support staff from the local accounting firms	❑ Yes ❑ No
17. Establish schedule of who is to provide who with one-to-one support during the data input four days	❑ Yes ❑ No
18. Update revenue and expenditure trend graphs, where necessary	❑ Yes ❑ No
19. Establish a Budget committee (CEO, two general managers, and CFO) and explain their responsibilities	❑ Yes ❑ No
Support budget holders during budget preparation	
20. Provide one-to-one support to budget holders	❑ Yes ❑ No
21. Provide a daily progress report to CEO of budget holders who are running late—the "shame and name" report	❑ Yes ❑ No
22. Provide incentives for prompt budget returns (e.g., movie vouchers)	❑ Yes ❑ No
23. Ensure budget holders have provided insightful commentary	❑ Yes ❑ No
24. Provide budget holders with comparison graphs so they can see how reasonable their forecast looks against the past trends	❑ Yes ❑ No
Complete quality assurance (QA) procedures	
25. Ensure all budget returns are in	❑ Yes ❑ No
26. Check all forecast key ratios for reasonableness of forecasts	❑ Yes ❑ No
27. Review all revenue and expenditure graphs to ensure the trends look reasonable	❑ Yes ❑ No
28. Ensure all key papers have been filed on the annual planning master file	❑ Yes ❑ No
29. Rework budgets where forecasts contain errors—with budget holders' permission	❑ Yes ❑ No

(continues)

Key Tasks	Is It Covered?
Complete quality assurance (QA) procedures *(Continued)*	
30. Check correct treatment of costs on major projects (particularly consulting fees)	❑ Yes ❑ No
31. Look for missed major expenditure items	❑ Yes ❑ No
Budget committee	
32. Advise budget holders of times for them to turn up and present their annual plan to the Budget committee	❑ Yes ❑ No
33. Budget committee have confirmed their attendance	❑ Yes ❑ No
34. Budget committee interviewed all relevant budget holders	❑ Yes ❑ No
35. Adjust annual plans based on feedback from the Budget committee	❑ Yes ❑ No
36. Budget committee confirm numbers annual plan	❑ Yes ❑ No
Presentation of annual plan to budget holders	
37. Delivery of presentation the final annual plan numbers to budget holders	❑ Yes ❑ No
Review process: Lessons learned	
38. Set up intranet-based feedback survey on annual plan process	❑ Yes ❑ No
39. Plan next quarterly rolling planning forecast run (this will replace the need for next year's annual planning cycle	❑ Yes ❑ No
40. Check for any timing differences when the last year-end numbers are finalized (budget holders have forecast prior to year-end so they did not know the final numbers)	❑ Yes ❑ No

APPENDIX D

Speeding Up the Annual Audit Process Checklist

Key Tasks	Tick Here If Covered
Planning meeting with auditors	
1. Preparation of agenda—it should include:	
a. Status of prior year significant audit findings	❑ Yes ❑ No
b. Unresolved internal control and accounting issues	❑ Yes ❑ No
c. Draft milestones should be discussed and agreement reached	❑ Yes ❑ No
d. Fine-tuning the content of this checklist	❑ Yes ❑ No
e. Proposed deadlines	❑ Yes ❑ No
f. Discussions of new accounting standards and policies	❑ Yes ❑ No
g. Procedures to alert each other to any potential issues or known obstacles that could affect the audit opinion	❑ Yes ❑ No
h. Role of internal audit team, their plan work, documentation, and degree of reliance that can be placed on their work	❑ Yes ❑ No

(continues)

Key Tasks	Tick Here If Covered
Planning meeting with auditors *(Continued)*	
i. "Information Needs" list	❑ Yes ❑ No
2. Schedule out desired dates for:	
a. Commencement and completion of interim audit field work	❑ Yes ❑ No
b. Scheduled audit progress meetings	❑ Yes ❑ No
c. Pre year-end meeting to address accounting issues with action plans and deadlines (where possible)	❑ Yes ❑ No
d. Sign off of the words in the financial statements	❑ Yes ❑ No
e. Commencement and completion of final audit field work	❑ Yes ❑ No
f. Exit audit meeting	❑ Yes ❑ No
g. Audit Committee meeting	❑ Yes ❑ No
h. Release of auditor signed financial statements	❑ Yes ❑ No
3. Ensure headquarters and field representatives attend this meeting with the auditors	❑ Yes ❑ No
Between planning meeting and first visit	
Formal agreement to deadlines in writing by CFO and auditors	❑ Yes ❑ No
1. Information Needs list	
a. Agreement on the "Information Needs" list—this list should contain all key items required by the auditors prior to the commencement of the final audit fieldwork	❑ Yes ❑ No
b. Itemize schedules and working papers for each financial statement component along with the agreed completion date	❑ Yes ❑ No
c. Schedule and working paper formats should be determined and agreed upon by both the Finance team and the auditor	❑ Yes ❑ No
d. All schedules that would take longer than two hours to prepare should be discussed with auditors to ensure the investment is worth it	❑ Yes ❑ No
e. Responsibility for the preparation of each schedule in the "Information Needs" list should be assigned to specific employees immediately by your office, and this information communicated to the auditor	❑ Yes ❑ No

Key Tasks	Tick Here If Covered
Between planning meeting and first visit *(Continued)*	
2. Role of internal audit team:	
a. Working papers of the internal audit completed and documented to meet the external auditors' standards so they can place some reliance on them and thus reduce their scopes	❑ Yes ❑ No
3. Update documentation of internal controls:	
a. Documenting the systems of internal controls	❑ Yes ❑ No
b. Significant changes in internal controls have been reported to the auditors	❑ Yes ❑ No
c. All work carried out by internal audit team should be documented	❑ Yes ❑ No
4. Communication with staff in your organization:	
a. Designate an audit coordinator	❑ Yes ❑ No
b. Designate a contact point in every function	❑ Yes ❑ No
c. Staff should be made aware of who is the audit coordinator	❑ Yes ❑ No
d. Have your staff mark their calendars when the auditor will be performing the interim and final fieldwork	❑ Yes ❑ No
e. Distribute the "Information Needs" list to the appropriate staff	❑ Yes ❑ No
f. Meet with staff a few weeks prior to the arrival of the auditors to assess their progress	❑ Yes ❑ No
g. Discuss conflict management procedures with staff during audit (the auditor's needs and the normal duties of your staff will create conflict)	❑ Yes ❑ No
Audit arrival interim	
1. Organize an off-site get-together at interim	❑ Yes ❑ No
2. An appropriately sized room, desks, phone, storage space, secure filing, adequate power points, parking spots, etc., should be arranged and ready for the auditor's arrival	❑ Yes ❑ No
3. Introduce the auditors to the audit coordinator and discuss the types of questions and concerns that can be brought to the coordinator's attention	❑ Yes ❑ No

(continues)

Key Tasks	Tick Here If Covered
Audit arrival interim *(Continued)*	
4. A contact list should be provided to the auditors. It should note the key people for each section, their phone numbers, and office locations	❑ Yes ❑ No
5. Assign individuals to locate documents for the auditors. Your staff should be able to gather information quicker and with less disruption than the auditors could	❑ Yes ❑ No
6. Reconfirm and hold the progress meetings	❑ Yes ❑ No
Pre year-end meeting to address accounting issues	
1. Raise all the likely accounting issues (discuss draft with management to agree to issues up front)	❑ Yes ❑ No
2. Obtain a sign-off from auditors as to what their opinion is	❑ Yes ❑ No
3. Discuss and agree to quantification of any differences of opinion	❑ Yes ❑ No
Assembling a well-structured financial statement file	
1. Supports all numbers in the financial statements	❑ Yes ❑ No
2. Supports all numbers presented in the notes	❑ Yes ❑ No
3. Includes all schedules and reports used to compile the financial statement numbers	❑ Yes ❑ No
4. Schedules and reports should tie directly to the accounting records	❑ Yes ❑ No
5. Organized in order of assets, liabilities, revenues, and expenses	❑ Yes ❑ No
6. Explanations of significant variances from year to year	❑ Yes ❑ No
7. Copies of all monthly management reports	❑ Yes ❑ No
Audit arrival final	
1. An appropriately sized room or desk space, phone, storage space, secure filing, adequate power points, parking spots, etc. should be arranged and ready for the auditor's arrival	❑ Yes ❑ No
2. Introduce the auditors to the audit coordinator and discuss the types of questions and concerns that should be brought to the coordinator's attention	❑ Yes ❑ No

Key Tasks	Tick Here If Covered
Audit arrival final *(Continued)*	
3. A contact list should be provided to the auditors. It should note the key people for each section, their phone numbers and office locations	❑ Yes ❑ No
4. Assign an individual to locate documents for the auditors. Your staff should be able to gather information quicker and with less disruption than the auditors could	❑ Yes ❑ No
5. Hand over the financial statement file to the auditors	❑ Yes ❑ No
6. Reconfirm and hold the progress meetings	❑ Yes ❑ No
Handling the audit adjustments and representations	
1. Provide management representation letters in prescribed format	❑ Yes ❑ No
2. Organize provision of legal representation letters	❑ Yes ❑ No
3. Posting of all final audit adjustments to the financial statements	❑ Yes ❑ No
Post-audit activities	
1. A meeting between the senior auditor and the audit coordinator should be held to discuss achievements, problems encountered, and possible solutions for next year	❑ Yes ❑ No
2. Organize post year-end party to celebrate the completion of a big task	❑ Yes ❑ No
3. Invite all those involved including the internal auditors	❑ Yes ❑ No

APPENDIX E

Part Two Checklist on More Wide-Ranging Changes Which Will Require a Significant Investment from the Finance Team

Key Tasks to Complete	Tick Here If Covered
Throw away the annual planning and associated monthly budget cycle	
Do you understand how to report without a monthly budget?	❑ Yes ❑ No
Have you read Jeremy Hope's work in this area?	❑ Yes ❑ No
Quarterly rolling planning/forecasting	
Have you sold the change through the emotional drivers?	❑ Yes ❑ No
Have you stopped forecasting at account code level and moved to category level?	❑ Yes ❑ No

Key Tasks to Complete	Tick Here If Covered
Quarterly rolling planning/forecasting *(Continued)*	
Are you going to hold a briefing workshop instead of issuing budget instructions?	❑ Yes ❑ No
Have you automated as many cost categories as possible (e.g., consumables, telecommunication, accommodation)?	❑ Yes ❑ No
Are you applying Pareto's 80/20 and going into detail for the major expenditure and revenue items (e.g., personnel costs should have much more detail, should forecast by major customer)?	❑ Yes ❑ No
Are your key assumptions easily identifiable in the budget model?	❑ Yes ❑ No
Have you planned to expand your annual planning support team so more one-to-one help can be offered?	❑ Yes ❑ No
Do you have a trend graph for every cost category?	❑ Yes ❑ No
Is the Budget committee ready for the lock-up each quarter?	❑ Yes ❑ No
Do budget holders understand the flexibility of a quarterly funding regime?	❑ Yes ❑ No
Have you bolted down your strategic direction for the next year before the ninth month (e.g., senior management team (SMT) go on an executive retreat)?	❑ Yes ❑ No
Have you embedded the "fast light touch" forecasting philosophy across the organization?	❑ Yes ❑ No
Does management understand why monthly forecast updates are not appropriate or necessary (except for companies in dynamically changing markets)?	❑ Yes ❑ No
Have you run a focus group workshop on quarterly rolling planning (QRP)?	❑ Yes ❑ No
Have you migrated away from Excel to a specialized forecasting application (e.g., winforecast, Cognos Planning, TM1)?	❑ Yes ❑ No
Do you have at least four to five in-house experts on the new planning application (do not forget the CFO)?	❑ Yes ❑ No
Are the quarterly forecasts done by budget holders (e.g., a bottom-up process)?	❑ Yes ❑ No
Is your monthly reporting comparing actuals versus most recent forecast for that month?	❑ Yes ❑ No

(continues)

Key Tasks to Complete	Tick Here If Covered
Quarterly rolling planning/forecasting *(Continued)*	
Have you educated budget holders to look for timing differences (e.g., actual plus remaining budget is not a correct forecast)?	❑ Yes ❑ No
Cost apportionment	
Do you keep head office costs where they are (e.g., avoiding apportioning them to the business units)?	❑ Yes ❑ No
Is product costing kept for one-off exercises?	❑ Yes ❑ No
Ban Excel	
Are you replacing daily, weekly, and monthly Excel routines with more robust solutions?	❑ Yes ❑ No
Is the team starting to re-skill in the 21st century solutions?	❑ Yes ❑ No
More emphasis on weekly reporting	
Are key performance indicators (KPIs) reported 24/7, daily, weekly?	❑ Yes ❑ No
Are yesterday's sales reported by 9 A.M. the following day?	❑ Yes ❑ No
Are key customers' sales reported on a weekly basis?	❑ Yes ❑ No
Do you report some weekly information of key direct costs?	❑ Yes ❑ No
Are you reporting weekly on late projects?	❑ Yes ❑ No
Are you reporting weekly on late reports?	❑ Yes ❑ No
Have the team listened to the QRP webcast by D. Parmenter on www.bettermanagement.com?	❑ Yes ❑ No
Have you read the white paper "quarterly rolling planning" by D. Parmenter on www.bettermanagement.com?	❑ Yes ❑ No
Developing winning KPIs and reporting them in a Balanced Scorecard (BSC)	
Do you understand the difference between the three types of performance measures (i.e., key results indicators (KRIs), performance indicators (PIs), and KPIs)?	❑ Yes ❑ No
Have the team listened to the KPI webcasts by D. Parmenter on www.bettermanagement.com?	❑ Yes ❑ No
Have you read the book *Key Performance Indicators: Developing, Implementing, and Using Winning KPIs* by D. Parmenter available from www.wiley.com?	❑ Yes ❑ No

Key Tasks to Complete	Tick Here If Covered
Developing winning KPIs and reporting them in a Balanced Scorecard (BSC) *(continued)*	
Do you understand the 10/80/10 rule?	❑ Yes ❑ No
Can you recall the characteristics of KPIs?	❑ Yes ❑ No
Do you and the SMT understand the 12-step process of implementing winning KPIs?	❑ Yes ❑ No
Do you and the SMT understand the critical success factors of the organization and the role they play in developing performance measures that work?	❑ Yes ❑ No
Do you have a dashboard for the Board of directors?	❑ Yes ❑ No
Do you have a balanced scorecard for management?	❑ Yes ❑ No
Do you have a balanced scorecard for teams?	❑ Yes ❑ No
Do you understand the significance of identifying the organization's critical success factors?	❑ Yes ❑ No
Do you have a staff icon-based monthly report covering the whole organization's performance on one page?	❑ Yes ❑ No
Have you sold the need for a KPI project through the emotional drivers?	❑ Yes ❑ No
Maximizing your accounting systems	
Have you invested in a planning and forecasting tool and migrated all forecasting and budgeting processes onto it?	❑ Yes ❑ No
Have you invested in your accounts payable systems (e.g., scanning equipment, electronic ordering and receipting)?	❑ Yes ❑ No
Have you invested in a reporting tool and migrated all reporting onto it?	❑ Yes ❑ No
Have you invested in a drill down front-end if it is not already part of your G/L?	❑ Yes ❑ No
Have you invested in your intranet and website so that customer statements, supplier remittances can be viewed by customers and suppliers, respectively, using password protection, 24 /7?	❑ Yes ❑ No
Implementing a new accounting system	
Have you got the CEO to send out the "you must attend the training session" letter (see Appendix I)?	❑ Yes ❑ No

(continues)

Key Tasks to Complete	Tick Here If Covered
Implementing a new accounting system *(Continued)*	
Have you organized a one-day focus group workshop on implementing a new accounting system?	❑ Yes ❑ No
Have you celebrated every small implementation success? The celebration alone is a great communication tool.	❑ Yes ❑ No
Have you sought the help of public relations (PR) support to help sell why budget holders should get behind the new system?	❑ Yes ❑ No
Have you sold the changes by the emotional drivers to the budget holders? Remember you do not sell by logic.	❑ Yes ❑ No
Have you run a focus group workshop?	❑ Yes ❑ No
Have you set up an "accounting systems newsletter" to cover the "gems" that are found from time to time in the system?	❑ Yes ❑ No
Have you resisted the temptation to customize the accounting system? Even one modification is one too many!	❑ Yes ❑ No
If you have customized the G/L have you made sure you have a copy of the code on all changes to the software put in a time capsule, in the company's bank?	❑ Yes ❑ No
Have you made it clear to budget holders that in this new world you have delegated the responsibility of maintaining their part of the G/L to them (e.g., budget holders are expected to monitor their part of the G/L, there will be no spring cleaning at month-end for any mispostings, budget holders will enter accruals directly into the G/L, etc.)?	❑ Yes ❑ No
Better use of the intranet	
Does your intranet include financial reports, at a company level, division, and department (outside the G/L)?	❑ Yes ❑ No
Do you have your accounting policies and procedures manual on the intranet?	❑ Yes ❑ No
Are your financial delegations on the intranet?	❑ Yes ❑ No
Is accounts receivable information on the intranet?	❑ Yes ❑ No
Does your intranet include the accounts payable statistics (e.g., managers who have most invoices outstanding)?	❑ Yes ❑ No
Can re-forecasting and budgeting be updated via the intranet?	❑ Yes ❑ No
Do you submit expense reports on-line and auto-route expense claims for approval?	❑ Yes ❑ No

Key Tasks to Complete	Tick Here If Covered
Holding Board meetings less frequently than once a month	
Have you commenced a marketing drive to restructure the operations of the Board, setting bi-monthly meetings?	❑ Yes ❑ No
Become a "warrior against waste"	
Have you read the "warrior against waste" section in Jeremy Hope's book *Reinventing the CFO*?	❑ Yes ❑ No
Have you finished any waste elimination projects?	❑ Yes ❑ No
Have you ordered Jeremy Hope's recent two books?	❑ Yes ❑ No
Have you read Jeremy Hope's published articles?	❑ Yes ❑ No
Are you setting aside two hours a month to read Jeremy's recent work?	❑ Yes ❑ No

APPENDIX F

How a Quarterly Rolling Forecast Can Be Laid Out in a Planning Tool

Example of a rolling forecasting model in a planning tool

Northland | Re-Forecast

	Q-2 Actuals	Q-1 Actuals	Month1	Month2	Month3	Current Quarter	Month4	Month5	Month6	lext Quarte
Period Ending	Mar 05	Jun 05	Jul 05	Aug 05	Sep 05		Oct 05	Nov 05	Dec 05	
Units Sold	0	0	507	508	509	1,524	170	171	171	
Sales $	0	0	0	0	0	0	0	0	0	
Cost of Sale	0	0	0	0	0	0	0	0	0	
GROSS PROFIT	0	0	0	0	0	0	0	0	0	
Marketing	0	0	0	0	0	0	0	0	0	
Salaries & Wages	0	0	0	0	0	0	0	0	0	
Personnel Expenses	0	0	0	0	0	0	0	0	0	
Travel & Accomodation	0	0	0	0	0	0	0	0	0	
Corporate Overheads	0	0	0	0	0	0	0	0	0	
Premises Plant & Equipment	0	0	0	0	0	0	0	0	0	
Depreciation & Amortisation	0	0	0	0	0	0	0	0	0	
TOTAL EXPENSES	0	0	0	0	0	0	0	0	0	
EBIT	0	0	0	0	0	0	0	0	0	
Interest Received/(Paid)	0	0	0	0	0	0	0	0	0	
Taxation	0	0	0	0	0	0	0	0	0	
NET PROFIT AFTER TAX	0	0	0	0	0	0	0	0	0	
Headcount - Salaried Staff	0	0	0	0	0	0	0	0	0	
Headcount - Wage Staff	0	0	0	0	0	0	0	0	0	
RATIOS										
Sales/Unit	0.00	0.00	0.00	0.00	0.00	0.00	0.00	0.00	0.00	
Gross Profit/Unit	0.00	0.00	0.00	0.00	0.00	0.00	0.00	0.00	0.00	
Net Profit/Unit	0.00	0.00	0.00	0.00	0.00	0.00	0.00	0.00	0.00	
Sales/Employee	0	0	0	0	0	0	0	0	0	

Source: COGNOS Inc

Example of how the model uses formula

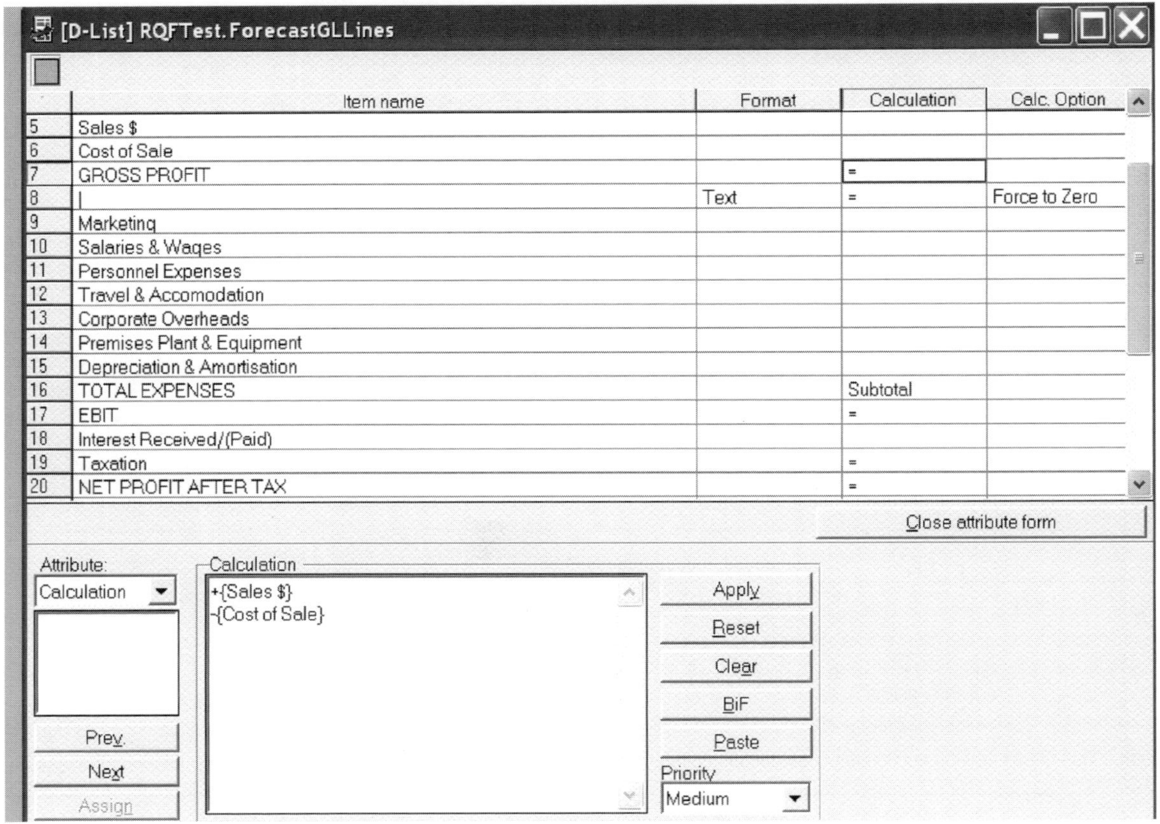

[D-List] RQFTest.ForecastGLLines

	Item name	Format	Calculation	Calc. Option
5	Sales $			
6	Cost of Sale			
7	GROSS PROFIT		=	
8		Text	=	Force to Zero
9	Marketing			
10	Salaries & Wages			
11	Personnel Expenses			
12	Travel & Accomodation			
13	Corporate Overheads			
14	Premises Plant & Equipment			
15	Depreciation & Amortisation			
16	TOTAL EXPENSES		Subtotal	
17	EBIT		=	
18	Interest Received/(Paid)			
19	Taxation		=	
20	NET PROFIT AFTER TAX		=	

Close attribute form

Attribute: Calculation

Calculation
+{Sales $}
-{Cost of Sale}

Apply
Reset
Clear
BiF
Paste
Priority: Medium

Prev.
Next
Assign

Products can be viewed as the unit sold or by other drivers

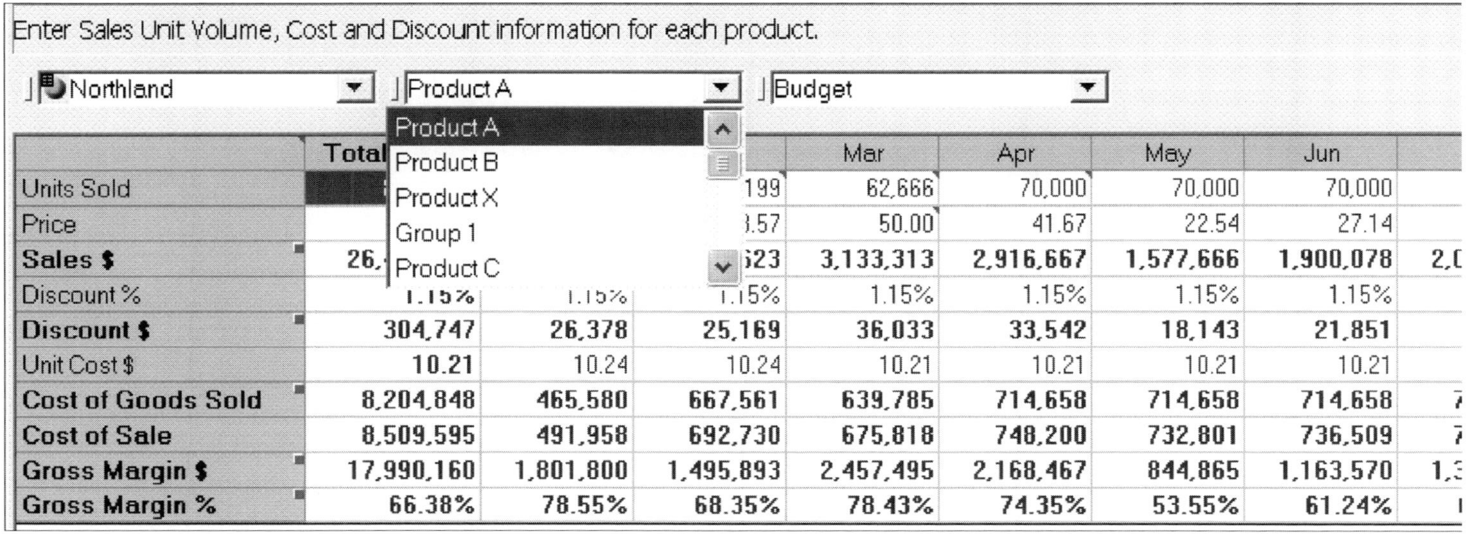

Enter Sales Unit Volume, Cost and Discount information for each product.

Northland | Product A | Budget

Product A
Product B
Product X
Group 1
Product C

	Total			Mar	Apr	May	Jun	
Units Sold			199	62,666	70,000	70,000	70,000	
Price			.57	50.00	41.67	22.54	27.14	
Sales $	**26,**		**523**	**3,133,313**	**2,916,667**	**1,577,666**	**1,900,078**	**2,0**
Discount %	1.15%	1.15%	1.15%	1.15%	1.15%	1.15%	1.15%	
Discount $	**304,747**	**26,378**	**25,169**	**36,033**	**33,542**	**18,143**	**21,851**	
Unit Cost $	**10.21**	10.24	10.24	10.21	10.21	10.21	10.21	
Cost of Goods Sold	**8,204,848**	**465,580**	**667,561**	**639,785**	**714,658**	**714,658**	**714,658**	**7**
Cost of Sale	**8,509,595**	**491,958**	**692,730**	**675,818**	**748,200**	**732,801**	**736,509**	**7**
Gross Margin $	**17,990,160**	**1,801,800**	**1,495,893**	**2,457,495**	**2,168,467**	**844,865**	**1,163,570**	**1,3**
Gross Margin %	**66.38%**	**78.55%**	**68.35%**	**78.43%**	**74.35%**	**53.55%**	**61.24%**	

Now we can look at product "A" in detail. We could also break down into key customers.

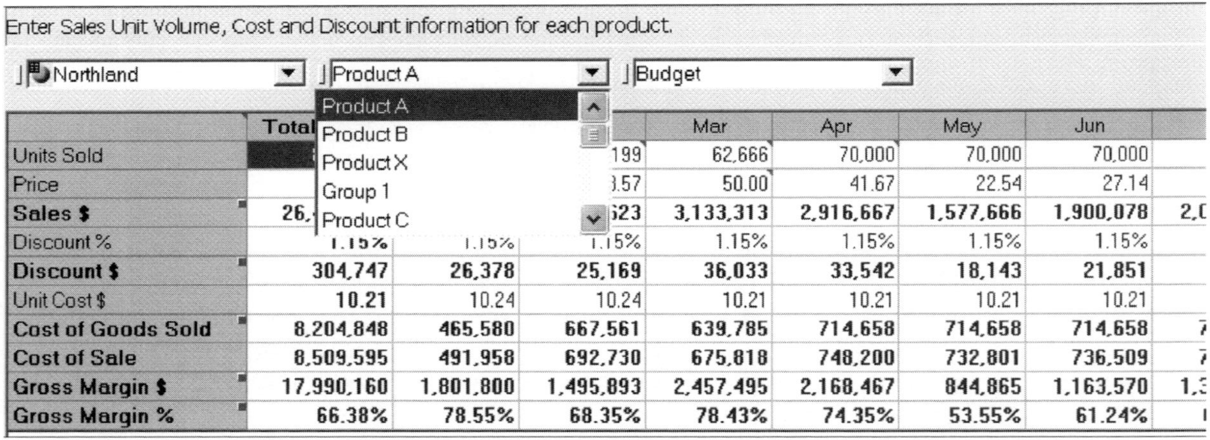

Enter Sales Unit Volume, Cost and Discount information for each product.

Northland | Product A | Budget

Product A
Product B
Product X
Group 1
Product C

	Total			Mar	Apr	May	Jun	
Units Sold			199	62,666	70,000	70,000	70,000	
Price			3.57	50.00	41.67	22.54	27.14	
Sales $	26,		523	3,133,313	2,916,667	1,577,666	1,900,078	2,0
Discount %	1.15%	1.15%	1.15%	1.15%	1.15%	1.15%	1.15%	
Discount $	304,747	26,378	25,169	36,033	33,542	18,143	21,851	
Unit Cost $	10.21	10.24	10.24	10.21	10.21	10.21	10.21	
Cost of Goods Sold	8,204,848	465,580	667,561	639,785	714,658	714,658	714,658	7
Cost of Sale	8,509,595	491,958	692,730	675,818	748,200	732,801	736,509	7
Gross Margin $	17,990,160	1,801,800	1,495,893	2,457,495	2,168,467	844,865	1,163,570	1,3
Gross Margin %	66.38%	78.55%	68.35%	78.43%	74.35%	53.55%	61.24%	

Payroll costs can be easily calculated by individual using a start and end month (when employees have given notice), personnel costs are then automatically calculated.

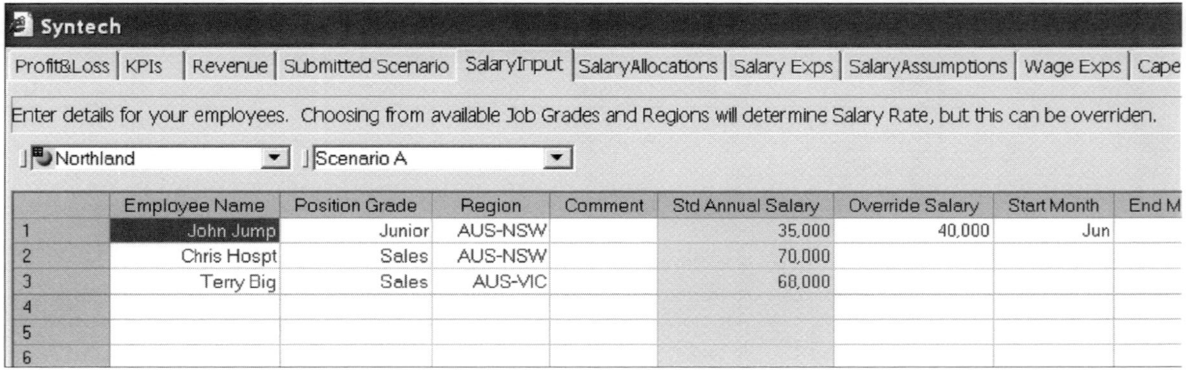

Syntech

Profit&Loss | KPIs | Revenue | Submitted Scenario | SalaryInput | SalaryAllocations | Salary Exps | SalaryAssumptions | Wage Exps | Cape

Enter details for your employees. Choosing from available Job Grades and Regions will determine Salary Rate, but this can be overriden.

Northland | Scenario A

	Employee Name	Position Grade	Region	Comment	Std Annual Salary	Override Salary	Start Month	End M
1	John Jump	Junior	AUS-NSW		35,000	40,000	Jun	
2	Chris Hospt	Sales	AUS-NSW		70,000			
3	Terry Big	Sales	AUS-VIC		68,000			
4								
5								
6								

APPENDIX G

Implementing a Quarterly Rolling Forecast Checklist

This checklist needs to be read in conjunction with the whitepaper written by David Parmenter on QRP available, free of charge, on www.better-management.com.

	Is It Covered?
Secure Senior Management Team (SMT) commitment	
1. Prepare comprehensive presentation to management	❑ Yes ❑ No
2. Big sell to management (historic evidence including costs, better practices, benefits to them) via a presentation	❑ Yes ❑ No
3. Get commitment for a "fast light touch" forecast process	❑ Yes ❑ No
4. Work closely with the Executive Assistants regarding calendar bookings so SMT are present during the first forecast	❑ Yes ❑ No
5. Ensure that management understands what is going to be delivered, and what their involvement is (expectation management)	❑ Yes ❑ No
6. Ensure that the CEO is very visible during the road show	❑ Yes ❑ No

(continues)

	Is It Covered?
Selection of a project team	
7. Ensure project team has no more than four members	❑ Yes ❑ No
8. Mix between people with forecasting, systems structure, and design expertise	❑ Yes ❑ No
9. Look for personality fit between team members	❑ Yes ❑ No
10. Have an end user or budget holder(s) on project team	❑ Yes ❑ No
11. Team leader assigned	❑ Yes ❑ No
Establish your quarterly pattern to best fit your needs and external requirements	
12. Avoiding peak workload periods or school holiday periods for QRP quarterly updates	❑ Yes ❑ No
13. Link QRP quarterly updates to monthly/quarterly/half yearly external reporting requirements	❑ Yes ❑ No
14. Determine when the forecast cycle is to be performed (e.g., commence second Monday in March, June, September, December)	❑ Yes ❑ No
15. Set pattern that fits with legal deadlines if public sector	❑ Yes ❑ No
16. Communicate dates to budget holders	❑ Yes ❑ No
Revisit last year's forecasting process and ascertain lessons learned	
17. Interview two to three members of the SMT for a debriefing	❑ Yes ❑ No
18. Interview four to six budget holders for a debriefing	❑ Yes ❑ No
19. Workshop with a focus group to ascertain hurdles and barriers	❑ Yes ❑ No
20. Report back findings to SMT and obtain sign-off for next phase	❑ Yes ❑ No
21. Gather historic information that can be used to help with the new forecasting system (e.g. trends, averages, etc.)	❑ Yes ❑ No
Evaluation of system requirements (including focus group meeting)	
22. Hold a focus group, one-day workshop, made up of a mix of key individuals around the different businesses and administrators who have a good understanding of operation issues	❑ Yes ❑ No

	Is It Covered?
Evaluation of system requirements (including focus group meeting) *(Continued)*	
23. Focus group workshop to ascertain the likely scenarios	❑ Yes ❑ No
24. Have one planning application demonstrated at the focus group workshop	❑ Yes ❑ No
25. Report on recommended planning application and how it is to be built	❑ Yes ❑ No
26. Road map for development drafted	❑ Yes ❑ No
27. Select at least four to five in-house staff to become experts on the forecasting system (do not forget the CFO) and ensure the selected staff are in the focus group	❑ Yes ❑ No
28. Assess the organization's skill set regarding implementation (extra training my be required to fill gaps)	❑ Yes ❑ No
Commence acquisition of planning application	
29. Appraise systems and short list to three before request for proposal (RFP)	❑ Yes ❑ No
30. Team to visit different sites of preferred solution	❑ Yes ❑ No
31. Establish selection criteria and short list down to three to five for the proposal	❑ Yes ❑ No
32. Reduce potential suppliers to the best two applications	❑ Yes ❑ No
Organize test of the best two applications by contracting the consultants to model some of the required key features (consultants paid)	
33. Request short-listed suppliers to demonstrate their application on some of the key features. Agree to two to three days of consulting fees and evaluate results (the winner is expected to offset these days from the quoted price)	❑ Yes ❑ No
34. Sign-off deal	❑ Yes ❑ No
35. Ensure key planning application consultants are locked-in to the project	❑ Yes ❑ No
Training of in-house designated experts on the new application	
36. Provide in-depth training to the four to five in-house staff who are to become experts on the forecasting system (do not forget the CFO)	❑ Yes ❑ No

(continues)

	Is It Covered?
Training of in-house designated experts on the new application *(Continued)*	
37. Organize off-site visits so they can see other applications and learn from their experience	❑ Yes ❑ No
Build new model using in-house teams with external advice	
38. More than one in-house staff member involved in design	❑ Yes ❑ No
39. Documentation of logic has been completed	❑ Yes ❑ No
40. Keep to Pareto's 80/20 (e.g., personnel costs should have much more detail as they are significant)	❑ Yes ❑ No
41. Based on key drivers ascertained through research and discussions with SMT	❑ Yes ❑ No
42. Brainstorm with SMT what their likely scenarios are	❑ Yes ❑ No
43. Ensure you can accommodate these in model design:	❑ Yes ❑ No
• Introduction of new products	❑ Yes ❑ No
• Close-down of an operation	❑ Yes ❑ No
• Delay of a major initiative	❑ Yes ❑ No
• Extrapolations on expenditure profiles that can be best computed by trending data	❑ Yes ❑ No
• Major shift in assumptions	❑ Yes ❑ No
44. Consultants give workshops and train but do not perform the modeling	❑ Yes ❑ No
45. Follow the KIS (keep it simple) principle	❑ Yes ❑ No
46. Make provision to accommodate budget holders calculations in model	❑ Yes ❑ No
47. Where relevant link forecasting tool to performance indicators	❑ Yes ❑ No
48. Ensure budget holders are directly involved in the forecasting process (e.g., no delegation permitted)	❑ Yes ❑ No
49. Lock in a short forecasting process	❑ Yes ❑ No
50. Deliver more interesting information from forecast process (e.g., trend graphs, performance measures)	❑ Yes ❑ No
51. During forecasting period (one or two weeks) update frequently how the budget holder numbers are progressing	❑ Yes ❑ No
52. Constantly market the success stories you are having	❑ Yes ❑ No

	Is It Covered?
Pilot planning application on two areas	
53. Set up new forecasting regime in two or three units, a quarter ahead, to iron out the bugs and to promote the efficiencies	❑ Yes ❑ No
54. Fine-tune system based on results and feedback	❑ Yes ❑ No
Road show of new rolling forecast application	
55. Prepare presentation (road test in front of public relations expert)	❑ Yes ❑ No
56. Test deliver especially the workshop exercises	❑ Yes ❑ No
57. Deliver road show	❑ Yes ❑ No
58. Improve road show, on the road, based on feedback	❑ Yes ❑ No
59. Explain that budget holders are encouraged to give realistic forecasts rather than what they think management wants to hear	❑ Yes ❑ No
Roll out training of planning application (using in-house experts)	
60. Find those staff who thrive with new technology and train them first	❑ Yes ❑ No
61. Learn from previous forecast mistakes and train staff to avoid them	❑ Yes ❑ No
62. Train all significant budget holders by "one-on-one" training	❑ Yes ❑ No
63. Set up from the outset a quarterly follow-up training course	❑ Yes ❑ No
64. Assess the training needs of the project champion (e.g., some training gaps may need to be filled)	❑ Yes ❑ No
Complete Quality Assurance (QA) processes on first rolling forecast	
65. Establish in-depth QA procedures	❑ Yes ❑ No
66. Set up index for the quarterly rolling forecast file and a standard layout for working papers	❑ Yes ❑ No
67. Provide reasonability checks	❑ Yes ❑ No
68. Audit the forecast application prior to use	❑ Yes ❑ No
69. Book in the calendars of the forecasting committee (CEO, two general managers, and CFO) the key dates when they need to be in committee to interview budget holders—book a year ahead	❑ Yes ❑ No

APPENDIX H

Performing a Quarterly Rolling Forecast Checklist

This checklist is designed to ensure you cover all the bases each time you run a forecast.

	Is It Covered?
Perform pre-work for quarterly run using new rolling forecast application	
1. Automate any additional expense categories you can (e.g., where trend analysis is as good or better than a budget holder's estimate)	❑ Yes ❑ No
2. Update standard costings for travel, accommodation, transfers, and daily allowances to all common destinations	❑ Yes ❑ No
3. Introduce continuous improvements based on prior quarter's surveys feedback	❑ Yes ❑ No
4. Complete payroll details and pre-populate all budget holders' schedules	❑ Yes ❑ No
5. Issue quarterly rolling forecast (QRF) timetable on the intranet	❑ Yes ❑ No

	Is It Covered?
Perform pre-work for quarterly run using new rolling forecast application *(Continued)*	
6. Obtain up-to-date demand forecasts from key customers where possible	❑ Yes ❑ No
7. Set key assumptions and materiality levels before the forecast round	❑ Yes ❑ No
8. Prepare presentation for budget holders (slides and handouts)	❑ Yes ❑ No
9. CEO invitation to attend quarterly rolling presentation sent stating permission is to be sought from CEO if not attending workshop	❑ Yes ❑ No
10. Deliver presentation explaining to all budget holders how it is going to be done, assumptions, lessons from last run, etc.	❑ Yes ❑ No
11. Organize additional local resources to help with one-to-one support (using local accounting firms—their staff would have to attend the workshop)	❑ Yes ❑ No
12. Provide briefing to new support staff from local accounting firms (if used)	❑ Yes ❑ No
13. Establish schedule of who is to provide which budget holder with one-to-one support during the forecast	❑ Yes ❑ No
14. Update revenue and expenditure trend graphs, where necessary	❑ Yes ❑ No
15. Have limited budget holder's forecast requirements to no more than 12 cost category lines	❑ Yes ❑ No
16. Process any changes highlighted from last forecast and audit the formulas forecast in the forecasting application	❑ Yes ❑ No
17. Remind forecasting committee (CEO, two general managers, and CFO) of their responsibilities	❑ Yes ❑ No
Support budget holders during forecast preparation	
18. Provide more one-to-one support	❑ Yes ❑ No
19. Provide a daily progress report to CEO of budget holders who are running late—the shame and name report	❑ Yes ❑ No
20. Provide incentives for prompt forecast returns (e.g., give movie vouchers)	❑ Yes ❑ No
21. Ensure budget holders have provided insightful commentary	❑ Yes ❑ No

(continues)

	Is It Covered?
Support budget holders during forecast preparation *(Continued)*	
22. Provide budget holders with comparison graphs so they can see how reasonable that forecast looks against the past trends	❑ Yes ❑ No
Complete Quality Assurance procedures	
23. Ensure all forecast returns are in	❑ Yes ❑ No
24. Check all key ratios for reasonableness	❑ Yes ❑ No
25. Review all revenue and expenditure graphs to ensure the trends look reasonable	❑ Yes ❑ No
26. Ensure all key papers have been filed on the master file	❑ Yes ❑ No
27. Rework forecasts where forecasts have known and agreed errors—with budget holders' permission	❑ Yes ❑ No
28. Check correct treatment of costs on all major projects	❑ Yes ❑ No
29. Interviews of budget holders by forecasting committee where the forecast is significantly different	❑ Yes ❑ No
30. Look for missed major expenditure items	❑ Yes ❑ No
Forecast committee	
31. Advise budget holders of times for them to turn up and present their case to the forecast committee (requesting additional funding, wanting to maintain unsubstantiated funding)	❑ Yes ❑ No
32. Forecasting committee confirmed their attendance	❑ Yes ❑ No
33. Forecasting committee interviewed all relevant budget holders	❑ Yes ❑ No
34. Adjust forecasts based on feedback from the Forecasting committee	❑ Yes ❑ No
35. Forecasting committee confirm forecast	❑ Yes ❑ No
Presentation of forecast to budget holders	
36. Delivery of presentation of the final forecast numbers to budget holders (this helps make the quarterly forecast contestable)	❑ Yes ❑ No ❑ Yes ❑ No
Review process: Lessons learned	
37. Set up intranet-based feedback survey on QRF process	❑ Yes ❑ No

	Is It Covered?
Review process: Lessons learned *(Continued)*	
38. Plan next quarterly forecast run	❑ Yes ❑ No
39. Ascertain budget holders who require special assistance next time	❑ Yes ❑ No
40. Check for any timing differences when the last month-end numbers are finalized (e.g., is there a major event that will now happen in the first month that was not forecast to occur and vice versa)	❑ Yes ❑ No
41. Update reporting application with new targets for the forthcoming three months for reporting against	❑ Yes ❑ No

APPENDIX I

Useful Letters and Memos

Memo from Accounts Payable Team Leader Sent to New Budget Holders

Date ______________

Dear ______________

Welcome from the accounts payable team

The accounts payable team is committed to adopting and implementing best practice. To this end we need to work in an effective partnership with all budget holders.

Practices in our organization may differ significantly from those you are used to.

We would like to meet with you for 20 minutes or so to go through our procedures, which will help you in your role as a budget holder. We have a short 20-minute PowerPoint presentation, which we will present on a laptop at your desk. Please advise us of a suitable time within the next few weeks.

In the meantime you might like to visit our intranet page on xxxxxxx.

We look forward to offering you a seamless service.

Kind regards,

AP Team Leader

Memo from CEO Sent to All Budget Holders

Date ____________

Dear ____________

Attending G/L training

You will all be aware that we have decided to implement a new accounting package. According to research these implementations are prone to failure.

The general ledger licenses and associated costs will be over $xxx,000 and thus it is imperative that we make this project a success and get it right the first time!

We are also using this implementation to alter radically the way we process accounting transactions. This means that we are implementing processes that will mean you are spending fewer nights and weekends working on administrative matters.

You will need to attend in person. So please select one course and e-mail back today. I will be taking a personal interest in this and will be monitoring course attendance and no-shows.

Should you feel that you are unable to attend please first contact me so we can discuss the reasons.

Kind regards,

CEO

Letter from Accounts Payable Team Leader to Suppliers

Date ______________

Dear ______________

We have thrown away the checkbook—and are at a loss as to how to pay you

We are a modern company and have now thrown away the checkbook, which is a "Charles Dickens technology." In fact the last check is mounted in a frame in the CEO's office. Other than trying to recycle that mounted check, little chance as the CEO is proud of its symbolic meaning, we have no means of paying you.

You should be aware that we have sent you a number of direct credit forms for completion.

One solution is that you complete this direct credit form today and fax it to us at xxxxxxxxxxx, another solution is that you direct debit us, alternatively we could start a barter system (I am joking!).

We value the relationship we have with your company and are looking at ways we can link our IT systems with yours so that we only process a transaction once between us. Our IT experts will be in contact with your IT experts sometime in the future.

Let's move into the 21st century together!

Kind regards,

AP Team Leader

Memo from CEO to Selected Staff to Set Up a Focus (Needed for QRP and KPIs Projects)

Date ____________

Invitation to attend a one day focus group to look at xxxx

It is important that we have a focus group workshop to kick start this assignment as:

- There are many pitfalls in such a project and many have failed to deliver in other companies
- A wide ownership is required and a focus group can have a huge impact on the selling process
- The foundation stones need to be understood and put in place early on in the project
- Focus group will give valuable input in how the implementation should best be done to maximize its impact

We are seeking a focus group selected from experienced staff covering the regions, branches, and head office and covering the different roles from administrators to the senior management team. I believe you would offer much to this exercise and request that you set aside the time to assist.

I welcome your support on this important project. The project team of xxxx, xxxx, xxx, and xxx will need and appreciate your support.

Please confirm availability to attend this focus group workshop, having discussed it with your manager. I look forward to meeting you at the workshop.

Kind regards,

CEO

Memo for a Member of the Team for Going the Extra Mile

Date ____________

Dear ____________

Re Completing project xxxx

I would like to comment on your exceptional skills you demonstrated in completing the xxxxx project on time and within budget. You managed all this while maintaining the routine day-to-day tasks!

Please accept this voucher as a small token of the organization's appreciation. I have discussed the recognition with the CEO who also would like to show their appreciation, in person. I have arranged a morning tea, at the CEO's office, next Tuesday at 10.30 A.M.

Kind regards,

xxxxxxx

Letter to a Supplier Who Has Gone the Extra Mile

Date ____________

Dear ____________

Re Breathtaking improvement

I would like to comment on the exceptional skill your staff and your contractors have demonstrated in the recent installation of xxxxxx. The finished product has exceeded my expectations and has been well worth the wait.

Should you need a reference, please feel free to give potential customers my number.

Kind regards,

xxxxxxx

APPENDIX J

Satisfaction Survey for an Accounting Team

FINANCE TEAM SATISFACTION QUESTIONNAIRE

The purpose of the satisfaction survey is to aid the finance team to deliver a quality service. In this questionnaire we are seeking to investigate your satisfaction with your relationship with the **Finance team since xxx.** Your response will help us make sure we deliver a quality service.

The comment fields are a very helpful part of a feedback to the finance team. Please invest time in making the comments as specific as possible and give examples where this is appropriate. Please return no later than xxth xx by e-mail to xxxxx@xxxxxxxxxxxx.

How satisfied are you with the Finance systems in the following areas?

Rating: 5 = Very satisfied, 4 = Satisfied, 3 = Neither satisfied nor dissatisfied, 2 = Dissatisfied, 1 = Very dissatisfied, X = Not applicable, cannot rate

Finance System	Code	Cannot Rate	Ease of Use	Ease of Accessing Data You Need	Adequacy of Reporting	Usefulness of Manual/Quick Reference Guide	Adequacy of Help Desk Support
Purchasing							
Accounts payable							
Accounts receivable							
General ledger							
Payroll services							
Forecasting system							
Payment of expenses							

How satisfied are you with the following Finance activities?

Rating: 5 = Very satisfied, 4 = Satisfied, 3 = Neither satisfied nor dissatisfied, 2 = Dissatisfied, 1 = Very dissatisfied, X = Not applicable, cannot rate

Finance Activities	Code	Cannot Rate	Timeliness	Accuracy (inc. QA)	Proactive/ Responsiveness	Expertise of Staff	Output (Fit for Purpose)
Processing of sales invoices							
Processing of purchase invoices							

How satisfied are you with the following Finance activities? *(Continued)*

Rating: 5 = Very satisfied, 4 = Satisfied, 3 = Neither satisfied nor dissatisfied, 2 = Dissatisfied, 1 = Very dissatisfied, X = Not applicable, cannot rate

Finance Activities	**Code**	**Cannot Rate**	**Timeliness**	**Accuracy (inc. QA)**	**Proactive/ Responsiveness**	**Expertise of Staff**	**Output (Fit for Purpose)**
Fixed assets processing/ reporting							
Payment of expenses							
Coordination of annual report							
Coordination of external auditors							
Coordination and support of budget process							
Coordination of forecasting the y/e position							
Advice to business units (on variance analysis, planning, financial implications of policy, etc.)							
Monthly financial information available to budget holders							
Monthly finance report to senior management							
One-to-one training							
Other (please specify):							
Other (please specify):							

(continues)

Please rate your satisfaction with Finance's working style (only rate those teams you have contact with).

Rating: 5 = Very satisfied, 4 = Satisfied, 3 = Neither satisfied nor dissatisfied, 2 = Dissatisfied, 1 = Very dissatisfied, X = Not applicable, cannot rate

How satisfied are you with the:	**Code**	**Accounts Payable**	**Accounts Receivable**	**Management Accounting**	**Payroll**	**Systems Accountants**
Team's accessibility and promptness in replying to your queries?						
Proactive role of the team in anticipating issues?						
Team's understanding of issues from your perspective?						
Team's service ethic (friendliness, approachability, positive attitude supportiveness, commitment to continuous improvement)?						
Degree of respect the team demonstrates toward you (e.g., arriving on time for meetings, delivering to deadlines, honoring promises, responding to e-mails)?						
Willingness to take ownership of issues (including responding constructively to criticism)?						
Teamwork and ability to redirect key issues to the appropriate person within the team?						
Decision making within the team (prompt, stand the test of time, rarely rescinded)						
Team's follow-through/ability to close issues?						

Please rate your satisfaction with the Finance's communication (only rate those teams you have contact with).

Rating: 5 = Very satisfied, 4 = Satisfied, 3 = Neither satisfied nor dissatisfied, 2 = Dissatisfied, 1 = Very dissatisfied, X = Not applicable, cannot rate

How satisfied are you with the:	**Code**	**Accounts Payable**	**Accounts Receivable**	**Management Accounting**	**Payroll**	**Systems Accountants**
Team's accessibility and promptness in replying to your queries?						
Frequency of face-to-face communication (e.g., not hiding behind e-mails)?						
Way we communicate operational/routine issues?						
Way we communicate complex issues?						
Overall effectiveness of our communication?						
Meetings that we host (keeping the meeting on track and on time)?						
Contribution we make to meetings you host (being prepared, our level of participation, and the follow-up action we undertake)?						
Presentations we deliver?						
Content of the Business group's intranet site?						
Reporting we give you?						

(continues)

Please provide a comment, **in this section,** to explain a 1 or 5 rating.

What do you consider to be the three main strengths of this service? *(If you have used the 5 rating please give examples.)*

What do you consider are three main areas for this service to develop? *(If you have used number 1 ratings, please give examples. Please also give suggestions of specific changes you would like, if appropriate.)*

Please insert your name. Your name will only be used for administrative purposes.	
If the findings of this survey were to be presented, would you be interested in attending the presentation?	**Yes/No (Delete as appropriate)**

Thank you for participating.

INDEX

Q

R

S